COMPETENCE
IN
COMMUNICATION

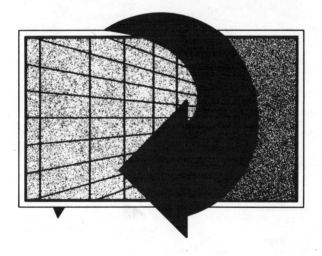

SOME PAST VOLUMES IN THE
SAGE FOCUS EDITIONS

COMPETENCE IN COMMUNICATION

A Multidisciplinary ──────Approach

edited by

Robert N. BOSTROM

SAGE PUBLICATIONS Beverly Hills London New Delhi

Copyright © 1984 by Sage Publications, Inc.

For information address:

SAGE Publications, Inc.
275 South Beverly Drive
Beverly Hills, California 90212

SAGE Publications India Pvt. Ltd.
C-236 Defence Colony
New Delhi 110 024, India

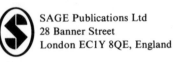

SAGE Publications Ltd
28 Banner Street
London EC1Y 8QE, England

Printed in the United States of America

Library of Congress Cataloging in Publication Data

Main entry under title:

Competence in communication.

(Sage focus editions ; v. 66)

1. Communicative competence. I. Bostrom, Robert N.
P37.5.C64C65   1984   001.51   83-24617
ISBN 0-8039-2200-0
ISBN 0-8039-2201-9 (pbk.)

FIRST PRINTING

Contents

Foreword

Almost everyone believes themselves to be at least a competent communicator; most even believe themselves to be skilled. In discussing communication competence, we are faced with a continuing problem: Most of us communicate on a daily basis, and few of us are aware of the difficulties that occur when they do occur. This is especially true of the forms of communication that involve large organizations, such as newspapers and broadcast networks.

The late Frank Rarig of the University of Minnesota was fond of recounting a commencement address once made by the eminent Danish theologian, Soren Kierkegaard, delivered to a class of young Lutheran divinity students about to enter the ministry. "You who are going to be missionaries," Kierkegaard said, "face a truly difficult job. To teach Christianity to non-Christians is one of the hardest tasks imaginable. But you who are to remain here in Denmark—and teach Christianity to Christians—ah, you have the most difficult task of all."[1]

Our difficulties are much the same. In a sense, it is very difficult to teach "communication" to communicators, and it is often extremely difficult for those who make their daily bread this way to believe that their activities are less than competent. Obviously, what is needed is some clear way of thinking about communication competency as a first step in evaluating what can be done against what is done. This is especially important in large organizational settings.

Most recent research on communication competence has focussed on interpersonal skills to exclusion of competence models in communication generally. In this collection, scholars in journalism, mass communication, organizational communication, and communication education examine the concept of competence from the particular approaches necessitated by the several disciplines. A competent journalist, for example, may necessarily be quite different from a competent interpersonal communicator. A competent bargainer is probably quite different from a competent mediator.

At the core of all notions of communication competence are certain fundamental assumptions about competence, primarily those of linguistic and verbal skill, interactional patterns, and interpersonal awareness. In addition, one of the fundamental assumptions is that many persons vary in their fundamental competence and that these variations can be observed with some regularity.

This collection begins, therefore, with a section on theoretical approaches to competence in which notions about the development of competence, the basic definitions of competence, and the ways that communication competence might interact with other competencies are discussed. As of now, no theoretical approach can be said to be dominate in our thinking about competence.

The second section of this book discusses the varying arenas in which competence can be said to be a factor in communication. These six chapters vary from mediated communication to antagonistic communication.

Our last chapter attempts to pull together and extrapolate principles from these varying approaches.

—Robert N. Bostrom

NOTE

1. I am indebted to Kenneth Berger for this fond recollection of Professor Rarig.

PART I

Theoretical Approaches to Communication Competence

1

A Conceptual Framework

RALPH E. COOLEY
DEBORAH A. ROACH

Although a substantial amount has been written (Allen & Brown, 1976; Bassett et al., 1978; Larson et al., 1978; Wood et al., 1977a; Wood et al., 1977b; Wood, 1981) to supply guidelines for the assessment of students' communicative competence, almost as many definitions of the concept of competence exist as there are authors. These definitions are not specific about the components of competence and leave undefined certain crucial concepts which are necessary to understand the nature of communication competence. The resulting confusion makes it difficult to translate the theories into either productive research or practice. It is time for a more specific statement that removes the confusion and allows communication scholars to begin productive research concerning the development of competence and its relation to classroom performance.

Three major issues must be resolved to develop a theory that productively illuminates the concept of competence. First, we must formulate statements that explicate the theory in a form which satisfies certain characteristics common to all well-formed theories: abstractness, empirical relevance, explicitness, and logical rigor. A theory of competence also must be structured in such a way that it is not just relevant to cross-cultural concerns but demands that cross-cultural phenomena be considered in explaining competence. Finally, such a theory must be explicit in its statement of relationships with other relevant constructs. The most important of these relational statements is the one between competence and performance. This relationship has not yet been satisfactorily developed and likewise remains a

EDITOR'S NOTE: This article represents the last effort of Ralph E. Cooley before his death on September 28, 1982. Long interested in the subject of competence from the particular viewpoint of the trained linguist, Cooley's notes and drafts have been compiled and rewritten by Ms. Roach, an associate at the University of Oklahoma.

major source of confusion. Current behavioral definitions of competence, which make performance an integral part of the concept, leave no clear way of assessing students' competence. Instead, only their performance can be assessed.

This chapter attempts to resolve these issues and to develop a conceptual framework for a theory of competence/performance that can support both research and practice. The chapter is divided into three parts. Part I presents a detailed discussion of the three issues mentioned above and develops the argument that they should be considered criteria for an adequate theory of competence/performance. Part II is a summary of current thinking on the issue of competence and is divided into three parts: (1) consideration of two conceptualizations that have had an impact on the competence literature, namely Noam Chomsky's notion of linguistic competence and Dell Hymes' notion of communicative competence; (2) a summary of the current notions of competence in the field of communication; and (3) a critique of these three conceptualizations as a function of the three theoretical criteria developed in Part I. Finally, in Part III we offer a conceptual framework for a theory of competence/performance. Hopefully such a framework will allow communication scholars to undertake productive research and form a theoretical base from which communication practitioners may make assessments of communication competence.

CRITERIA

THEORETICAL FOUNDATIONS FOR EXPLANATION AND ASSESSMENT

Reynolds (1971) notes three desirable characteristics of statements of scientific knowledge: abstractness (independence of time and space), intersubjectivity (agreement about meaning among relevant scientists), and empirical relevance (the statements can be compared to empirical findings). In addition, he breaks intersubjectivity into two specific characteristics: explicitness, or "description in necessary detail and with terms selected to ensure that the audience agrees on the meaning of the concepts" (p. 18), and rigorousness, or "use of logical systems that are shared and accepted by the relevant scientists to ensure agreement on the predictions and explanations of the theory" (p. 18). These four characteristics, abstractness, explicitness, rigor, and empirical relevance, are the foundations for the issues of explanation and assessment.

Any theory of competence that is constructed according to these criteria must be both general enough to account for a wide number of cases, yet specific enough concerning its statements about behaviors that it can apply to individual instances. In effect, it must focus on both levels of explanation:

the general level that addresses human behavior overall (for example, "What are the components of competence? How do they fit together?), and the specific level that allows for the generation of causal statements as explanations for individual behaviors (i.e.,What components are responsible for those behaviors?). The level of specific explanation should be an operationalization of the general explanatory level. Through generalizations such as this, individual variation in human behavior may be accounted for.

In addition to the contribution that such a theory of competence/ performance could make to a clearer understanding of human behavior, such a theory likewise could contribute to a more solid foundation for the assessment of communication competence—a vital concern to educators in the field of communication. However, any assessment of competence must be theoretically based in order to have meaning and, to the extent that it generates specific explanations, each case of assessment should supply data with which the general power of the theory can be tested. Thus, *through the development of a theory of competence, more meaningful assessments of competence might be accomplished*; and, in turn, the theoretical statements may be tested for their value as a composite structure through which human behavior might clearly be explained and understood.

CROSS-CULTURAL RELEVANCE

As Larson et al. have noted, in the course of normal development children become competent as a matter of course (1978, p. 2). Although in one sense of the argument this statement is true, in another it is not. The "truth" in the Larson et al. argument lies in the understanding that competence is the end result of normal development; the "falseness" resides in the realization that the statement does not hold in cross-cultural encounters. It is this second sense that makes competence the educational issue that it is today and demands that a theory of competence *attend to cross-cultural issues.* Communication behaviors that are the reflection of an individual's competence are culturally specific and, hence, bound by the culture in which they are acted out. As a result, behaviors that are understood as reflections of competence in one culture are not necessarily understood as competent in another. In addition, a representative observer can only assign the label "competent" out of his or her own cultural experience. Hence, communication behaviors are culturally specific from two perspectives, *that of the communication source and that of the observer.* Indeed, an individual who is becoming competent as a function of the acquisition of knowledge about his or her culture's norms is not simultaneously gaining competence in the eyes of another who has different values, attitudes, and beliefs as a function of his or her culture's norms. Thus, such an individual may be judged as incompetent by an observer from another culture, should the latter be unfamiliar with the situational norms for behavior of the former. Such an assessment of competence would be inappropriate, for a great deal of difference exists between a judgment of "incompetent" and a judgment of "incompetent in one culture but competent in another."

Two further cross-cultural issues are relevant to a theory of competence that supposes to account for communication behaviors in a single culture: the breadth and depth of the impact of culture on communication behavior, and the salience of particular communication behaviors to members of different cultures. The developers of the concept of communication competence in this country (with the exception of Hymes) have specified competence in terms of white, middle class behaviors. Such behaviors, however, are not necessarily salient to non-white, other-than-middle-class, urban and rural Americans. Labov, Cohen, Robins, and Lewis (1968, Vol. 2), for example, have revealed the wide variance between school norms and street norms in urban Black society. In addition, communicative patterns have been found to differ among many areas of rural America and the generalized urban populations. However, rural minorities can be expected to differ even more. Dumont and Wax (1969) report that the goals, norms, and values of rural Northeastern Oklahoma Cherokees not only differ from urban norms and values, but also differ from rural whites in the same area. Indeed, cross-cultural research points to the wide variety of norms for communication behavior existing among the many cultural groups in this country and to the differential salience of those norms among individual cultural groups.

We must also consider the impact of an individual's cultural background on his or her behavior. A large body of research exists (Labov et al., 1968, vol. 1; Kochman, 1978; Cooley & Lujan, 1982; Siler & Labadie-Wondergem, 1982; Dobkins, 1974; Lujan & Dobkins, 1978, etc.) which indicates that behaviors evidenced by members of different cultures are not simply surface representations of their cultural background, but rather are deeply tied to the values and self-identity supplied by their culture. Such behaviors are not easily changed, and efforts to effect such change must be approached with a great deal of concern for the individual.

In summary, data exist which demonstrate that the behaviors that are part of communication competence are culturally specific, that competent behaviors in one culture are not necessarily salient or relevant to competence in another culture, and that communication behaviors are deeply seated representations of cultural values and identities. Any theory of competence that is intended to account for behavior in the multicultural reality of American education (to say nothing of being generalizable to other parts of the world) must take these data into consideration. Thus, *cross-cultural issues become the test case for a theory of competence.* If we hope to derive a theory that achieves either level of explanatory adequacy and founds useful assessment techniques, we must create a conceptual base in which a wide range of social/cultural constructs are considered as constitutive elements of competence.

PERFORMANCE

The third issue that needs to be addressed in the formulation of a theory of competence is the explicit statement of the relationship between competence and performance. McCroskey (1982) points out the current confusion concerning this issue in the field of communication. As he noted, various authors have equated competence and performance in their definitions, despite the need for a conceptual separation of the two. McCroskey argues further that "performance of behaviors judged to be competent is neither a necessary nor sufficient condition for a judgment of communication competence" (p. 3). However, this statement alone is not a solution to the problem. The issue remains that despite the method of measurement we use—whether formal or informal—we have only performance (of various sorts) to measure. Competence itself is neither perceivable nor measurable; it can only be inferred. Thus, unless our observations of communicative behaviors are founded in a theory that explicitly defines the boundaries of the two constructs (competence at the level of hypothetical construct—performance on the plane of perception) and the relationship between the two, we will have little guidance in making accurate inferences concerning communicative competence.

In summary, we have argued that a theory that is to contribute to our understanding of competence must

(1) be characterized by abstractness, explicitness, empirical relevance, and logical rigor, if it is to explain behavior and contribute to useful assessment;
(2) be responsive to the issues of culturally specific instantiation of competence, the impact of the culture on behavior, and the salience of one culture's norms to members of another culture; and
(3) specify the relationship between competence and performance.

These three issues should, in fact, be considered criteria for the evaluation of any conceptualization of competence. To the extent that any conceptualization of competence does not satisfy each of the three criteria, it obfuscates our understanding of human communication.

PREVIOUS FORMULATIONS OF COMPETENCE AND PERFORMANCE

LINGUISTIC/SOCIOLINGUISTIC

Chomsky's Formulation. The notions of competence and performance have been addressed in linguistic circles for decades (Weinreich et at., 1968, p. 104), although the current labels for these concepts have been applied only recently. Historically, linguists were interested in the notions of competence and performance not for their own sake but because of their relevance to an understanding of the nature of language and the ways in which linguists might successfully study language concepts. Indeed, the notions of competence and performance have had considerable impact on linguists' understanding of language as an object of study. Social scientists, however, only recently have developed an interest in their relevance to communication issues.

The linguist who has had the greatest impact on social scientists is Noam Chomsky, who is best noted for his work with transformational grammar. Chomsky's dichotomously formulated notions of competence and performance not only have shaped much of linguistic theory for nearly two decades, but also have had a tremendous impact on social scientists who were interested in language phenomena. Chomsky's background in the discipline of philosophy (see Chomsky, 1966) led him to the belief that linguistics contributed to an understanding of humans as rational beings. As a function of this belief, the notion of competence became an essential component in his theory of grammar and linked that theory with his understanding of the human mind. His notion of competence was formulated in a parsimonious, elegant statement: Competence is "the speaker-hearer's knowledge of his language" (Chomsky, 1965, p. 4). For Chomsky, the speaker-hearer is ideal—an autonomous individual

> in a completely homogeneous speech community, who knows its language perfectly and is unaffected by such grammatically irrelevant conditions as memory limitations, distractions, shifts of attention and interest, and errors (random or characteristic) in applying his knowledge of the language in actual performance [p. 3].

Chomsky separated competence, which he felt was the proper domain of linguistic inquiry, from performance, which he placed outside of the domain of linguistic theory and investigation (Chomsky, 1967, pp. 397-398). Consequently, performance was not an area of major concern for Chomsky, although he did address it briefly as "the actual use of language in concrete situations" (Chomsky, 1965, p. 4).

Hymes's Reformulation. In 1971 and 1972, Dell Hymes took Chomsky's conceptualizations of competence and performance to task. Criticizing the formulation of competence for its theoretical and pragmatic weaknesses, Hymes found it inadequate on the grounds that it did not realistically account for actual language behavior (Hymes, 1972a, p. 271). For Hymes, such a narrow formulation could not account for the wide range of variation that is present in the interactions that occur in actual everyday communication. Indeed, such a formulation kept investigators from seeing the normal heterogeneity that exits in every speech community (Weinreich et al., 1968, p. 125).

Hymes also found the concept of competence inadequate on other grounds. In particular, he charged that Chomsky's formulation omitted considerations of the relevance of social/cultural factors to a speaker's knowledge of language. Such phenomena as the use of different pronouns (e.g, *tu* and *vous)* to signal familiarity or formality in French, grammatical structures and lexical forms to show different levels of respect in Japanese, or the use of different languages to indicate an understanding of rank differential (common in Spanish American communities) played an important role in Hymes's notion of a speaker's competence. For Chomsky they did not. He ignored the notion of sociality and, thus, defined competence as relating to the community only in the sense of the community's homogeneity—a notion that has been shown to be in error (Weinreich et al., 1968).

For Hymes, the notion of performance also played an eminent role in the study of human communication. Its salience for him is reflected in his writings concerning the inadequacies in Chomsky's formulation. Of specific concern was Chomsky's loose formulation of the notion of performance, which included both the ability to use language and its actual use (Hymes, 1972a, pp. 282-283), without theoretically differentiating between the two. Thus, investigators who wished to address situationally bound differential behaviors (which, for Hymes, were an essential part of ability to use language) were faced with a particularly perplexing theoretical problem. Chomsky's theory of competence could not account for such phenomena because of the asociality of that theory; however, no theory of performance existed to account for them either.

Based on ideas inherent in this critique, Hymes reformulated the notion of competence. Expanding the label to *communicative competence*, he formulated the concept as follows:

> I should take competence as the general term for the capabilities of a person. Competence is dependent on both (tacit) *knowledge* and (ability for) *use*. Knowledge is *distinct*, then from both competence (as its part) and from systemic possibility (to which its relation is an empirical matter).

The specification of ability for use as part of competence allows for the role of noncognitive factors, such as motivation, as partly determining competence. In speaking of competence, it is especially important not to separate cognitive from affective and volitive [Hymes, 1972a, pp. 282-283].

This reformulation went beyond the narrowness of Chomsky's notion to allow for the inclusion of communicative behaviors other than sentence-bound verbal structures (for example, the inclusion of nonverbal behaviors, turn-taking, and the organization of public presentations). Further, it allowed for the inclusion of social/cultural factors as well as a more complete account of the process by which communicative competence is developed, as Hymes reflects in the following:

A normal child acquires knowledge of sentences, not only as grammatical, but also as appropriate. He or she acquires competence as to when to speak, when not, and as to what to talk about with whom, when, where, in what manner. In short, a child becomes able to accomplish a repertoire of speech acts, to take part in speech events, and to evaluate their accomplishments by others. *This competence, moreover, is integral with attitudes, values, and motivations concerning language, its features and uses* [Hymes, 1972a, p. 277; emphasis added].

Hymes attempted to differentiate between competence and performance by restricting the latter term to "actual use and actual events" (p. 283). Such a distinction had major implications for understanding language behavior for it took into account "the interaction between competence (knowledge, ability for use), the competence of others, and the cybernetic and emergent properties of events themselves" (p. 283). Thus, to properly understand and appreciate an individual's communicative performance, one must understand its relation to that individual's competence, which underlies it; the competence of the person with whom she or he is communicating; and the necessity of an understanding by all parties of the salient properties of the interaction event.[1] Hymes's formulation allowed for the inclusion of cognitive, social, and other noncognitive factors as explicit, constitutive features of competence. As a result, differential context-bound communication could be related to theory.

COMPETENCE IN THE FIELD OF COMMUNICATION

Definitional Statements. Unlike the previous formulations of competence and performance which attempted to construct theoretically grounded statements and assertions, formulations of competence by scholars in our discipline have been motivated primarily by *pedagogical* concerns. As Wiemann and Backlund (1980) have noted in their review of the work in competence, there is both a "lack of definitional and theoretical consistency" (p. 186) and confusion over the separation of the notions of competence and performance. They separated current definitions into two specific categories: those that take the cognitive perspective, and those that take the behavioral perspective. Communication definitions belong in the latter category, which ties competence and performance together (p. 187). Wiemann and Backlund (1980) argue that the cognitive and behavioral perspectives must be combined and offer the differentiation between *knowing* and *knowing how to* as a way of accomplishing this combination. Adopting Wiemann's earlier definition, their view of competence is as follows:

> The ability of an interactant to choose among available communicative behaviors in order that he(she) may successfully accomplish his(her) own interpersonal goals during an encounter while maintaining the face and line of his(her) fellow interactant within the constraints of the situation [p. 188].

Others (Larson et al., 1978; Backlund, 1977) take the same general behavioral approach. For example, Larson et al. (1978, p. 24) state, "We have chosen to define communication competence as the ability to demonstrate knowledge of the communicative behavior socially appropriate in a given situation."

Many of the behavioral positions depend heavily on a narrow interpretation of Hymes's discussion of competence and performance (Hymes, 1971), taking ability for use as a performance construct. Allen and Brown (1976) and their associates are an example. Citing both Hymes (1971) and his seminal article (Hymes, 1972a) on competence, they clearly take a sociolinguistic perspective. One such associate, Naremore (1976), notes that competence is "knowledge of the rules for what is appropriate language use in a given situation" (p. 23). She also writes as follows:

> The child who is learning roles and norms is learning how to employ the language code to meet the demands of communication situations not in a novel, individual fashion, but in the same fashion as others in the community. Communication roles and norms are defined by the culture [p. 17].

For this group, competence "involves an awareness of the transactions that occur between people...[it] is tied to the actual performance of language in

social contexts" (Allen & Brown, 1976, p. 248). In addition, they note the
following:

> 1) The exercise of competence depends upon an available repertoire of experi-
> ences; 2) It requires that the individual make critical choices from that reper-
> toire; 3) It is revealed when suitable behaviors are brought to bear in
> performing desired tasks; and 4) It is sustained when individuals are able to
> evaluate their performance behaviors objectively [p. 249].

Other than occasional references to performance such as these, the concept
of competence is only sketchily discussed.

Competency Lists. In addition to the scholars who have been interested in
defining competence, there are others who have been interested in the
assessment of communication competence, usually in the form of lists of
minimal competencies (see Bassett et al., 1978; the SCA Guidelines; Wood
et al., 1977a; Wood et al., 1977b; Wood, 1981; Allen and Brown also fit in
this category to some degree). These formulations of competence have been
based on extensive reviews of the literature (Bassett et al., 1978; Wood et
al., 1977a; Wood et al., 1977b; Wood, 1981), reports on the work of
different task forces (Bassett et al., 1978; Wood et al., 1977a; Wood et al.,
1977b; Wood, 1981), and correspondence with state coordinators of
language arts programs (Bassett et al., 1978).

For both Bassett and his associates, and Wood and her associates,
competence is the demonstration of those skills that must be developed by
students at all educational levels for the effective accomplishment of work,
citizenship, and daily life (Bassett et al., 1978, pp. 296-297; Wood, 1981,
p. 286). These skills, or competencies, are presented as generalized lists
constructed according to certain criteria. Wood (1981) offers this:

> Only those speaking-listening skills that met the following criteria were
> included: the skill had to be functional, educational (appropriate for classroom
> instruction), and general (related to children and youth from all over the coun-
> try) [pp. 286-287].

Although time and space will not allow a detailed list of the competencies, it should be noted that the content varies among the lists. For example,
Wood presents a lengthy list organized around five specific functional categories: controlling, feeling, informing, ritualizing, and imagining (Wood et
al., 1977a; Wood et al., 1977b; Wood, 1981). Bassett and his associates list
a smaller set of behaviors organized around four categories: communication

codes, oral message evaluation, basic speech communication skills, and human relations (SCA Guidelines). Allen and Brown (1976) present a list that is organized around thirteen instructional categories, but which follows the same five functional categories that Wood used (pp. 260-272).

Specific statements concerning individual competencies also vary widely, but all are written in a form that presents the skill as an observable activity and that focuses the observer's attention on the presence or absence of the activity. All of the lists are derived from pragmatic sources, as we have noted, and none of them has an overt relation to a theory of competence. Also worth noting is that the structure of the statements in these lists of minimal competencies depends on the assumption that performance is part and parcel of the competence construct.

CRITIQUE

Chomsky and Hymes. We argued earlier that a theory of competence/performance must be capable of (1) a general level of explanation, (2) a specific level of explanation, and (3) yielding the capability for assessment. Applying these criteria to Chomsky's formulation of linguistic competence, we find that its major theoretical flaw is its inability to explain[2]. Specifically, Chomsky's formulation is insufficient in its specificity concerning the components of linguistic competence. As a result, it can neither generate specific explanations, nor can it contribute to assessment. Further, it is constructed from a cognitive perspective and, thus, is not concerned with the notion of performance. As a result, it can generate neither general nor specific assessment techniques.

Although Hymes cogently brings to our attention the problems with Chomsky's formulation and offers us important clues towards their solution, he likewise presents a less than detailed formulation from which we can work. His main contributions are the inclusion of social and other noncognitive features as constitutive of competence, and the idea that ability for use is part of competence and not performance. Nevertheless, because his formulation lacks both detail and specific statements of its relation to performance, it lacks explanatory power at either the general or the specific level. In addition, Hymes's formulation cannot yield theoretically based assessment instruments. His formulation, like Chomsky's, is more a definition than a statement of theory.

When we consider Chomsky's notion of linguistic competence in light of its concern with cross-cultural issues, we find that it comes up short in this area also. As Hymes noted, Chomsky's essentially asocial definition of linguistic competence has no room in it for the concepts of a heterogeneous speech community, situation, and differential speech behaviors and, thus, is incapable of dealing with cross-cultural interaction. Hymes's definition (with its accompanying explanation) comes a great deal closer to the mark. As we have noted, Hymes is concerned with accounting for cross-cultural issues throughout his discussion of competence. Hymes again falls short, however, because he does not translate that concern into specific ideas of those social/cultural factors that constitute competence and their relations to the other categories (i.e., cognitive, volitive, etc.).

Communication Conceptualizations of Competence. To the extent that these two formulations have served as models for the field of communication, we, likewise, have constructed formulations with the same set of problems. Not only are our formulations definitional in nature, they lack detailed information about the components of competence, specific statements of its relation to other critical constructs, and explanatory power at the general and specific levels. Further, they cannot inform us as to what to assess or how to go about the task. Finally, although existing conceptualizations are behavioral in perspective, an important link is still missing. The specific relationship between competence and performance remains unstated. Without such a statement, theoretically grounded assessment is unlikely.

Existing conceptualizations of competence are clearly unable to achieve explanatory and assessment power. Although a combination of the behavioral and cognitive perspectives, as Wiemann and Backlund (1980) suggest, may aid in the explanations of competence and performance, it will not do so unless we are specific in our explication of the constructs that we take from each perspective. We also must take care in approaching the degree of relationship between these constructs. Indeed, the relationship between competence and performance must be clearly stated before we can begin to achieve theory-grounded assessment and supply data to test the theory.

When we examine current communication conceptualizations of competence in light of their relevance to cross-cultural concerns, we find that there is little concern for cross-cultural issues. Because the specific competencies described in the minimal competency lists are written as generalized statements that are based on the values, beliefs, and communication strategies of white, middle class America, they become culture-specific criteria for an assessment of competence. Further, each statement presents the skill or "competence" as an observable activity that represents an ability which is either present or absent. The combination of these two features results in a list of skills that does not match the observable reality of everyday American life. In addition, such lists consider neither the validity of the existence of other cultures and subcultures nor their impact on their members' communication patterns.

The manner of presentation of the individual skills encourages measurement of the competency in terms of its presence or absence and discourages attention to the degree of its acquisition.[3] The presence of skills that serve the same function in other cultures as the skill being measured in the white culture is not likely to be counted positively, nor is the partial acquisition of the white, middle class skill. This type of misevaluation can lead to inappropriate pedagogical planning. As an example of this danger, we need only think back to the many remedial programs of the sixties that are based on the conclusion that children who spoke black English did not "have language" (Labov, 1970). That conclusion was the result of linguistic evaluations that could not allow any dialects except white ones to be counted positively. Further, lists constructed in this manner encourage misevaluations that punish children in very subtle but powerful ways (Michaels & Cook-Guperz, 1979).

Existing definitional statements of competence likewise overlook the importance of cross-cultural issues. Although they acknowledge the existence of such concepts as social context (Allen & Brown, 1976), situation (Wiemann & Backlund, 1980; Larson et al., 1978; Naremore, 1976), and appropriateness (Larson et al., 1978; Naremore, 1976), they fail to note that each of these terms is instantiated differently in different cultures. Thus, current definitions are devoid of critical conceptual differentiations as well as of the specificity that is needed to distinguish between their corresponding theoretical constructs. As a result, they are certain to be interpreted from the standpoint of the white, middle class culture, exactly as they are in the lists of competencies we discussed earlier. If these concepts are to be useful to us in research and practice, we need to define them in such a way that the possibility for more than one instantiation is explicit.

These criticisms all speak to the same issue: the lack of a clear, theoretically founded definition of competence. We have, at this time, either holistic definitions of competence or theoretically unfounded pedagogical material. Concern over communication competence in our field has concentrated on the issue of assessment without much concern for explanation at either level. However, valid and reliable assessment cannot take place without being founded in a theory that allows for both general and specific explanation. Current conceptions of competence are theoretically weak, their boundaries are undefined, and their relation to other relevant communication concepts is unstated.

A CONCEPTUAL FRAMEWORK FOR COMPETENCE

In spite of these criticisms, the notion of competence can be valuable to the field of communication as a heuristic device for making sense out of human behavior. Such a notion, however, must be defined carefully and clearly so that we can understand its boundaries and content. In addition, it must explicitly include cross-cultural phenomena in its field of concern. Finally, because we only have performance as input to decisions concerning competence and because statements about an individual's competence are always (and can only be) inferences drawn from our perceptions of her or his performance, the theory must contain an explicit statement of the relationship between competence and performance.

CRITERIA FOR A THEORY OF COMPETENCE

In order to begin a discussion concerning potential criteria governing the contents of a theory of competence, several issues must be addressed. First, what set of construct categories should the theory contain? As competence is inferred from observations of individuals, the theory must account for the physiological and psychological makeup of the person being assessed.[4] Thus, a place must exist for a set of physiological differences due to age, sex, and the like. The theory must also include a set of psychological constructs of at least four types: cognitive constructs such as IQ, cognitive style, and so on; affective constructs such as emotional state, communication apprehension, and mood; personality constructs such as extroversion/introversion, locus of control, Machiavellianism, and dogmatism; and motivation. These two physiological and four psychological categories provide a minimum specification of individual factors which affect competence.[5]

The theory must also provide a place for a set of social/cultural constructs. Communication takes place in situations that are culturally defined (Hymes, 1972b) and are accompanied by sets of culturally determined norms. Sociolinguistic research (Labov, 1972; Ervin-Tripp, 1973; Joos, 1960) has indicated that situation has a powerful impact on communicative behavior. Any theory of communication competence that intends to account for behavior in everyday life must include social constructs such as situation, norms, values, beliefs, and attitudes as constitutive features of competence. In the assessment of communication competence, the social/cultural domain is, in addition, the proper place in which one must acknowledge the impact of the observer (and his or her competence) on the individual being assessed. Sociological variables such as perceived status, power, and authority may impact on a given performance and its subsequent assessment.[6]

Second, the theory must specify the relationships between the constructs it contains. We see the individual as operating within a culture that defines norms for behavior in all of the relevant situations and supplies a structure for passing values, beliefs, and attitudes to each succeeding generation. Individuals differ according to their physiological and psychological makeup and, therefore, their behaviors will be somewhat different from one another. The individuals in an interaction jointly create a set of behaviors which (most of the time) fall within the boundaries of the norms in order to accomplish their own ends. In other words, members act within a social/cultural matrix using their physiological and psychological resources to accomplish goals. The individual, as a psychological entity, operates within the context[7] of his or her physiological abilities and the resulting psychological and physiological entity operates in the context of a social/cultural environment.[8] To be more exact, the set of physiological constructs act as a context for the sets of psychological constructs, and the set of social/cultural constructs operate as a context for both the others.[9]

Finally, a theory of competence must account for communication behaviors in the entire range of situations in which humans ordinarily find themselves. It must also supply principles for understanding how they adjust their communication behaviors to satisfy situations that are new to them. A theory of this scope is necessary to account for both the contrived situations that we must often use in our research and teaching and the naturally occurring situations that make up the overwhelming majority of human life. More importantly, such a scope is necessary if we intend to derive a theory-based list of communication skills appropriate to the many facets of everyday life.

DEFINITION OF COMPETENCE

In a general sense, competence may be defined as *the knowledge of appropriate communication patterns in a given situation and the ability to use the knowledge*. In a specific sense, competence is composed of individual physiological and psychological abilities and social/cultural knowledge. The social/cultural knowledge serves as data and context for the individual's psychological abilities, which also operate in the context of his or her physiological abilities. This definition recognizes the central role of culture in competence. Culture specifies knowledge and situationally bound rules for use. It also recognizes the role of the individual. Individual members, depending on their own physiological and psychological abilities, use this knowledge and these rules to generate unique behaviors that fall within culturally approved bounds and so can be recognized by other members of that culture as competent. Thus, competence is culturally specific in two senses. The knowledge that an individual has is generated through his or her participation in a cultural group. In addition, the recognition of degree of competence by an outside observer can only be determined if that observer is also a member of that culture. Knowledge is social property, owned by the community. Ability to use it, on the other hand, is the property of the individual.[10]

CONCEPTUAL COMPONENTS OF COMPETENCE

Our general definition of competence includes a number of concepts which are, themselves, in need of definition: communication patterns, appropriate, situation, and ability to use.

Communication Patterns. We mean this term to encompass the entire range of communication behavior: language structure from below the sentence level to larger levels of discourse, turn-taking, and the like, and the nonverbal behaviors that accompany them or stand in their stead.

Appropriate. The concept of appropriate behavior has caused a great deal of difficulty for scholars from the beginning of our interest in competence. For our purposes, appropriateness will be defined in terms of cultural determination; that is to say, each culture sets forth rules that determine which of the many possible communication patterns are acceptable and appropriate for any given situation. Further, the culture sets forth a set of rules that supply meanings in that situation for each of the possible communication patterns that a member might use. Hymes (1972b, p. 60) labels these rule sets norms for interaction and norms for interpretation, respectively. These rule types must be kept heuristically separate, for the strategic choices of patterns that are available to any member in a given situation depends on his or her understanding of the meanings attached to each (knowledge of the norms for interpretation) and his or her intended goals. The choice among available strategies leads to perceptions of effectiveness. Such a differentiation may function as a way to separate the concepts of competence and effectiveness.

Situation. Situation is also a difficult construct that can only be understood through its relation to culture. A situation is defined here to be an event having physical, psychological, and interactional features that make it distinguishable from other situations and that, somewhat redundantly, render it significant to the participants. While this terminology stands as a reasonable definition of the general idea of situation, it is complicated by the fact that what counts as a situation is determined by the culture and will differ from culture to culture. Thus, storytelling counts as a member of the general class "instructional situation" in some cultures while in others it may be classified as an "entertainment situation."

Ability to Use. Hymes separates ability to use from performance, apparently intending the phrase to cover the noncognitive aspects of competence. The ability to use, for us, has a somewhat broader scope but is still separate from performance. The term is used here to mean those individual factors for which psychological constructs account, such as intelligence, motivation, personality, empathy, and the like that enable a member to process, retain, and use social/cultural knowledge to produce situation—appropriate communication behaviors. Ability to use that knowledge is demonstrated and instantiated in regular levels of performance, but is not itself performance. Competence is the basis for performance, but remains separate from it.

COMPETENCE AND PERFORMANCE

The separation of these two constructs is a difficult issue for scholars who take the behavioral perspective, perhaps because it smacks of mentalism. Unless, the two can be separated, however, the construct becomes nothing more than performance. An argument on this position can be constructed as follows. If competence and performance are the same, then we can draw two conclusions: First, a competent individual is one who can perform in an appropriate manner. Whereas this conclusion is trivial, the second one—its negative—is not. An individual who does not perform in an appropriate way is *not* competent. This statement may or may not be true, but we are left, both as researchers and as practitioners, with no way of determining its truth. Further—and more importantly—if competence and performance are the same, we have no way of determining the reasons for the inappropriate behavior.

Thus, a theory that separates competence and performance and states the relationship between the two supplies a way to explain human behavior. Thus, we take performance, as Chomsky and Hymes have observed, to be "actual behavior in actual cases." Further, if we omit isolated cases as data, we understand competence to be the foundation for performance. However, the situation is far more complicated than these statements reveal. First competence and performance are theoretical issues, and the relationship between them (as we have just stated it) is simply a theoretical one. However, a relevant relationship exists between our observations (rigorous or casual) of behavior and "perceived competence," and that relationship rests upon inference. We observe performance, not competence, and we infer some state of underlying competence that we take to explain that performance. Competence, as here conceptualized, is broken down into knowledge and ability to use. Performance has no further breakdown, and hence cannot be equated with competence—either pragmatically or theoretically.

Again, if we do not equate competence and performance, we can pose two conclusions. First, regular appropriate behavior is evidence from which we *infer* that an individual is competent. As before, the negative is more revealing: Lack of regular appropriate behavior is evidence from which we *infer* that an individual is not competent. We cannot, however, determine why without further examination. Regular inappropriate behavior could be due to lack of knowledge or of the ability to use it.[11] The utility of this formulation of the details and internal relationships in competence and performance is that it explicitly specifies both the data and the explanation, and allows us to make more accurate assessments of both knowledge and the ability to use it.

CRITIQUE AND CONCLUSION

To this point, we have presented a formulation of competence that goes beyond current formulations in scope and detail. It combines the cognitive and behavioral approaches, taking from the first the recognition of knowledge and ability for use, and from the second the understanding that knowledge is social and the explicit statement of the need for performance as an essential part of the conceptual framework. Before concluding our discussion, however, it seems appropriate that we examine our formulation in light of the three criteria that we proposed at the beginning of this chapter.

At the level of a conceptual framework, our formulation meets the criteria of theory construction in that it has the characteristics of abstractness, empirical relevance, intersubjectivity, and logical rigor. Its concepts are labeled and defined in such a way that they are independent of time and place (abstractness), and yet they are presented in sufficient detail that they are capable of being compared to empirical findings (empirical relevance). The separation of competence into knowledge and ability to use that knowledge is especially pertinent to this characteristic; for, with this separation, the framework suggests an approach to research and assessment that clearly differentiates what one knows from how one goes about using that knowledge. This differentiation requires unambiguous categorization of data. Further, the specification of performance as data for inferring perceived competence (with our conception of competence serving as a heuristic device for understanding and organizing our perceptions) supplies explicit guidelines on how to process our observations of empirical findings.

By defining the concepts of the framework in detail and by carefully proposing a set of relationships between them, this formulation also satisfies the characteristic of intersubjectivity. The subcategory of explicitness is met by the detail (conceptual and ostensive definitions of the factors that constitute knowledge and ability for use), and logical rigor is met by the statements of relationship between the categories of physiological, psychological (i.e., ability for use) and social/cultural (knowledge) factors.

By specifying that knowledge is a shared, community property (i.e., social/cultural in nature) and that knowledge includes repertoires of behaviors, our formulation acknowledges the centrality of cross-cultural concerns in the notion of competence. Because knowledge is determined by the culture, both research into competence and assessment of competence must take into account the content of that knowledge for the culture of the individuals being assessed. Further, it is understood that culture has a powerful impact on behavior and that no behavior is salient to competence in all cultures. Thus, this conceptual framework satisfies the criterion of cross-cultural relevance.

Finally, the conceptual framework that we offer does, in fact, separate competence from performance. Following Hymes, we separate the two conceptually by including ability to use knowledge as a component of competence. Thus, both "knowing" and "knowing how to" are competence issues, while "doing" is a performance issue. However, we go further than Hymes by specifying the hypothetical nature of the competence construct as opposed to the concrete nature of the performance construct. The two are related in that performance supplies the data from which we form (i.e., infer) our perceptions of competence. Thus, a careful conceptualization of competence is necessary as a heuristic device to guide that process to inference. As a result of such a distinction, this conceptual framework satisfies the last criterion—the need for a clear distinction between competence and performance.

Like all initial statements, this conceptualization is far from complete. However, it offers an initial framework for the detailed explications of the relevant components of competence. While a considerable amount of insightful data analysis already exists in the literature, a great deal of research remains to be done before this task can be completed. The conceptual framework that we present offers guidelines for the choice of tasks and for a means of achieving them.

NOTES

1. Note that "the other person's competence" can only mean "as interpreted by the member being judged." Hence, the last two terms are specifications of the first (that member's competence). While such a distinction is not required in Hymes (1972a), it is consistent with a distinction he draws between "norms of interaction" and "norms of interpretation" (1972b). These two sets must be part of the knowledge that is part of competence. Note also that the interpretation that we give to Hymes' quotation requires an understanding of the relationship between competence and performance. While this interpretation is consistent with Hymes' thinking, we have not yet found a discussion of this relationship in his work.

2. It must be noted here that neither Chomsky nor Hymes intended to present a full-blown theory of competence. However, the criticisms offered here are still relevant because these two

conceptualizations have been repeatedly cited and used as models by authors who do intend such a theory.

3. See Black, 1979, for a detailed discussion of this phenomenon.

4. It is outside of the scope of this chapter, to discuss the same factors as they are applicable to a judge of someone else's competence. Suffice it to say that the relevance of these factors to judging competence is not new and must be dealt with from a theoretical position also.

5. Many speech pathologies are socially defined. For example, "creak," which counts as a treatable phenomenon in this country, is an appropriate voice quality in certain British dialects. Nodules on the vocal folds are a desired condition for Indonesian shadow-puppet masters, a highly prestigious profession (Ian Catford, personal conversation).

6. We do not attempt to offer anything like an exhaustive list of specific constructs. At this point the relevance of any individual construct to competence is a matter for empirical investigation. It is likely that the constructs, once they are determined, should be ordered according to their impact on competence. What that order should be also remains to be determined. The constructs listed under each category serve only as illustrations of the possible contents of that category.

7. Context is a more appropriate notion than constraint. Constraint implies restrictions on behavior. Context allows for the notion of creative use of resources.

8. The reader will note that there are important similarities between our position and the position offered by Coordinated Management of Meaning theorists (see Harris, 1979; Cronen, Pearce et al. 1982; and Pearce & Cronen, 1980). There are also important differences. One of the most significant differences is in the definition of system, which we understand in the broader sense of culture and which they see in a narrower sense of the interpersonal or organizational system. Thus, participants can move in and out of the Pearce et al. system, but they cannot do so within ours.

9. The relationships we have stated here do not take into account the construction of the social/cultural matrix, only its relationship to the others once it is "constructed." We are not talking about the generation of culture/society, but about the impact of what has already been generated on the individual.

10. The differentiation of knowledge as social property and ability as individual property suggests that before we can test individuals' competence, we must look to the society to see what the content of the knowledge is.

11. McCroskey (1982) and Wiemann & Backlund (1980) attempt to capture this distinction by distinguishing between "knowing" and "knowing how to." However, because they confuse those terms with competence and performance, "knowing" and "knowing how to" do not help us to understand the complexities of competence.

REFERENCES

Allen, R.R., & Brown, K.L. (Eds.) *Developing competence in children: A report of the Speech Communication Association's national project on speech communication competencies.* Skokie, IL: National Textbook Company, 1976.

Backlund, P.M. *Issues in communication competency theory.* Paper presented at the annual meeting of the Speech Communication Association, Washington, DC, 1977.

Bassett, R.E., Whittington, N., & Staton-Spicer, A. The basics in speaking and listening for high school graduates: What should be assessed? *Communication Education,* 1978, *27,* 293-303.

Black, J.K. Assessing kindergarten children's communication competence. In O.K. Garnica and M.L. King (Eds.), *Language, children and society: The effect of social factors on children learning to communicate*. Oxford: Pergamon, 1979.

Chomsky, N. *Aspects of the theory of syntax*. Cambridge, MA: MIT Press, 1965.

Chomsky, N. *Cartesian linguistics*. New York: Harper & Row, 1966.

Chomsky, N. *Current issues in linguistic theory*. The Hague: Mouton, 1967.

Cooley, R.E., & Lujan, P. A structural analysis of speeches by Native American students. In F. Barkin, E. Brandt, & J. Ornstein-Galacia (Eds.) *Bilingualism and language contact: Spanish, English, and Native American languages*. New York: Teachers College Press, 1982.

Cronen, V.E., Pearce, W.B., & Harris, L. The coordinated management of meaning: A theory of communication. In Frank E.X. Dance (Ed.) *Human communication theory*. New York: Harper & Row, 1982.

Dobkins, D. The rhetoric of John Ridge: The crisis of Cherokee removal. Unpublished masters thesis, Department of Speech Communication, University of Arkansas, 1974.

Dumont, R.V., Jr., & Wax, M.L. Cherokee school society and the intercultural classroom. *Human Organization*, 1969, *28*, 217-225.

Ervin-Tripp, S. An analysis of the interaction of language, topic, and listener. In A.S. Dil (Ed.) *Language Acquisition and Communicative Choice: Essays by Susan M. Ervin-Tripp*. Stanford: Stanford University Press, 1973.

Harris, L. *Communication competence: An argument for a systemic view*. Paper presented at the annual meeting of the International Communication Association. Acapulco, Mexico, 1979.

Hymes, D. Competence and performance in linguistic theory. In R. Huxley & E. Ingram (Eds.) *Language acquisition: Models and methods*. London: Academic Press, 1971.

Hymes, D. On communicative competence. In J.B. Pride & J. Holmes (Eds.) *Sociolinguistics: Selected readings*. Baltimore: Penguin, 1972. (a)

Hymes, D. Models of the interaction of language and social life. In J.J. Gumperz & D. Hymes (Eds.) *Directions in sociolinguistics: The ethnography of speaking*. New York: Holt, Reinhart and Winston, 1972. (b)

Joos, M. The isolation of styles. In *The Georgetown monograph series on language and linguistics*, 1960, *12*, 107-113.

Kochman, T. Toward an ethnography of Black American speech behavior. In M. Lourie & N.F. Conklin (Eds.) *A pluralistic nation: The language issue in the United States*. Rowley, MA: Newbury House, 1978.

Labov, W., Cohen, P., Robins, C., & Lewis, J. *A study of the non-standard English of Negro and Puerto-Rican speakers in New York City: Volume I & Volume II* (Cooperative Research Project No. 3288). New York: Columbia University, 1968.

Labov, W. The logic of non-standard English. In F. Williams (Ed.) *Language and poverty: Perspectives on a theme*. Chicago: Markham, 1970.

Labov, W. Methodology. In Dingwall, W.O. (Ed.) *Linguistic Science*. College Park: The University of Maryland Press, 1972.

Larson, C., Backlund, P., Redmond, M., & Barbour, A. *Assessing functional communication*. ERIC: Ed 153275, March 1978.

Lujan, P., & Dobkins, D. *Communicative reticence: Native Americans in the college classroom*. Paper presented at the annual meeting of the Speech Communication Association. Minneapolis, Minnesota, 1978.

McCroskey, J.C. Communication competence and performance: A research and pedagogical perspective. *Communication Education*, 1982, *31*, 1-7.

Michaels, S., & Cook-Gumperz, J. A study of sharing time with first grade students: Discourse narratives in the classroom. In C. Chiarello et al. (Eds.) *Proceedings of the Fifth Annual*

Meeting of the Berkeley Linguistics Society, 1979. Berkeley, CA: Berkeley Linguistics Society, 1979.

Naremore, R.C. The learning of communication roles and norms. In. R.R. Allen & K.L. Brown (Eds.), *Developing competence in children: A report of the Speech Communication Association's national project on speech communication competencies.* Skokie, IL: National Textbook Company, 1976.

Pearce, W.B., & Cronen, V.E. *Communication, action, and meaning: The creation of social realities.* New York: Praeger, 1980.

Reynolds, P.D. *A primer in theory construction.* Indianapolis, IN: Bobbs-Merrill Educational Publishing, 1971.

Speech Communication Association guidelines for minimal competencies in speaking and listening for high school students. Falls Church, VA: Speech Communication Association.

Siler, I.C., & Labadie-Wondergem, D. Cultural factors in the organization of speeches by Native Americans. In F. Barkin, E. Brandt, & J. Ornstein-Galicia (Eds.) *Bilingualism and language contact: Spanish, English, and Native American languages.* New York: Teachers College Press, 1982.

Wiemann, J.M. & Backlund, P. Current theory and research in communicative competence. *Review of Educational Research*, 1980, *50*, 185-198.

Weinreich, U., Labov, W., & Herzog, M.I. Empirical foundations for a theory of language change. In W.P. Lehmann, & Y. Malkiel (Eds.) *Directions for historical linguistics: A symposium.* Austin, TX: University of Texas Press, 1968.

Wood, B.S., Brown, K., Ecroyd, D., Hopper, R., McCambridge, M., & Nance, T. *Development of functional communication competencies: Pre-kindergarten-grade 6.* ERIC: Ed 137858, 1977. (a)

Wood, B.S., Brown, K., Ecroyd, D., Hopper, R., McCambridge, M., & Nance, T. *Development of functional communication competencies: Grades 7-12.* Eric: Ed 137859, 1977. (b)

Wood, B.S. *Children and communication: Verbal and nonverbal language development* (2nd ed.). Englewood Cliffs, NJ: Prentice-Hall, 1981.

2

Managing Interpersonal Relationships

Social Cognitive and Strategic Determinants of Competence

JAMES L. APPLEGATE
GREGORY B. LEICHTY

Perhaps no aspect of human existence is as perplexing as our social relationships. These relationships can be sources of security or anxiety, material success or failure, happiness or sorrow. Given their importance it is not surprising that considerable popular writing and scientific research has been devoted to studying how social relationships are developed, maintained, and dissolved. In this chapter we describe and critique a large body of relationship research tied to Altman and Talyor's (1973) social penetration model of relationship development. Following this we briefly describe a "constructivist" theory of communication and argue for its utility as an approach to relational studies in overcoming many of the limitations of traditional relationship research. We believe the later perspective provides a more comprehensive theoretical base from which to study the general social cognitive and communicative processes that undergird the competent negotiation of social relationships.

We should note that our review of traditional relationship research focuses on studies of relationship development. Growing numbers of researchers are turning their attention to the processes of relationship dissolution or disengagement (e.g., see Duck, 1982a; Knapp, 1978). We feel our criticisms research on development are applicable to dissolution research adopting a model of dissolution that is basically social penetration in reverse (see Duck, 1982b, for a critique of these positions). Some recent work has

AUTHORS' NOTE: This chapter was partially supported by the University of Kentucky Research Foundation.

pointed to the need to ground dissolution research in more basic understandings of the communication processes which characterize it (Duck, 1983; Duck et at., forthcoming; McCall, 1982). Such research is consistent with our general argument that relationship development, maintenance, disengagement, and dissolution are best seen as implicit accomplishments within multifunctional communicative interactions. Competent relationship management is dependent upon individuals' ability to effectively integrate relationship goals within everyday communications designed as well to inform, persuade, comfort, and/or manage impressions of relational partners.

THE SOCIAL PENETRATION MODEL OF RELATIONAL DEVELOPMENT

While a number of approaches are available for the study of acquaintance and relational development, the social penetration theory of Altman and Taylor (1973) has received more theoretical elaboration than its competitors. The framework of this theory is also broad enough to encompass a number of smaller theories that are confined to particular stages of acquaintance, or focus on specific behavioral developments such as self-disclosure or reciprocity of exchange. This discussion incorporates attribution perspectives and filter theories of information processing under the umbrella of the social penetration paradigm. Even though these smaller theories are usually considered separately, they are compatible with and subject to the weaknesses of social penetration theory.

Altman and Taylor (1973) characterize initial exchange between strangers as narrow and superficial. Strangers initially talk on a rather narrow set of topics and are careful only to disclose the outer nonintimate layers of their personalities. As a relationship between two persons develops, however, the exchange characteristically broadens and includes the disclosure of increasingly intimate or core aspects of one's personality. The quantitative and qualitative transformations of this exchange facilitate the mutual penetration of personalities as a relationship progresses. Relational partners are presumed to acquire increasing amounts of intimate and nonintimate information about each other as the relationship proceeds through the developmental cycle. The process of information exchange is thought to proceed more quickly in the early stages of relational development. Exchange of intimate information tends to involve greater risks and is done with greater discretion (Altman & Taylor, 1973).

According to social penetration theory, persons anticipate rewards from mutual association that they are unable to attain individually and are thus motivated to form social relationships. From this perspective a relationship represents "mutual agreement, implicit or explicit, between people to interact in order to maximize rewards" (Roloff, 1976, p. 182). While the types of rewards sought in relationships are quite varied, the theory assumes that a relationship will be maintained only for as long as each relational partner anticipates that his or her desired rewards will be available at reasonable costs in the future. Concurrently, the impetus to form relationships or to escalate existing ones, can fluctuate as a function of several factors. The potential rewards of relational escalation may become more salient to an individual following changes in location, personal crises, or changes in one's self concept (Miller & Steinberg, 1975).

From this perspective the formation, maintenance, and dissolution of relationships depends on how the relational partners calculate the reward/cost ratios of existing and anticipated interaction. Persons presumably make relational decisions on the basis of whether or not these ratios are favorable. In theory, a person evaluates the rewards and costs of the present interaction with the intent of determining whether the rewards are greater than the costs. In addition, the person forecasts or assesses the probable reward/cost ratios of future interaction with the same person at the next more intimate relational stage. If both the evaluation of present interaction and the forecasts of future interaction with a person are favorable, the individual should decide to proceed to the next level of intimacy. Of course, actual relational escalation is always contingent on the other person's acceptance of the move.

Social penetration theory assumes that the calculation of profit/cost ratios continues for the duration of a social relationship, and that these calculations are the basis for each movement toward or way from a given level of intimacy. If either of the ratios become unfavorable at some point, the individual has a number of options depending on the stage of the relationship. If this occurs early in interaction, the other person can easily be filtered out of a field of potential partners. A relationship can also be frozen at the existing stage of development or it can be deescalated. According to social penetration theory, the individual progressively chooses a few intimates from a large field of potential intimates via these processes of evaluation and forecasting the costs and rewards of interaction.

Given the importance of these calculation processes, a considerable amount of attention has been given to *how* persons calculate reward/cost ratios and decide whether they are favorable or infavorable. This has included research into how decision making may be qualitatively different depending on the stage of a relationship. A second line of research has examined how persons go about changing a relational trajectory once they have made a decision to do so.

Under the first line of research, Thibaut and Kelley (1959) developed a conceptual framework to describe how a person evaluates reward/cost ratios and forecasts. According to Thibaut and Kelley, this is done by comparing ratios and forecasts to two standards, a comparison level (CL), and a comparison level of alternatives (CLalt). An individual's comparison level represents what a person feels she or he should receive in a relationship based on her or his past experience. A person's comparison level of alternatives represents the lowest profit ratio a person is will to accept on the basis of his or her estimate of rewards available in other relationships. Using these variables we can predict the stability of a relationship and the satisfaction that each partner derives from the relationship. This is done by comparing each person's present and anticipated outcomes with each individual's CL and CLalt (Miller & Parks, 1982; Roloff, 1981).

Considerable attention has also been directed to how persons process information while they construct profit ratios and forecast the relative rewardingness of future interaction. Person perception research has shown that forecasts frequently appear to be made on the basis of very limited amounts of stimulus information about the other person (see the review of research in Schneider et al., 1979). Such information often consists of a mere scanning of the other person's appearance, a brief observation of the person's behavior in one or two social contexts, or utilization of information that has been received about the person from third parties. Person-perception researchers have been particularly interested in how persons use such limited information sets to create an overall impression of the other person and make additional inferences about the target person's response characteristics.

Impression formation research suggests the construction of profit forecasts are made possible by the use of implicit theories of personality (Bruner & Tagiuri, 1954). These implicit theories are beliefs about sets of perceived relationships between behaviors and underlying invariances in persons' personalities. Persons are thought to use these theories to infer personality traits from observed appearances and behaviors. Future behaviors of the target person are then forecast from these personality traits. The implicit personality theories help the perceiver infer additional information about the other person, as well as to organize the accumulated beliefs into an overall impression that can be evaluated.

Most relational development research assumes that assessment of the specific response propensities of the other person are heavily influenced by initial evaluations of the other person (i.e., interpersonal attitudes). The perceiver's global affective evaluation of the stimulus person is thought to serve as the primary determinant of whether a person decides to pursue, escalate, freeze, or retreat from a given relationship. Attitude research posits that persons will make positive forecasts of future interaction for persons they like and negative forecasts of future interaction with people they dislike (see O'Keefe, 1980, for an analysis of this research).

Given the theoretical importance of interpersonal attitudes, an extensive body of research has sought to determine what sorts of attributes lead to an overall positive evaluation of a person. A number of studies indicate that we tend to be attracted to persons whom we believe possess attitudes, interests, beliefs and values similar to our own (Morton & Douglas, 1981). However, several competing theories exist to explain *why* similarity is attractive.

Reinforcement theory suggests that cognitive similarity is attractive because it provides an individual with social validation of his or her beliefs and opinions about social reality (Duck, 1976). Alternatively, balance theory suggests that similarity is attractive because it keeps persons' interpersonal cognitions comfortably balanced (Heider, 1958). Others suggest that similarity is attractive because it makes for easier communication and synchronization of interaction, or that similarity makes understanding and prediction of the other person easier (Schneider et al., 1979).

These conclusions about the attractiveness of similarity, however, are tempered with the recognition that interpersonal attraction is not a unitary phenomena. The attractiveness of an attribute also depends on the developmental stage of a relationship. Levinger and Snoek (1972) point out that criteria for liking based on a first impression are qualitatively different from liking assessments based upon rewarding interactions with a person over an extended period of time. It also is apparent that acquaintance can be treated as a process with qualitatively different stages. These stages are characterized by the kinds of information that persons in a relationship attend to and give off (Duck, 1973, 1976).

The developmental view of relational information processing suggests that the perceiver uses the level of information that fits with his or her purposes at the given stage of interaction. Early in interaction, decisions are made on the basis of physical appearance and status cues that are readily available. In the latter stages of acquaintance, information about the other person's underlying personality is increasingly sought and inferred. This developmental view of information processing recognizes that interpersonal attraction is not a simple function of any kind of information. The informativeness of a given type of information at a particular stage of acquaintance must also be taken into account.

The developmental view of acquaintance also highlights the necessity of treating acquaintance as a skilled performance. Mutual attraction alone does not guarantee that relational escalation will occur. Each person must skillfully encode and decode information in a way that is appropriate to the given stage of a relationship. Researchers generally have abandoned the relatively simple assumption that individuals form relationships by matching up with persons on factors that are antecedent to the acquaintance process itself. Accordingly, increasing attention has been given to how individuals strategically control the rate of relational escalation.

Self-disclosure has received enormous attention as one of the primary mechanisms that individuals use to manage self presentation and control the trajectory of a relationship (Deregla & Grzelak, 1979). A person wanting to escalate a relationship must simultaneously convey a positive image of self and still convey his or her intentions of being trusting and trustworthy. Early conceptions that free self-disclosure would automatically escalate a relationship were abandoned as it became apparent that indiscriminate disclosure often does more harm than good. In any case of disclosure of potentially negative information, there is a trade-off between the benefits one gains by disclosing and conveying that one is honest and trusting and the potential negative impact of the information disclosed (Ajzen, 1977).

It has also become clear that self-disclosure is not a discrete variable. The context of self-disclosure changes and the goals of disclosure can be pursued with a large number of strategies (Roloff, 1976). These discoveries pointed to the importance of considering communication strategies within the context of situated interaction. The person wanting to disclose information needs to be able to do so in ways that are consistent with the norms that apply to a given context. The discloser must also be able to forecast whether positive or negative attributions will result from the disclosed information.

A CRITIQUE OF THE TRADITIONAL MODEL

The social penetration account of relational development has become increasingly sophisticated as developmental processes of relationships have been considered. A reasonable amount of empirical data supporting the theory has also accumulated. Recently, however, a number of the assumptions of the model have been seriously challenged (Applegate, 1983; Berger & Roloff, 1982; Burke & Springer, 1981; Crockett & Friedman, 1980; Delia, 1980; Duck et al., forthcoming). We offer a selective review of these criticisms and offer an alternative view of relationship development suggested by them.

RELATIONSHIP DEVELOPMENT IS AN IMPLICIT PROCESS

The most prevalent criticism of mainstream relationship research is that it paints an overly conscious and rationalistic picture of relational negotiation.

The heavy use of laboratory investigations and experimental methods that force individuals to explicitly consider relational variables has helped to foster such a view. They also have deprived the area of rich descriptive data depiciting historical, cultural, and individual variations in the ways various types of relationships (especially nonintimate ones) emerge as an implicit feature of daily activities (Berger & Roloff, 1982; Delia, 1980; Deaux, 1978; Duck, 1980; Hinde, 1979; Kimmel, 1979).

An inordinate amount of research has been devoted to studying attraction issues based on initial impressions in first encounters. The "longitudinal" research that does exist has originated for the most part in retrospective accounts of the development of commitment in heterosexual relationships. Moreover, little attention has been given to the frequency with which the phenomena typically studied in controlled settings actually occur in everyday life. Without such frequency data we have little indication of whether a particular phenomena has much relevance to an explanation of recurring behaviors in relationships.

We believe that longitudinal analyses of relationships in everyday life will, and common sense does, suggest that vast majority of our relationships are developed and maintained as implicit features of daily activities. Some theorists have offered perspectives addressing relationship development in such a way (see Berger & Roloff, 1982; Delia, 1980; McCall, 1970). However, the bulk of relationship research has ignored the fact that the majority of relationships we establish (e.g., plumbers and homeowners, doctors and patients, students and teachers, supervisors and subordinates) are not dependent for their existence on traditional relational variables like self-disclosure, increasing intimacy, or even positive affect. Rather, competent management of such relationships requires the ability to implicitly negotiate a variety of types of relationships in the course of communicating about healing, teaching, repairing pipes, and turning a profit. To analyze many everyday relationships with these traditional variables is to impose dimensions on interactants' communication that are at best tangential to the actual organization of their interactions.

Moreover, even in relationships where intimacy, positive global affect, relational control, and so on might have expected relevance (e.g., with close friends, spouses, dating couples) these qualities of relationships typically are implicitly accomplished and maintained as we communicate in the course of deciding what restaurants to frequent, cleaning house, and/or dressing the children for school. Individuals' ability to integrate relational goals for intimacy, supportiveness, and love within strategic performance that comfort, inform, instruct, persuade, and manage impressions is, in our view, central to relationship development and the maintenance of mutuality in relationship definitions. We know little about what enables people to construct such integrated strategic efforts or how they are constructed largely because of the tendency in traditional research to extract relationships from the social contexts in which they exist and make them explicit foci for subjects.

RELATIONSHIPS FOLLOW MULTIPLE TRAJECTORIES

Traditional relationship research, tied to the notion of social penetration has fostered a narrow conception of the differing forms relationship development may take. A survey of the bulk of relationship research would suggest that all relationships follow the same trajectory. Like astronauts strapped into a fully automated rocket, relational partners are seen as locked into a trajectory carrying them from impersonal to personal levels: from acquaintance to intimacy. Progress is fueled by increasing self-disclosure and positive affect. Partners' only choices are to provide the appropriate mix of self-disclosure and affect for different stages of the flight or bail out. Implicit in this idea of relationship development is the notion that relationships are driven by a strain toward total integration of partners' selves. The function of relationships is to convince persons of the genuineness, dependability, and reality of other persons. Persons are led inevitably to integrate greater portions of their selves into the foci of the relationship making the relationship less vulnerable to unmasking. In addition this strain toward totality and intimacy is motivated by a need to conserve cognitive energy. It is argued a few intimate relationships provide a more efficient method of gaining dependable support for our various role-identities. Hence, it is easier to satisfy our identity-support and relational needs in a few relationships than in a large number of them.

While there is no doubt that some relationships reflect a path of development similar to that outlined in traditional theory, we find the model deficient in at least two respects. First, the model encourages researchers to treat communication as epiphenomenal to the process of relational development. That is, communication behaviors are studied as realizations of a particular relational trajectory rather than as the medium through which relational goals and paths to those goals are negotiated and pursued. We argue (and this argument is developed in detail in the latter half of this chapter) that adequate explanation of the process of relationship negotiation should begin with analyses of the communicative goals of interactions. The multifunctional nature of communication is a well-documented truism. Clark and Delia (1979) suggest that every interaction is organized around at least three types of goals: instrumental (e.g., persuasive, informational, instructional), identity/impression management, and relational. Research in social cognition and communication suggests the specific nature of the goals embodied in our definitions of social situations directly influence the organization of strategic behavior (Cohen, 1981; Higgins et al., 1981; McCann & Higgins, forthcoming; O'Keefe & Delia, 1982). Moreover, there is evidence of group and individual differences in the importance assigned to different types of goals (e.g., instrumental vs. relational) as well as to types of instrumental, identity, and relational goals typically informing interaction (McCann & Higgins, forthcoming).

Such research suggests that studies of the relational function of communication begin with assessments of the *variety* of relational goals informing communication as well as their explicitness and salience in relation to other types of communicative goals—this, rather than assuming the goal of social penetration as a salient feature of most (if not all) communication in relationships. Some theorists have offered perspectives which explicitly address relational goals and definitions as negotiated products of multifunctional communications rather than treating communications as the product of a particular relational trajectory (e.g., McCall, 1970). Such as orientation allows study of relationships in which goals of intimacy and intimacy and penetration are explicit but casts such relationships within a broader framework treating relational trajectories themselves as variables for study.

Our second objection to the narrow conception of relational trajectories encouraged by traditional research is that it encourages a much too orderly conception of development even for those relationships in which intimacy and social penetration are the general goals (e.g., dating couples thinking about marriage). Huston, Surra, Fitzgerald, and Cate (1981) have found a variety of developmental patterns for courtship relationships and in the way self-disclosure, perceived similarities, conflict, and mutual participation in different types of activities affect the pattern of development. Moreover, Duck, Miell, and Miell (forthcoming) argue that individual differences in social cognitive and communicative ability affect the way in which intimacy is achieved or whether or not it is achieved at all. Again, the argument here is that even relationships generally oriented to social penetration evidence various paths of development is part due to the differences in communicative ability of interactants.

RELATIONAL DEVELOPMENT IS AN ACCOMMODATIVE PROCESS

O'Keefe and Delia (1982) argue that most impression formation research reflects an assimilative bias emphasizing the role of the perceiver's cognitive system in reconstructing, inferring, and organizing information about others. Such a bias has led researchers to neglect the role of situations and the behavior of others in determining what dimensions of judgment perceivers deem salient for a situation and in effecting change in the nature and organization of perceivers' cognitive organization that facilitate accommodation to new information across time. A similar criticism can be leveled at traditional approaches to relationship development.

Traditional relationship research has focused on how perceivers' reconstruct information about others and attempted to identify the criteria applied to make relationship decisions (e.g., similarity, reward/cost potential). Typically such approaches have implied a static conception of perceivers' self-concepts and goals. The result is conceptions of relationship development closely tied to matching and filtering hypotheses.

This orientation has led researchers to neglect the central role of communication in negotiating identities and relationships. We know little about how particular situational constraints, instrumental goals, and types of behavior by partners affect the elicitation and modification of perceivers' relational goals or their decisions about which aspects of self to disclose in a given context, or relationship. We have little to say about how and why relational partners alter their self concepts or their beliefs and strategic responses to one another in accommodating to new information provided in communication. Finally, and perhaps most disturbing, we have little knowledge about what contributes to differences in individuals' strategic flexibility in meeting the changing demands of an ongoing relationship. Any adequate approach to relationship development must offer a way of explaining accommodation and change as well as differences in individuals' ability to strategically make such accommodations.

A related criticism of traditional models of relationships development is their tendency to disregard social-structural constraints to which individuals' must accommodate. Much writing on interpersonal attraction assumes that persons have a great deal of choice about whom to interact with. While this assumption may be fairly accurate in a high school, it does not apply to many contexts. We frequently find it necessary to establish friendly relations with persons we don't particularly like (Kurth, 1970). Kin relationships also involve very little choice but are still very important relationships for most people. Friendship patterns are affected as well be the number of social roles one acquires. Marriage and parenthood both appear to significantly alter a person's friendship network (Dickens & Perlman, 1981). A more realistic model of relational development would presumably devote at least some attention to how persons accommodate to these social-structural constraints.

AN ALTERNATIVE FRAMEWORK FOR RELATIONSHIP
STUDIES

We now briefly overview a "constructivist" theory of communication and argue for its utility in studying relationship development in a way that overcomes many of the limitations of traditional relationship research outlined above. Over the last 15 years, constructivist theory has spawned an important research tradition in the field of speech communication (for a comprehensive overview see Delia et al., 1982). The thrust of this work has been the integration of research on interpersonal construct system development within the general study of social cognition and communication behavior. Communication, by this account, is not epiphenomenal to construal processes but rather an independent phenomena influenced by and influencing application and development of personal constructs, social scripts, perspective-taking processes, and the like (for recent work offering similar interactive accounts of the relationship between social cognition and communication, see Athay & Darely, 1981; Duck et al., forthcoming; McCann & Higgins, forthcoming.)

The logic of the constructivist epistemology is hierarchic and developmental in nature embracing the comparative conception of development forwarded by Werner (1957; also see Werner & Kaplan, 1963) which is captured succinctly in his orthogenetic principle: "Whenever development occurs, it proceeds from a state of relative globality and lack of differentiation to a state of increasing differentiation, articulation, and hierarchic integration" (1957, p. 126). Specific assessments of relationships between and individual differences in the quality of communication behavior and social cognition are approached through comparative analysis within a series of parallel developmental axes derived from this principle. The analysis of social cognition is grounded in an integration of Kelly's (1955) theory of interpersonal constructs with Werner's developmental approach. An elaboration of this conception of communication and its relationship to interpersonal constructs follows.

COMMUNICATION AS FUNCTIONAL BEHAVIOR

At the heart of the constructivist conception of communication is the contention that messages *do* things. People typically do not communicate to be listener-adaptive, evidence the behavioral correlates of labile cognitive structure, and so on. Rather, talk is directly tied to interaction goals such as comforting, persuading, or negotiating relationships (O'Keefe & Delia, 1982). The functions communication messages serve may be explicit (closely tied to the intentions of the interactants) or implicit (embedded in tacit situational knowledge).

Constructivist theory has integrated aspects of symbolic interactionist theory in sociology, including W.I. Thomas's conception of the "definition of the situation" (see Ball, 1972; Blumer, 1969) and a variety of sociolinguistic analyses (e.g., Bernstein, 1974; Halliday, 1973; Hymes, 1974) to construct a beginning taxonomy of communicative functions. Clark and Delia (1979) argue that every communicative transaction involves the overt and/or tacit negotiation of identities and relationship definitions between interactants. Moreover, the transaction may (and typically odes) involve pursuit of instrumental goals (e.g., persuading, comforting, transmitting information).

Utilizing a variety of data gathering techniques including naturalistic observation, structured interactive communication tasks, and open-ended responses to hypothetical situations, researchers have generated a corpus of strategies employed by children, adolescents, and adults to accomplish interaction goals. Hierarchic coding systems have been derived from analysis of these strategies reflecting axes of development consistent with Wernerian developmental theory. This work has provided a picture of developmental and individual differences in (1) the listener-adaptiveness of persuasive strategies (e.g., Applegate, 1982a; Clark & Delia, 1977; Delia & Clark, 1977; Delia et al., 1979; B. O'Keefe & Delia, 1979); (2) the referential adequacy of information giving strategies (e.g., Hale, 1980, 1982); (3) the person-centeredness of regulative and interpersonal comforting strategies (e.g., Applegate, 1980a, 1980b; Applegate et al., forthcoming; Applegate & Delia, 1980; Burleson, 1982); and (4) the relative sophistication of impression management strategies in meeting cultural guidelines for politeness and "face" needs (for a general analysis of such strategic demands see Brown & Levinson, 1978; for constructivist applications see Kline 1981; Kline & Ceropski, forthcoming; also see Applegate, 1982a, 1982b). Such developmental differences have been found across a variety of social contexts for all ages (e.g., the family, school, peer groups, work settings).

INTERPERSONAL CONSTRUCTS AND COMMUNICATION

Constructivist theory suggests that differences in the quality of strategic behavior are strongly influenced by the quality of communicators' understanding of people. That "person knowledge" is in turn largely achieved through application of constructs. The bulk of research (including that referenced above) has attempted to establish relationships between interpersonal construct system development along particular axes (e.g., globality-differentiation, concreteness-abstractness, diffuseness-integration) and strategy quality.

In contrast to the limited success of research attempting to relate communication behavior to global measures of empathy, perspective-taking, and/or role-taking (see the general review of Shantz, 1981), constructivist research efforts have evidenced consistent success in relating developmental differences in the quality of child and adult communication strategies to specific developments in the differentiation, abstractness, integration, and comprehensiveness, and so on of the interpersonal construct system. For example, in the research referenced previously, individual's with more differentiated, abstract (dispositionally oriented) and comprehensive constructs have been shown to use a greater number of alternative strategies that are more listener-adaptive in pursuing persuasive goals. Parents with more advanced systems employ more person-centered strategies in regulating children's behavior and helping them deal with interpersonal problems—strategies that better recognize and elaborate individual feelings, beliefs, and the like as salient features of social contexts and encourage the child to engage in autonomous reflection. Increased differentiation and abstractness of constructs also has been tied to greater awareness of and strategic sophistication in impression management.

Researchers recently have acknowledged the influence of various types of social cognitive schemes, scripts, and the like on communication (e.g., O'Keefe & Delia, 1982; O'Keefe et al., 1980). However, personal constructs still are viewed as central structures underlying social perception processes (e.g., social inference and evaluation, perspective-taking, impression organization) and thus a central foundation for the formulation of communication strategies.

INTERACTION GOALS AND THE "DEFINITION OF THE SITUATION"

While previous research has consistently found direct relationships between interpersonal construct system development and communication behavior, it has led also to a theoretical explanation for that relationship that is somewhat more complex. It is an extremely suggestive explanation for investigation of ties between personal constructs, communication, and the development of interpersonal relationships—one that enlarges the scope of the theory and enables it to address many of the limitations of current approaches to relationship development.[1]

In this view, communication behavior is most directly influenced by situated communication-relevant beliefs organized within the interactant's "definition of the situation." One usually has some expected definition as one enters the situation that is modified as one accommodates to the behavior of others. Included in this changing definition are impressions of self and other, a definition of the relationship that exists with the other, and beliefs about type of context, expectations for behavior in that context, and the like. Also included either as explicit intentions or tacitly embedded in beliefs about self, other, and/or the situation, are identity, relational, and instrumental interaction goals (Clark & Delia, 1979). Moreover, the interactant typically has some beliefs about his or her partner's definition of the situation (e.g., the other's impression of him or her, self-concept, goals).[2]

Not all beliefs embodied in situational definitions are communication-relevant. Only those that suggest interaction goals means of achieving and/ or obstacles to those goals and hence have implications for strategic behavior are relevant. That Joe's socks do not match and that I believe him to be sloppy may not be relevant for strategic behavior designed to persuade him to loan his Mercedes. On the other hand much of the person knowledge acquired through application of personal constructs is communication-relevant. Moreover, differences in the quality of person knowledge produced by application of a more differentiated, integrated construct system should enable the individual to recognize more of what could or should be influencing their goals and strategic behavior. A more advanced perceiver might understand that Joe's socks are part of general behavior pattern that reflects not only sloppiness but a desire to be seen as nonmaterialistic. That information, unavailable to a less integrative perceiver, could be relevant to the persuasive effort. More advanced person knowledge can affect not only how interaction goals are pursued but what goal(s) are perceived. If the persuader understands that Joe feels his friends are more attracted to his possessions than to him, the persuader would understand that in addition to trying to persuade Joe it would be good to reassure Joe that their friendship is not materially based. Such understandings lay the foundation for a more complex, integrated, multifunctional strategic effort. It is in this somewhat indirect way—through its potential influence on the number and quality of communication-relevant beliefs—that construct development is thought to influence strategic behavior.

To date there has been little effort to relate personal construct development to the quality of situated communication-relevant beliefs (cf. O'Keefe et al., 1983). Some previous research has indirectly addressed the issue by asking subjects to provide rationales for the strategies they employ (e.g., Applegate, 1980a, 1980b, 1982b). Such rationales display the goals that inform behavior and beliefs about self, others, situation and the like, which are perceived as useful or obstructive to goal attainment. These studies show that individuals with more advanced interpersonal construct systems more consistently tend to (1) point to beliefs about the subjective perspectives of others (e.g., their self-image, perception of the subject, feelings) as influential in strategic organization; and (2) recognize multiple goals in the situation (e.g., spontaneously indicate that identity and relationship goals were also influential in the formulation of persuasive strategies).

Future research that (1) directly examines the impact of differences in the quality of person knowledge produced by construct system development on communication-relevant beliefs (of which interaction goals are themselves a subset) and (2) casts analysis of strategic behavior in terms of the multiple implicit and explicit functions it fulfills can enlarge the scope of our analysis of communication in at least two ways. First, we take seriously the multi-functional nature of communication and orient toward strategic *complexity* and *integration* as important variables for research. Here the concern is not the degree of listener-adaptation or self-disclosure evidenced in the form of a particular strategy but rather the extent to which that strategy and others employed in the situation reflect an integrated effort to meet the multiple implicit and explicit identity relational and instrumental goals presented by/perceived in the situation (e.g., relative sophistication in organizing a strategic effort so as to persuade a peer to reform his drinking behavior while maintaining the existing supportive, equalitarian relationship, and without spoiling his self-image as a good parent).

Obviously situations vary in the types and number of goals and obstacles they present. Similarly, individuals will vary in the typical types and number of goals and obstacles they typically perceive as present and in their ability to construct integrated strategic responses to what they perceive. It is just those individual differences that we now study in their own right as they are influenced by construct system development.

Second this framework points to strategic *flexibility* as a central feature of communication ability. Obviously, when we consider the variety of goals interactants have and the variation in situational constraints they confront we recognize that no one form of strategy is consistently functional. At times tying persuasive requests to the individual needs of the persuade (i.e., being highly listener-adaptive) may be less sensible than simply issuing a command. Similarly, having the strategic skills necessary to self-disclose appropriately does not preclude recognizing the need to "stonewall" information skillfully at times.

Individual differences in strategic flexibility should be expected not only in behavior across contexts but also within contexts as interactants' are confronted with new information requiring strategic accommodation. Such variations in behavior within and across situations are common and reflect ability to range across the possible levels/types of persuasive, identity management, and relational strategies to accomplish situated goals. Such flexibility as a product of development is suggested in Werner's principle of "developmental stratification" (the ability to operate at different levels depending on situational demands). It argues for accepting Tschudi and Rommetiveit's (1982) suggestion that Kelly's sociality corollary might (and we would argue should) be interpreted as meaning, "To extent that one person construes the construction process of another, he may, *if he so chooses,* play a role in a social process involving the other" (p. 257). That choice, implemented in strategic behavior, will be a product of goals and other communication-relevant beliefs embodied in the individual's definition of the situation.

We have suggested application of this conception of personal constructs, interaction goals, and strategic organization would be useful for researchers interested in a analysis of relationship development. We now attempt to make good that claim.

AN APPLICATION TO RELATIONSHIP RESEARCH

Longitudinal studies of different types of relationships examining the effect of interpersonal construct system development on communication-relevant beliefs/goals and strategic behavior can address systematically the implicit, multipathed, accommodative features of relationship development outlined here. Direct examination of relationship relevant goals and beliefs can define the multiple trajectories of relationships. Leichty's (1983) comparison of attributions to friendship and supervisor-subordinate relationships suggests, for example, that in work relationships (unlike friendships) subordinates incorporate almost no "person-centered" qualities (e.g., mutual emotional support, self-concept validation, partners' personal qualities) in their descriptions of the focus of the relationship regardless of the length of association with the supervisor. Yet comparison across the two types of relationships reflect similar levels of relational satisfaction. The results suggest different paths as well as different determinants of development. Such differences can only be captured through direct examination of relationship relevant goals and beliefs embodied in situational definitions.

Study of group and individual differences in the paths and determinants of particular types of relationship development related to social cognitive and communicative skill in producing more functionally complex, integrated, and flexible strategic behavior is another important area of research. The development of many types of relationships (those heavily scripted by straightforward, simple cultural and institutional norms) may be unaffected by differences in development. However, in less scripted relationships the quality of personal constructs and person knowledge may affect the nature of development. Leichty (1983) found that while offering activity-centered and instrumental goals for friendships, more advanced perceivers tended over time to incorporate person-centered (see above) goals as well. The latter goals were seldom included in the relational attributions of their less advanced peers. In Burke and Springer's (1981) study construct differentiation related significantly to the variability of behavioral intentions toward friends and roommates. More generally, advanced perceivers evidence greater explicit concern for relationship maintenance/development in their definitions of communicate situations (Applegate, 1980b, 1982a). Research in this area is limited and very exploratory, but encourages further investigation of relationship between personal construct development and the types of goals and information that individuals define as relevant to relationship development.

In addition, some past research defining the role of personal construct quality in social perception processes suggests possible individual differences in determinants of relationship development. For example, differentiated perceivers are less reliant on global evaluations in the organization of their beliefs about others (O'Keefe & Delia, 1981; O'Keefe, 1980). This may explain in part Burke and Springer's (1981) finding that increasingly global evaluations of relational partners (liking) is a less salient determinant of relationship development for differentiated perceivers.

Other impression-formation research has related construct development and ability to integrate inconsistent information to accommodate to basic differences in values and background between self and others, and to less use of simplifying social schemes in understanding patterns of interpersonal relationships (see Delia et al., 1982). These findings alone suggest at least two important questions for research on relational development. Do these abilities to accommodate to inconsistencies and dissimilarities in others reduce the salience of "similarity" as a determinant of development, or at the least orient more advanced perceivers to different types of similarity? Second, does construct development produce relational definitions and goals (especially in institutional settings) that are more frequently at variance with cultural/institutional norms (i.e., are less scripted)?

Such research questions, examining the effects of personal constructs on the nature of communication-relevant (and more specifically relationship relevant) beliefs are one important part of a constructivist agenda for research on relationship development. A second, equally important item is analysis of communication behavior itself.

The same methods of strategy elicitation and analysis used successfully to identify the quality of persuasive, comforting, and referential efforts individually can be used to assess differences in the degree to which and the ways in which relational goals are addressed in strategic messages. Typically such goals will be implicit features of multifunctional messages. The findings of Applegate (1980b, 1982a) and Kline (1981) suggest systematic relationships between construct development, interaction goals, and the formulation of more complex strategic efforts that incorporate relationship and identity goals as implicit features of persuasive messages. Continued examination of relationship development in the context of multifunctional messages will allow researchers to capture its implicit accomplishment in everyday talk and assess the impact of individual differences in ability to construct complex and integrated messages on that process. Moreover, differences in the degree to which individuals and social groups explicitly address relational concerns becomes, in itself, an interesting relational variable (see Komarovsky, 1962; Philipsen, 1975).

Multifunctional analyses also allow researchers to assess the impact of differences in strategic skill in pursuing other communicative goals on relational development. Clark (1979) has shown how relational concerns affect the form of persuasive strategies. Conversely, differences in the way impressions are managed, comfort is offered, persuasive goals are pursued, and/or information is transmitted should be expected to dramatically affect relationships between individuals—often in ways at odds with their particular relational goals. Differences in strategic ability in these areas has been related to construct development. However, their implications for relationship development have not been addressed.

Let us conclude with one final advantage of this particular constructivist conception of relationships. It focuses attention on individual differences in strategic flexibility in (1) accommodating to the variety of goals that emerge across and within relationships and (2) negotiating conflicts between the relational expectations of self, others, and those embedded in cultural and institutional contexts. There is no more important variable for research examining relationship development.

Explorations of the contribution of interpersonal construct system development on this accommodative skill are called for. Given the demonstrated relation of construct quality to perspective-taking, ability to integrate diverse and inconsistent information about people, listener-adaptive communication skills, and awareness of communication-relevant cultural rules outlined previously, relationships between strategic flexibility and construct differentiation, abstractness, integration, permeability, and comprehensiveness should be expected.

However, research on flexibility and accommodation must not neglect the ways in which exposure to varieties of relationships, immersion in relational conflicts, and confrontation with particular behavior patterns serve to alter relational goals and definitions, the application of constructs, and ultimately the content and structure of the construct system itself. The effect of contexts and communication on individuals' self-concepts, constructs for perceiving others, and their relational definitions and goals has been neglected in research on relationship development. A focus on the causes and effects of strategic flexibility and accommodation will at least allow researchers to address the issue.

This application of constructivist theory to the study of relationship development is admittedly brief and speculative. Nevertheless, the general success of the theory in establishing relationships between construct development and a variety of social perception and communication processes, the encouraging results of recent exploratory research on relationship development, and the conceptual tools if offers for tackling the limitations of traditional research on relationships argue for its viability as an alternate framework within which to cast future research. It ties competent relationship management to the development of (1) social cognitive skills producing situational definitions with a more complex and integrated understanding of communication-relevant factors and (2) the ability to construct more integrated and flexible strategic responses to others in the negotiation of the implicit and explicit instrumental, identity *and* relational goals of situated actors.

NOTES

1. In analysis of this issue and its implications for relationship research we are indebted to B. O'Keefe and Delia (1982) for the insights provided by their general exploration of relationships between social cognition and message production.

2. Several researchers (e.g., Laing et al., 1966) have shown metacognition to operate at even more abstract levels involving assessments of "what I think you think *I* think," "what I think you think I think you think," and the like.

REFERENCES

Ajzen I. Information processing approaches to interpersonal attraction. In S.W. Duck (Ed.), *Theory and practice in interpersonal attraction.* New York: Academic Press, 1977.

Altman, I. & Taylor, D. *Social penetration: The development of interpersonal relationships.* Chicago: Holt, Rinehart and Winston, 1973.

Applegate, J.L. Person and position-centered teacher communication in a day-care center: A case study triangulating interview and naturalistic methods. In N.K. Denzin (Ed.) *Studies in symbolic interaction* (vol. 3). Greenwich, CT: JAI Press, 1980. (a)

Applegate, J.L. Adaptive communication in educational contexts: A study of teachers' communicative strategies. *Communication Education,* 1980, *29,* 158-170. (b)

Applegate, J.L. The impact of construct system development on communication and impression formation in persuasive contexts. *Communication Monographs,* 1982, *49,* 277-289. (a)

Applegate, J.L. *Construct system development and identity-management skills in persuasive contexts.* Paper presented at the meeting of the Western Speech Communication Association, Denver, 1982. (b)

Applegate, J.L. *Constructs, interaction goals, and communication in relationship development.* Paper presented to the Fourth International Congress on Personal Construct Psychology, Boston, 1983.

Applegate, J.L., Burke, J.A., Burleson, B.R., Delia J.G., & Kline, S.L. Reflection-enhancing parental communication. In I.E. Sigel (Ed.) *Parental belief systems: The psychological consequences for children.* Hillsdale, NJ: Erlbaum, forthcoming.

Applegate, J.L. & Delia J.G. Person-centered speech, psychological development, and the contexts of language usage. In R. St. Clair & H. Giles (Eds.) *The social and psychological contexts of language.* Hillsdale, NJ: Erlbaum, 1980.

Athay, M. & Darley, J.M. Toward an interaction-centered theory of personality. In N. Cantor & J.F. Kihlstrom (Eds.) *Personality, cognition, and social interaction*. Hillsdale, NJ: Erlbaum, 1981.

Ball, D.W. The definition of the situation: Some theorectical and methodological consequences of taking W.I. Thomas seriously. *Journal for the Theory of Social Behavior*, 1972, *2*, 61-82.

Berger, C.R., & Roloff, M.E. Thinking about friends and lovers: Social cognition and relational trajectories. In M.E. Roloff & C.R. Berger (Eds.) *Social cognition and communication*. Beverly Hills, Sage, 1982.

Bernstein B. *Class, codes, and control: Theoretical studies towards sociology of language* (Rev. ed.). New York: Schocken Books, 1974.

Blumer, H. *Symbolic interactionism: Perspective and method*. Englewood Cliffs, NJ: Prentice-Hall, 1969.

Brown, P. & Levinson, S. Universals in language usage: Politeness phenomena. In E.N. Goody (Ed.), *Questions and politeness: Strategies in social interaction*. Cambridge: Cambridge University Press, 1978.

Bruner, J.S., & Tagiuri, R. Person perception. In G. Lindsay (Ed.) *Handbook of social psychology* (vol. 2). Reading, MA: Addison-Wesley, 1954.

Burke, J.A., & Springer, E.V. *Roommate relations: On the variability of behavioral intentions*. Paper presented at the meeting of International Communication Association, Minneapolis, 1981.

Burleson, B.R. The development of comforting skills in childhood and adolescence. *Child Development*, 1982, *53*, 1578-1588.

Clark, R.A. The impact on selection of persuasive strategies of self interest and desire for liking. *Communication Monographs*, 1979, *46*, 257-273.

Clark, R.A., & Delia, J.G. Cognitive complexity, social perspective-taking and functional persuasive skills in second to ninth-grade children. *Human Communication Research*, 1977, *3*, 128-134.

Clark, R.A. & Delia, J.G. Topoi and rhetorical competence. *Quarterly Journal of Speech*, 1979, *65*, 187-206.

Cohen, C.E. Goals and schemata in person perception: Making sense from the behavior stream. In N. Cantor & J.F. Kihlstrom (Eds.), *Personality cognition and social interaction*. Hillsdale, NJ Erlbaum, 1981.

Crockett, W.H., & Friedman, P. Theoretical explorations of the processes of initial interactions. *Western Journal of Speech Communication*, 1980, *44*, 86-92.

Deaux, K. Looking at behavior. *Personality and Social Psychology Bulletin*, 1978, *4*, 207-211.

Delia, J.G. Some tentative thoughts concerning the study of interpersonal relationships and their development. *Western Journal of Speech Communication*, 1980, *44*, 97-103.

Delia, J.G. & Clark, R.A. Cognitive complexity, social perception, and the development of listener-adaptive communication in six-, eight-, ten-, and twelve-year-old boys. *Communication Monographs*, 1977, *44*, 326-345.

Delia, J.G., Kline, S.L., & Burleson, B.R. The development of persuasive communication strategies in kindergarteners through twelfth-graders. *Communication Monographs*, 1979, *46*, 241-256.

Delia, J.G., O'Keefe, B.J., & O'Keefe, D.J. The constructivist approach to communication. In Frank E.X. Dance (Ed.) *Human communication theory*. New York: Harper & Row, 1982.

Derlega, V.J. & Grzelak, J. Appropriateness of self-disclosure. In Gordon Chelune (Ed.) *Self-disclosure*. San Francisco: Jossey-Bass, 1979.

Dickens, W.J. & Perlman, D. Friendship over the life-cycle. In S. Duck & R. Gilmour (Eds.) *Personal relationships 2: Developing personal relationships.* New York: Academic Press, 1981.

Duck S. *Personal relationships and personal constructs: A study of friendship formation:* New York: John Wiley, 1973.

Duck, S. Interpersonal communication in developing acquaintance. In G.R. Miller (Ed.) *Explorations in interpersonal communication.* Beverly Hills, CA: Sage, 1976.

Duck, S.W. Personal relationships research in the 1980's: Towards an understanding of complex human sociality. *Western Journal of Speech Communication,* 1980, *44,* 114-119.

Duck S.W. (Ed.), *Personal relationships 4: Dissolving personal relationships.* New York: Academic Press, 1982. (a)

Duck, S.W. A topography of relationship disengagement and dissolution. In S.W. Duck (Ed.) *Personal relationship 4: Dissolving personal relationships.* New York: Academic, 1982. (b)

Duck S.W. *Attraction, acquaintance, filtering and communication . . . but not necessarily in that order.* Paper presented to the Fourth International Congress on Personal Construct Psychology, Boston, 1983.

Duck S.W., Miell, D.E., & Miell, D.K. Social cognitive and communicative aspects of relationship growth and decline. In H.E. Sypher & J.L. Applegate (Eds.) *Interpersonal communication in children and adults.* Beverly Hills, CA: Sage, forthcoming.

Hale, C.L. Cognitive complexity-simplicity as a determinant of communication effectiveness. *Communication Monographs,* 1980, *47,* 304-311.

Hale, C.L. An investigation of the relationship between cognitive complexity and listener-adapted communication. *Central States Speech Journal,* 1982, *33,* 339-344.

Halliday, M.A.K. *Explorations in the functions of language.* London: Edward Arnold, 1973.

Heider, F. *The psychology of interpersonal relations.* New York: John Wiley, 1958.

Higgins, E.T., Fondcaro, R., & McCann, C.D. Rules and roles: The "communication game" and speaker-listener processes. In W.P. Dickson (Ed.) *Children's oral communication skills.* New York: Academic Press, 1981.

Hinde, R. *Towards understanding relationships.* New York: Academic Press, 1979.

Huston, T.L., Surra, C.A., Fitzgerald, N.M., & Cate, R.M. From courtship to marriage: Mate selection as an interpersonal process. In S. Duck & R. Gilmour (Eds.) *Personal relationships 2: Developing personal relationships.* New York: Academic Press, 1981.

Hymes, D. *Foundations of sociolinguistics: An ethnographic approach.* Philadelphia: University of Pennsylvania Press, 1974.

Kelly, G.A. *The psychology of personal constructs* (2 vols.). New York: Norton, 1955.

Kimmel, D. Relationship initiation and development: A life-span developmental approach. In R. Huston & R. Burgess (Eds.) *Social exchange and developing relationships.* New York: Academic Press, 1979.

Kline, S.L. *Individual differences in the accomplishment of face-support in persuasive communication.* Unpublished doctoral dissertation, University of Illinois at Urbana-Champaign, 1981.

Kline, S.L., & Ceropski, J.M. Person-centered communication in medical practice. In J.T. Wood & G.M. Phillips (Eds.) *Human decision-making.* Carbondale: Southern Illinois University Press, forthcoming.

Knapp, M.L. *Social intercourse.* Boston: Allyn & Bacon, 1978.

Komarovsky, M. *Blue-collar marriage.* New York: Vintage, 1962.

Kurth, S.B. Friendship and friendly relations. In G.J. McCall, M.M. McCall, N.K. Denzin, G.D. Suttles, & S.B. Kurth (Eds.) *Social relationships*. Chicago: Aldine, 1970.

Laing, R.D., Phillipson, H., & Lee, H.R. *Interpersonal perception*. New York: Springer, 1966.

Leichty, G. *The effects of interpersonal construct system development on attributions to two types of interpersonal relationships*. Unpublished M.A. thesis, University of Kentucky, 1983.

Levinger, G., & Snoek, D. *Attraction in relationships: A new look at interpersonal attraction*. Morristown, NY: General Learning Press, 1972.

McCall, G. Becoming unrelated: The management of bond dissolution. In S.W. Duck (Ed.), *Personal relationships 4: Dissolving personal relationships*. New York: Academic Press, 1982.

McCall, M. Boundary rules in relationships and encounters. In G. McCall (Ed.) *Social relationships*. Chicago: Aldine, 1970.

McCann, C.D., & Higgins, E.T. Individual differences in communication: Social cognitive determinants and consequences. In H.E. Sypher & J.L. Applegate (Eds.) *Interpersonal communication in children and adults*. Beverly Hills, CA: Sage forthcoming.

Miller, G., & Parks, M. Communication in dissolving relationships. In S. Duck (Ed.) *Personal relationships 4: Dissolving personal relationships*. New York: Academic Press, 1982.

Miller, G., & Steinberg, M. *Between people: A new analysis of interpersonal communication*. Palo Alto, CA: Science Research Associates, 1975.

Morton, T., & Douglas, M. Growth of relationships. In S. Duck & R. Gilmour (Eds.) *Personal relationships 2: Developing personal relationships*. New York: Academic Press, 1981.

O'Keefe, B.J. & Delia, J.G. Construct comprehensiveness and cognitive complexity as predictors of the number and strategic adaptation of arguments and appeals in a persuasive message. *Communication Monographs*, 1979, *46*, 231-240.

O'Keefe, B.J. & Delia, J.G. Impression formation processes and message production. In M.E. Roloff & C.R. Berger (Eds.) *Social cognition and communication*. Beverly Hills, CA: Sage, 1982.

O'Keefe, B.J. Delia, J.G. & O'Keefe, D.J. Interaction analysis and the analysis of interactional organization. In N.K. Denzin (Ed.) *Studies in symbolic interaction* (vol. 3), Greenwich, CT: JAI Press, 1980.

O'Keefe, B.J., Murphy, M., Meyers, R., & Babrow, A. *The development of persuasive communication skills: The influence of developments in interpersonal constructs on the ability to generate communication-relevant beliefs and on level of persuasive strategy*. Paper presented at the meeting of the International Communication Association, Dallas, 1983.

O'Keefe, D.J. The relationship of attitudes and behavior: A constructivist analysis. In D.P. Cushman & R. McPhee (Eds.) *Message-attitude-behavior relationship*. New York: Academic Press, 1980.

O'Keefe, D.J. & Delia, J.G. Cognitive complexity and the relationship of attitudes and behavioral intentions. *Communication Monographs*, 1981, *48*, 146-157.

Philipsen, G. Speaking like a man in teamsterville: Cultural patterns of role enactment in an urban neighborhood. *Quarterly Journal of Speech*, 1975, *61*, 13-22.

Roloff, M. Communication strategies, relationships, and relational change. In G. Miller (Ed.) *Explorations in interpersonal communication*. Beverly Hills, CA: Sage, 1976.

Roloff, M. *Interpersonal communication: The social exchange approach*. Beverly Hills, CA: Sage 1981.

Schneider, D., Hastorf, A., & Ellsworth, P. *Person perception* (2nd ed.). Reading, MA: Addison-Wesley, 1979.

Shantz, C.U. The role of role-taking in children's referential communication. In W.P. Dickson (Ed.) *Children's oral communication skills.* New York: Academic Press, 1981.

Thibaut, J., & Kelley, H. *The social psychology of groups.* New York: John Wiley, 1959.

Tschudi, F., & Rommetveit, R. Sociality, intersubjectivity, and social processes: The sociality corollary. In J.C. Mancuso & J.R. Adams-Wevver (Eds.) *The construing person.* New York: Praeger, 1982.

Werner, H. The concept of development from a comparative and organismic point of view. In D.B. Harris (Ed.) *The concept of development.* Minneapolis: University of Minnesota Press, 1957.

Werner, H., & Kaplan, B. *Symbol formation.* New York: John Wiley, 1963.

3

Basic Communication Fidelity

A Fundamental Approach

WILLIAM G. POWERS
DAVID N. LOWRY

As business and industrial management has begun to realize that the primary element associated with successful management is communication skill, their concerns have focused upon communication competence. As counselors and ministers have begun to realize that the primary element associated with successful marriage is communication skill, their concerns have focused upon communication competence. As psychologists and psychiatrists have begun to realize that the primary element to successful adaptation in life is communication skill, their concerns have focused upon communication competence. As education researchers and theorists have realized the primary element in social and professional success is communication skill their concerns have focused upon communication competence. Correctly or incorrectly, these concerns have brought communication competence to the forefront of intellectual investigation.

Actually communication competence concerns have been academically active since Aristotle in a cyclic manner under a wide variety of nomenclatures. During the past fifteen years, a generalized societal discontent has impacted the educational arena and produced a relatively strong "back-to-basics" thrust. This movement has reinvigorated interest and created an upward bend of the cycle utilizing such concepts as communication effectiveness (Brandt, 1979; Freimuth, 1976; Gunderson & Hopper, 1976; Miller, 1975), communication competence (Backlund, 1978; Krauss & Glucksberg, 1969; Weimann, 1977), functional communication (Larsen, 1978; Larsen et al., 1978) and interpersonal competence (Bienvenu, 1971; Bochner and Kelly, 1974; Weinstein, 1969). The vast majority of concern regardless of nomenclature has focused upon the ultimate outcome of "success" whether in a persuasive, professional, or social form. Success has a will-o'-the-wisp flavor that has varied dramatically.

Conceptually and operationally the idea of communication success has been impacted by concepts of organizational, societal, or relational norms in most of the above work (such norms are typically assumed within the form of verbal/nonverbal behaviors that are treated as communicative). Within each of the models cited above (and probably in other chapters of this book) appears a recurring but undeveloped prerequisite to any reasonable notion of communication success. For the purpose of this chapter, it shall be identified as Basic Communication Fidelity (BCF).[1] Conceptually, BCF represents a most elemental aspect—it is defined as the degree of congruence between the cognitions of two or more individuals following a communication event. It is reasoned that the communication of cognitions by one person in such a manner as to result in congruent cognitions being constructed by the recipients of that communication is essential. Many communication success models contain components that seem inherently (although sometimes indirectly) related to BCF. For example, conceptual components such as the ability to demonstrate (Backlund, 1978), to inform (Allen & Brown, 1976; Wells, 1973), clarity of expression (Bienvenu, 1971), basic speech communication skills (Bassett et al., 1978), and empathy (Bochner and Kelly, 1974; Wiemann, 1977) all point toward the essential nature of the BCF construct. Although little previous effort has been devoted to conceptual and operational expansion of this concept, it is self-evident that without basic fidelity in communication events socially successful interactions are accidental, if not impossible.

A common approach recently used among researchers in communication competence is the "questionnaire" approach (Rubin, 1982). Here a questionnaire is devised and individuals are asked whether or not they are competent communicators. Little evidence exists to support either the truthfulness of these questionnaire responses or the basic validity of these tests. A more fruitful approach would be to have other persons use questionnaire responses (Stohl, 1983). However, even this kind of questionnaire study needs some kind of validating criterion against which the evaluations can be compared.

One of the more interesting and potentially fruitful aspects is that, unlike previous conceptualizations, BCF is not concerned with the social appropri-

TABLE 3.1
BCF Outcomes Following Communication Behavior

	Cognition of Source	Cognition of Reciever
1.	$E = mc^2$	$E = mc^2$
2.	$E = mc^2$	$E = mc^2$
3.	$E = mc^3$	$E = mc^3$
4.	$E = mc^3$	$E = mc^2$

ateness or accuracy of the initial source cognition nor the ultimate receiver cognition but rather focuses upon those factors specifically addressing the issue of congruent cognitions between source and receiver following communication behavior by the source. Through the development of a "basics" approach, more specificity will be available in distinguishing actual communication problems. Utilization of the BCF construct suggests four primary outcomes are possible. Table 3.1 details those outcomes.

Theoretically, cognitions of the source and receiver may be classified as accurate/appropriate or inaccurate/inappropriate on the basis of contemporary knowledge, standards, and sociocultural criteria. For example, under certain conditions, $E = mc^2$ is an accurate cognition while $E = mc^3$ is inaccurate. On a different level, appreciation for another's act of kindness is an appropriate cognition while nonappreciation is an inappropriate cognition. This classification represents the assertion of a "social reality" agreed to by the members of a community and plays a major role in traditional judgments of communication competence. Utilizing the BCF construct, outcome 1 would indeed, represent competent communication. However, outcome 4 would not represent competent communication due to the lack of congruity between the cognitions of source and receiver. Further, in addition to the communication problem in outcome 4, the source also has an inaccurate/inappropriate perspective of social reality—a problem distinct from the communication of such a cognition.

Conversely, within a more conventional competence framework, outcomes 2 and 3 would result in judgments of noncompetent communication as a function of the inaccurate/inappropriate classification of the receiver's cognition. Yet only outcome 2 actually represents a basic communication problem—incongruent cognitions of the source and receiver. Of principal importance is the realization that outcome 3 represents a high fidelity of communication even though the source cognition was initially inaccurate/inappropriate and the receiver cognition ultimately inaccurate/inappropriate.

Thus, the BCF construct provides some insight into the potential foci of instructional and therapeutic strategies. Within the confines of this model, many psychologically disturbed or intellectually handicapped individuals are basically high fidelity communicators in spite of their inaccurate/inappropriate cognitions of social reality (outcome 3). In a similar vein, many mentally "normal" individuals have inaccurate/inappropriate cognitions of social reality yet are also basically high fidelity communicators (outcome 3). The latter group, however, would typically be classified as noncompetent communicators. On the other hand, a significant portion of the population have accurate/appropriate source cognitions yet are indeed low fidelity communicators (outcome 2). These two groups of "normal" individuals are typically classified as one and the same. Differentiation of groups would allow communication training efforts to be placed where they could resolve an actual problem. The inaccurate/inappropriate source cognition group should be the focus of educational, cultural, and possibly psychological exposure. The group having distinctive communication fidelity problems should be the focus of generic communication skill development, education, and training.

Further differentiation of problem areas may be made clear by adding components to the basic BCF model. Figure 3.1 depicts an outcome framework with the variables of social reality and communication behavior added. Social reality (A) represents accuracy/appropriateness as determined by current knowledge and sociocultural conventions.

Cognition-source represents the individual view of social reality held by and desired to be communicated by the source. Communication behavior refers to verbal and nonverbal acts utilized by the source to represent the source's cognition to another. Cognition-receiver represents the cognition constructed by another following the source's communication behavior. It is the degree of congruency, moving from one component to the next, that yields information regarding the specific nature of problems that occur in human interaction. Following are a series of five generalizations reflecting potential properties of the source that would appear to have a bearing upon an individual's BCF level.[2]

(1) The individual must have access to signals, and symbols within the receiver's framework and knowledge of associated denotative and connotative meanings. The greater such access and knowledge, the greater the potential for BCF.

(2) A source must have linguistic capabilities in order to arrange the signals and symbols in a manner comprehensible to a receiver. The greater the syntactic capability the greater the potential for BCF.

(3) A source must have information-processing skills including perceptual accuracy, decoding, encoding, neurological transmission, logic, intelligence, and many more. The greater the information processing skills, the greater the potential for BCF.

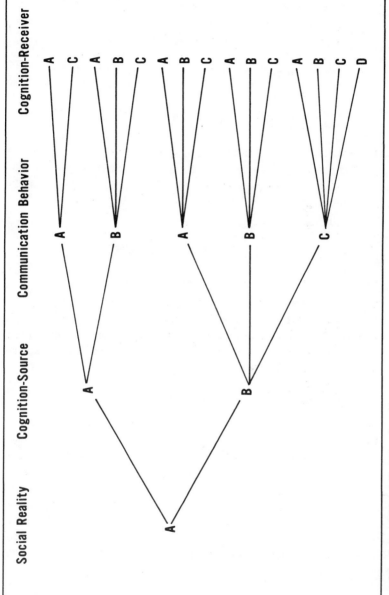

Social Reality   Cognition-Source   Communication Behavior   Cognition-Receiver

Figure 3.1   Communication Framework

61

(4) A source must have an accurate awareness of culture, society, and the communication context in which the messages will be transmitted. The greater the cultural, societal, and contextual awareness, the greater the potential for BCF.

(5) A source must have sufficient physical and speech production capacities. Should one not be able to gesture or to correctly pronounce words, a receiver has minimal opportunity to develop cognitions congruent with those of a source. The greater the physical and speech production adequacy, the greater the potential for BCF.

Given the model of BCF and the generalizations described above, a conceptual foundation has been laid for the exploration of components within the model. The following section summarizes the progression of the research program and details the most current project.

THE RESEARCH PROGRAM

Initial testing of the BCF model has focussed upon the source cognition-receiver cognition link of the model (see Figure 3.1). Two primary issues have been addressed: (1) measurement, and (2) meaningfulness. Studies conducted to this point are summarized below with a more detailed explication of the latest work.[3]

STUDY 1 (POWERS, 1978)

An obvious measurement restriction was the inability to discern cognitions in their raw form. Thus the challenge was to select or develop a known "social reality" that would stimulate the construction of a source cognition. That stimulus had to be simplistic enough to minimize error in cognition development by the source yet complex enough to maximize the potential to discriminate between sources' communication fidelity. The stimuli also needed to be amenable to objective, data-based, evaluation of source-receiver congruency. Rather than relying upon language to describe a social reality to a source, the decision was made to develop social realities of graphic forms. Earlier work by Leavitt and Mueller (1951) and Lieb-Brilhart (1965) suggested the potential to utilize connected geometric shapes. This format has been utilized in classrooms to demonstrate principles of feedback and nonverbal communication.

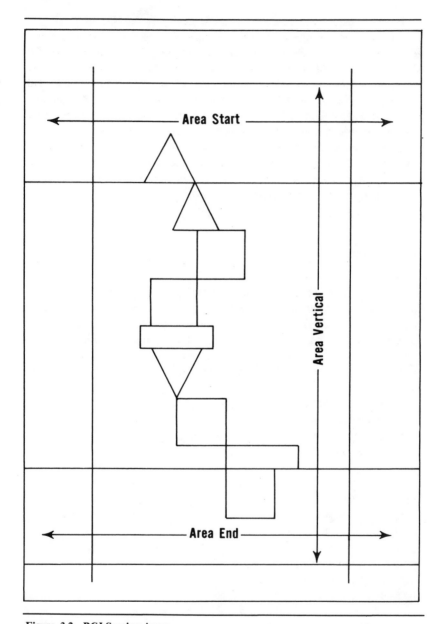

Figure 3.2   BCJ Scoring Areas

From the basic communication class 42 randomly selected subjects were asked to rate the potential difficulty in communicating each of fifteen different formats. The selected format (Figure 3.2) yielded data representing the closest approximation to a normal distribution. In order to ascertain the congruency between the source's cognition and the social reality represented by the geometric format, 100 students from the same population were given a copy of the image and asked to reproduce it on a blank sheet of paper. One student produced a mirror image and two students produced miniature versions. The remaining 97 percent congruently reproduced the format on the basis of size, shape, and relationship criteria. Thus, it was reasoned that in the vast majority of cases it was possible to stimulate a cognition congruent with a social reality of connected geometric forms.

STUDY 2 (POWERS, 1979a)

The next issue to be resolved was the viability of using the geometric format to derive data-based measurement of BCF. Essentially, the procedure consisted of (1) giving a source the desired cognition; (2) having that source communicate the cognition to others; (3) having the receivers reproduce their cognitions during the communication event; (4) scoring the reproduced cognitions against the original form; and (5) assigning a BCF score to the source.

Recognizing that receiving skills varied among individuals, the initial work utilized a minimum of 20 receivers for each source with the average congruency score representing the source's BCF score. It was reasoned that congruency scoring could be broken down into six basic categories. Five of the six categories reflected relatively simple cognitive and behavioral activity. The sixth category—"the relationship between each form"—clearly represented more complex cognitive and behavioral demands. The scoring values were weighted to include this difficulty perspective: 1 point for each congruent geometric shape, 1 point for connecting all geometric forms, 1 point for placement of starting form within Area Start, 1 point for placement of ending form within Area End, 1 point for placement of the entire set of forms within Area Vertical, and 2 points for each congruent relationship between two geometric forms (see Figure 3.2). The average receiver score represented each source's BCF score (having a potential range of 0.0-29.0).

From basic communication classes 32 randomly selected subjects were instructed to communicate the format on videotape so that it could be duplicated by a group of peers. A five-minute time limit was imposed for the communication behavior. The following semester, each videotape was randomly assigned to 1 of 32 sections of basic communication classes. Each group of receivers (ranging in number from 20-27 subjects) were instructed to listen closely and draw the images presented by the communicator. Following the communication event, receivers were instructed to complete a research packet containing measures related to ascertaining the potential impact of BCF.

Two coders were trained in scoring procedures and scored the same 51 receiver forms (r = .91). They then were allowed to proceed to independently code the remaining forms. BCF scores for each of the 32 sources were derived ($\overline{X}$ = 15.5, S.D. = 4.223).

The relatively low number of subjects in this sample produced a BCF distribution approximating a normal curve. Low, moderate, and high BCF groups were formed on the basis of a ±1 standard deviation from the mean. Receiver apprehension did not differ across groups of receivers; however, the high BCF group produced less state anxiety in the receivers than did the moderate or low groups. Additional measures traditionally associated with communication competence concepts (credibility and interpersonal attraction) were included in the research packet. Multivariate analysis of variance was followed by discriminant analyses for each perception variable set to ascertain the broad impact and potential meaningfulness of the BCF variable and classification procedures. Significant differences were indicated between the low and high BCF groups on the credibility perception variable set with the perceived competence dimension as the dominant contributor to explained variance (35 percent). Within the interpersonal attraction variable set, significant differences were indicated between the low and moderate BCF groups and between the low and high BCF groups. Task and social attraction were the dominant contributors accounting for 33 percent and 10 percent, respectively, of the explained variance. The direction of impact on credibility and task attraction was as expected. The higher the BCF, the most positive the perceptual evaluation. Interestingly, the direction was inverted with the social attraction variable.

At this stage two tentative conclusions were possible. First, it appeared that BCF was measurable on an objective data-based foundation. Second, the research suggested that BCF influenced participant receiver's perceptions of the source's competence and their task attraction toward the source. The conceptual nature of these two dominant impact variables suggested the methodology clearly involved a task-orientation function. Further development and assessment was indicated.

STUDY 3 (POWERS & LOWRY, 1980a)

To further investigate the impact of BCF, a project was conducted using nonparticipants as subjects. It was reasoned that the BCF had pedagogical implications. The teacher has a cognition, communicates it to students, and students then develop a cognition. One index of successful teaching is congruity of student-teacher cognitions.

Four advanced Ph.D. candidates in education viewed each of the original 32 videotapes. The evaluators were informed that each tape was made by an undergraduate major in the College of Education soon to be engaged in student teaching. Evaluators were not given the actual format used by the sources but were told that all sources were trying to communicate the same format to a group of freshmen. Evaluators were not allowed to draw the format. Following each videotape, evaluations encompassing each source's overall potential for success as teachers of science and math and of fine arts within each educational level were made. The average success potential in each area was then correlated with each source's BCF score. Correlations between each source's average success potential and respective BCF score ranged over the nine areas from .43 to .56. The moderate, but significant relationship between externally derived BCF scores and perceptions of teacher success based upon non-participant observation of communication behavior seemed encouraging. It appeared that the perceptual impact associated with the BCF task was generalizable beyond participant perceptions to include nonparticipant or "observer" perceptions. The relative complementarity of correlations across educational levels and content material suggested a generality of application to the educational task.

STUDY 4 (POWERS, 1979b)

This research aimed to ascertain whether one group of receivers could consistently and reliably respond to the communication behaviors of a succession of sources. It was reasoned that once receivers learned a single format, the BCF scoring procedures would no longer discriminate between sources. Thus, the first task was to compile a series of geometric formats that were all consistent in terms of difficulty, but also all different in terms of arrangement. A group of 50 students from basic communication classes initially rated the difficulty of 36 new geometric formats. Nine formats fell within ±.5 standard deviations of the mean perceived difficulty ratings. A source (whose BCF score in Study 2 was 15.1) was then videotaped attempting to communicate each of the formats. The videotapes were randomly assigned to one of nine randomly selected sections of the basic communication course where students served as receivers. Analysis of the data indicated four formats produced BCF scores that were not significantly different from each other.

Next, the relationship factor within each geometric format was then reversed to produce eight stimuli formats equivalent in difficulty. Then, 20 sources and 21 receivers were randomly selected from volunteers associated with basic communication classes. Formats were randomly assigned to sources and the standard videotapes made of each source's communication behavior. The group of receivers were first exposed to a series of four training videotapes using one source and four formats not utilized in the study to acquaint receivers with the task and minimize a learning effect of repeated exposure. The 20 videotapes were then shown to the receivers in a random order. All receivers simultaneously completed the BCF task for each source (initial test). This was followed immediately by a second administration (immediate retest). A third administration was completed one week later (delayed retest). Analysis of the data indicated that while BCF scores significantly increased with each administration, the correlations between administrations dropped no lower than .96. Thus while within-source learning occurred as a function of repeated viewing of the same tapes over time, the relationship between individual source scores remained fairly constant.

Using only initial administration data, scores were arranged in the time sequence or order of presentation. Significant differences were not indicated between BCF scores using split halves, split thirds, or split fourths of the speaking group. On the basis of these results, it appeared that a single group of receivers could be utilized to ascertain BCF scores for a variety of speakers.

The potential to utilize a smaller group of receivers for any given source was tested by randomly deleting one receiver, recomputing BCF scores, and calculating the correlation between the BCF scores computed from 21 receivers with the scores obtained from 20 receivers. This process was continued with two deletions, three deletions, and so on until only 1 receiver remained. Correlations between BCF scores obtained by the entire group of 21 receivers and the reduced receiver groups remained greater than .92 until less than 4 receivers remained. It was tentatively concluded that the size of the receiving body used to calculate source BCF scores could be reduced with little impact on the distribution of BCF scores.

STUDY 5 (POWERS & LOWRY, 1980b)

The latest study examined the earlier established conceptual generalizations regarding BCF. It was reasoned that individuals using English as a first language (EFL) should achieve higher BCF scores and more favorable perceptions than individuals using English as a second language (ESL). This would be consistent with generalizations 1, 2, 4, and 5 posited in the conceptual model. Based upon the earlier research (Studies 2 and 3), it was further reasoned that BCF scores should be linearly related in a positive manner with participant perceptions. The high number of international teaching fellows' and students' complaints regarding their communication prompted concern. Standard procedures were utilized to obtain 42 source tapes (21 EFL and 21 ESL).[4] With the speakers appearing randomly, 10 EFL students completed the receiver's task and a research packet over two days of viewing. The research packet contained measures of perceived overall competence, task attraction, social attraction, vocalic quality, and subjective probability estimates of success as a student communicating with teacher,s with other students in class, and with other students out of class; and subjective probability estimates of success as a teacher in communicating with other teachers, students in class, and students out of class. In addition, subjective probability estimates of the likelihood that students would seek out the source (as teacher) for assistance with difficult material and assistance with personal problems were obtained.

An analysis of variance indicated the EFL group ($\bar{X}$ = 20.0) achieved significantly greater (F = 10.407, df = 40, p .05) BCF scores than did the ESL group ($\bar{X}$ = 15.9). Thus the basic conceptual generalizations received support.

A modified stepwise multiple regression analysis treating BCF, EFL/ESL and their interaction as predictor variables was performed on each perceptual variable. Significant models were generated in each case. Variance accounted for by the models ranged from .56 to .76. Only in the case of projected success as a student did the EFL/ESL variable contribute significantly to a model. In no case did the interaction variable contribute significantly to a model. The variance accounted for by the significant contribution of BCF ranged from .38 to .56. These analyses suggest the BCF variable overcame the potential effect of nationality and English learning emphasis. Scattergrams for the separate groups of EFL and ESL subjects indicate the linear plots positively correspond between both groups. This study suggests strongly that initial perceptions by participants in a communication event are impacted by the BCF variable.

The procedure used earlier (random deletion of 1 . . . n receivers) to test for the viability of reduction within the receiver groups was again followed. Correlations between reduced-receiver BCF scores and the base BCF score (10 receivers) remained above .95 (df = 41) until the receiver group size was reduced below 4. Thus additional support was indicated for the feasibility of reducing the receiver group size.

At this point in the progression of the research program, BCF scores have been obtained for 92 sources. Recognizing that different procedures were used to compute BCF scores and different populations, descriptive statistics for the overall data array are as follows: $\overline{X}$ = 17.0, S = 19.603, SC = 4.427. While a normal distribution is approximated, it would appear the actual mean score will be slightly higher than the theoretical mean (15.0). The difference appears to be a function of the utilization of one group of receivers over a succession of sources rather than independent groups of receivers for each source.

As one decreases the size of the receiver group, one increases the potential for dissimilar receiving skills when comparing source scores derived from different receiving groups. It is suggested that future work obtain an estimate of receiving skills relative to a base group of receivers which must then be matched by other receiving groups prior to source data comparison. Research has commenced to standardize these procedures.

DISCUSSION

The conceptual implications of the BCF model are relatively clear. As the basic components of communication fidelity are delineated, educators will achieve increased accuracy in determining particular problem areas. Thus, the most appropriate treatment administered by the most appropriate group for any given problem may eventually be applied. While not denying the role of communication in any of the links within the model, it is evident that some problems heretofore designated as "communication" problems may be better resolved by trained personnel in specific areas of education and psychology. The BCF model will allow increased specificity for teachers in describing the communication process to our students and also allow us to focus our educational efforts upon specific links within the model (Brandt & Powers, 1980).

The current data base suggests that BCF is a meaningful variable. Perceptions were moderately positively related to BCF scores: People who do well in the BCF task are perceived to have higher teacher potential than people who do not do as well. Future field research should assess whether those perceptions are maintained in ongoing classrooms.

NOTES

1. Previous work identified this concept as Technical Communication Competence. In order to avoid confusion with the academic area of Technical and Scientific Communication, the concept is now referred to as Basic Communication Fidelity.

2. The initial research focusses on source BCF and future research should examine receiver BCF.

3. Detailed statements regarding methodological procedures and statistical analysis used in each of the following studies are available from the first author.

4. Copies of BCF videotapes used in this study are available at cost from the first author.

REFERENCES

Backlund, P. Defining communication competence. In C. Larson, P. Backlund, M. Redmond, & A. Barbour, *Assessing Functional Communication*. SCA/ERIC, RCS, 1978, p. 26.

Bienvenu, M.J., Sr. An interpersonal communication inventory. *Journal of Communication*, 1971, *21*, 381-388.

Bochner, A.P. & Kelly, C.W. Interpersonal competence: Rationale, philosophy, and implementation of a conceptual framework. *Speech Teacher*, 1974, *23*, 288.

Brandt, D.R. On linking social performance with social competence: Some relations between communicative style and attribution of interpersonal attractiveness. *Human Communication Research*, 1979, *5*(3), 223-237.

Brandt, D.R. & Powers, W.G. An approach to developing communicative competence in scientific technical communicators. *Journal of Technical Writing and Communication*, 1980, *10*(3), 213-221.

Freimuth, V.S. The effects of communication apprehension on communication effectiveness. *Human Communication Research*, 1976, *2*(3), 289-298.

Gunderson, D.F. & Hopper, R. Relationships between speech delivery and speech effectiveness. *Communication Monographs*, 1976, *43*(2), 158-164.

Krauss, R. & Glucksberg. The development of communicative competence as a function of age. *Child Development*, 1969, *40*, 255-266.

Larson, C.E. Problems in assessing functional communication. *Communication Education*, 1978, *27*, 304-309.

Larson, C., Backlund, P., Redmond, M., & Barbour, A. *Assessing functional communication*. SCA/ERIC, RCS, 1978.

Leavitt, H.J. & Mueller, R.A.H. Some effects of feedback on communication. *Human Relations*, 1951, *4*, 401-410.

Lieb-Brilhart, B. The relationship between some aspects of communicative speaking and communicative listening. *Journal of Communication*, 1965, 35-46.

Lieb-Brilhart, B. & Brown, K.L. *Communication Education*, 1978, *27*(3).

Miller, D.T. The effect of dialect and ethnicity on communicator effectiveness. *Speech Monographs*, 1975, *42*(1), 69-74.

Powers, W.G. Cognition generation accuracy: Technical communication competence. Communication Research Laboratory Report #101578, North Texas State University, 1978.

Powers, W.G. *Technical communication competence: A preliminary report*. Paper presented at the annual meeting of the Texas Speech Communication Association, Arlington, Texas, 1979.(a)

Powers, W.G. Procedural investigations in project basic communication fidelity. Communication Research Laboratory Report #51579, North Texas State University, 1979.(b)

Powers, W.G. & Lowry, D.N. *Technical communication competence and projected teacher success.* Paper presented at the annual meeting of the International Communication Association, Acapulco, Mexico, 1980.(a)

Powers, W.G. & Lowry, D.N. Basic communication fidelity, English language learning, and projected instructional success. Communication Research Laboratory Report #103180, North Texas State University, 1980.(b)

Rubin, R. Assessing speaking and listening at the college level. *Communication Education,* 1982, *31,* 19-32.

Stohl, C. The development of a communicative competence scale. In R. Bostrom (Ed.) *Communication yearbook 7.* Beverly Hills, CA: Sage, 1983.

Weimann, John M. Explication and test of a model of communicative competence. *Human Communication Research,* 1977, *3*(3), 197.

Weinstein, E.A. The development of interpersonal competence. In D. Goslin (Ed.) *Handbook of socialization theory and research.* Chicago: Rand McNally, 1969.

PART II

Competence in Specific Settings

4

The Search for a Competent Press

Fundamental Assumptions

MICHAEL KIRKHORN

Accompanied by three other reporters, the *Chicago Tribune*'s Floyd Gibbons went to Samara in August 1921 "to see the people die." When he had collected enough grisly detail to compose a vivid report of the "indescribable suffering" that famine had brought to the Russian town, "in his forthright Chicago manner" he strode through streets littered with dead and dying victims until he found a Western Union office: "Send that to Riga," he told the clerk. As his colleague George Seldes recalled, "since there was still one telegraph operator alive in that town with no telegrams to send, he clicked out Gibbons' words, thousands of them." Gibbons had another scoop.

The other three—accomplished reporters—"were completely broken up by what they saw." Scruples or sorrow inhibited any desire they may have felt to cable their articles from Samara or, Seldes speculated, they possessed "imagination enough" to keep them from reporting from the midst of famine. The unimaginative, single-minded journalistic zealot, Gibbons, captured a "big world story" that might have been theirs as well.

Seldes described Gibbons as

the best reporter of his time, one of the best of all times, in the old sense. That meant graduation from the city ward route, police court news, and stealing pictures from the homes of suicides and murderers, or pennies from the eyes of the dead if for some reason they were needed for a story. Floyd was tough physically and he had a tough mind. It was frequently brilliant in a hard way. That is why he got his scoop in Samara.

Unlike the "new generation of foreign correspondents" then emerging in Europe, reporters "who were not ashamed of a college education, who believed in background stories as well as headlines," Gibbons remained "the police reporter of Chicago *in excelsis,* covering the world as he would a ward. He was of the stuff of plays and movies. He was of the days when the legs were mightier than the brain" (Seldes, 1953).

Seldes's dismissal of Gibbons was premature, but the motive is understandable. For more than a century American Journalists have been telling each other that scourers like Gibbons should be replaced by better educated reporters who are more sensitive to the meaning of events. The operation has been partly but not completely successful: Standards have improved; thoughtfulness and sensitivity are widely applied; but if Gibbons should reappear tomorrow morning, by noon he would have a hundred job offers and within a week he would have revived his career—reporting from perilous and inaccessible locations, outrunning and outsmarting the competition, chugging through the sand on a Citroen tractor in search of the lost city of the Sahara, filing stories from Timbuktoo. Gibbons dared to go anywhere, he was fearless, he could dramatize events and he always got the story. He was a master of the lower journalistic competence—not low in a despicable way for his courage and resourcefulness were admirable, but even to his contemporaries his reporting often seemed opportunistic and sensationalizing. No reporter could be called incompetent who, anticipating a German submarine attack, equipped himself with an inflatable suit, boarded the *Laconia,* survived the attack (finding a place in a lifeboat with a Chicago couple so he would have a local angle), was rescued, and cabled his story before his hair thawed. But this is a competence that requires a large stage and is not of much use behind the scenes.

The search for a higher competence in journalism has been accentuated in recent years by critics who wish to encourage discussion of moral considerations that may be involved in journalistic practice. Journalists, even those who have been active in the reform of journalism ethics (mainly through restrictive rule making), are not always comfortable with talk about morality, which seems intended to impose new responsibilities on journalism. The demand that journalists consider the larger rights and wrongs of their practice goads them but does not seem to inspire them. One reason for this reluctance is that the lower competence—get the story first, worry later about proprieties and consequences—still serves its purpose. It is a useful purpose if one accepts the idea that too much calculation may inhibit journalists, thereby restricting the flow of information through society.

The archaic lower competence and the unevolved higher competence exist side by side—and have for some time. When Bill Bolitho, considered by many to be the finest reporter of his generation, died in 1930 at the age of 39, Heywood Broun wrote this:

> From the standpoint of the old-fashioned school Bolitho could hardly be called a newspaperman at all, let alone a leader in the first rank. There still endure graybeards who detest frills and shake their heads to say that news is all and that anything else which creeps into a paper is so much folly. But these graybeards employ a tight and tenuous definition of news. They mean no more than the report of the thing which has happened. . . . Such a definition would have excluded William Bolitho almost completely. He was far more interested in the explanation than in the event. Many had better eyes to see and ears to hear but less of analytic power. . . . Yet news must be a deeper and more significant thing than a mere recital of names, addresses and the doctor's diagnosis. Causes, however far beneath the surface they may lie, are distinctly within the province of journalism. That is, if journalism is to be a kingdom and not a little parish [Kirkhorn, 1982].

We still argue in the same terms over the definition of news. Journalism seems perpetually uncertain about its identity. The purpose of this chapter is to examine this uncertainty and to try to determine where the current debate over the competence of journalists will carry us—back to reassuringly familiar routines and habits or toward an encompassing definition that corresponds to the situation of the democratic press: extensive and varied, powerfully influential (although perhaps not in ways its members suppose), carrying on its work in an era characterized by opportunity and discovery and by unprecedented danger. Obviously, journalists must become something more than swingers of the searchlight which, for Walter Lippmann, symbolized the job of the press—revealing events and personalities as they emerged. But it remains unclear what the new journalistic identities will be. One definition of the news is that it is *new*. What is excitingly and frighteningly new in our time is the magnitude of the challenge to mankind—the opportunity for creation balanced against the possibility of destruction. By responding to the challenges they publicize through "coverage," those who control our public communication and are employed by its agencies may be able to find some more inclusive and therefore more serviceable conception of competence—a conception that would carry journalism beyond habit, ritual, and jumpy inattention while retaining the useful and necessary parts of its tradition.

If competence is defined as the ability to perform with acceptable proficiency a series of routine assignments, then most journalists are competent. Most are able to obtain information from recognized sources and relay that information more or less accurately to the public. Most editors understand the necessity of painstaking and judicious editing; and as graphics and presentation of the news have become more important, editors have included those skills in their range of competence. The framework for all this deligence is the code of "objectivity" which has many sources—among them, very influentially, Walter Lippmann's prescriptions, expressed in the 1920s in *Public Opinion* and its sequel, *The Phantom Public.* Lippmann assumed that the press would be competent only if its activities were restricted to the careful transmitting of what little information its reporters could find out. Ulterior intentions—didacticism, preachiness, philosophical sentiments such as adherence to the Jeffersonian idea that men were essentially good—would ruin competence. Even less capable was the public reading the news reports: "We must assume that a public is inexpert in its curiosity, intermittent, that it discerns only gross distinctions, is slow to be aroused and quickly diverted; that since it acts by aligning itself, it personalizes whatever it considers, and is interested only when events have been melodramatized as conflict." The upshot was that since the press was incapable of providing complete information, and the people had neither the time nor energy nor interest to use that information were it available, experts with other, more complete information should govern in the public interest (Lippmann, 1927).

This distrust of the body of citizens has persisted in the American press. Even where it has not, objectivity has prevailed. Objectivity has had scads of detractors, and even its advocates advocate somewhat apologetically, asserting that "complete" objectivity may be impossible but its approximation—fairness—is possible (as though it were possible to be fair about a question that defies objective analysis). But as an enduring prejudice—and for lack of anything better—objectivity remains the code of the American press; and young reporters and editors are taught that, respecting events, impartiality and neutrality are high virtues. Those who energetically pursue these goals are rewarded. In a section of the *Scripps-Howard News* devoted to praise for "pacesetters" who had done outstanding work for the communication group's various publications, a young editor was commended for writing "lively and accurate" headlines that "showcase" articles. A photographer was singled out for "speeding around southern California in pursuit of the latest happenings." A newspaper graphics artist was "prolific" and "a perfectionist." The city editors who must inspire and incite this activity were praised by Charles E. Scripps, chairman of the E.W. Scripps Co., for having discovered motivation: "I remember when city editors dealt with their staffs on a sink-or-swim basis. Now I see you're concerned with people skills, and the development and nurturing of talent." Maddy Ross, special project editor of the *Pittsburgh Press,* observed that the motivation of employes had been considered a "soft topic" but "in the new vernacular of journalism, motivation is not for plant-hanging quiche eaters but for tough, grizzled editors. It gets results (Scripps-Howard News, 1983)."

This celebration of adequacy and all that prompts it is typical. Young staff members who are promoted in any news organization usually are praised for being busy, enthused, careful with the facts, alert, and concerned about their communities. If these qualities summed up *are* journalistic competence, then training and motivation should ensure it. But competence is something more than adequate performance. It cannot be measured solely by its utility. If it could, journalism would provide fewer problems for observers and critics both within and without its walls who are troubled by the values journalists espouse or fail to espouse and by their working assumptions and standards of behavior.

Quite often, the wall around the newsroom does help decide questions of competence; and when it does, journalism usually is the loser. At a conference on the responsibilities of journalists, held late in 1982 at the University of Notre Dame, four panelists were asked to consider a hypothetical ethical problem in which a snoopy "investigative" reporter tries to decide whether to publish a story about a state official who had been seen along with a couple of women in the company of a contractor who was building a road for the state. Two of the panelists were Notre Dame philosophy teachers— the Reverend Edward Malloy and the Reverend Oliver Williams; one, Lisa Sowle Cahill, taught philosophy at Boston College; the fourth panelist was John G. Craig, Jr., editor of the *Pittsburgh Post-Gazette.* Craig, applying the practicalities of his trade, said the reporter's conjectures would support a small story on an inside page. The professors' demurrers suggested that they held a larger view of journalistic competence. Malloy suggested that the reporter's *identity* was a factor; nothing more than a "town tattle," the reporter was disguised by the "heroic image of the investigative reporter" and because of this aura was permitted to presume to hurry into print stories that were "circumstantial, rushed, and one-sided." Williams said reporters should be "fair and compassionate" and practice "conscious care to make the world more humane." Cahill suggested that a story penetrating an individual's right to privacy could be justified only when a "proven threat to the public good" sufficient to justify the violation existed (Kirkhorn, 1983).

By inference, then, a reporter constructed by the three professors presumably would possess the skills without which he could not be called a reporter: He would be able to obtain information from interviews, study of documents, and observation; he would be able to decide the worth of the information, write down all that could be proven fair, factual, and relevant, and pass his story along to an editor. But there would be other items of competence. The reporter would be a bit introspective. Am I, he would ask, overstepping here because I am caught up with my own romantic identity— certified sleuth for the hometown newspaper? Capable of compassion, he would have enough imagination to understand what might lead an official to betray a public trust, even if he intended—unlike Gibbons' colleagues—to write the story. Thoughtful and studious, he would know enough law and philosophy to be able to ask himself, "By what standard of justice am I permitted to ruin this man's life?" These considerations carry us beyond the necessities of journalistic work and may suggest that the reporter would operate better as paragon while in fact all sorts of useful work is done by people who never have bothered to analyze their occupational identifies, who have simply assumed them, as Seldes said Gibbons had learned to "play the part of Richard Harding Davis brilliantly." Introspection, compassion, and caring may be inhibiting. Next to the predicament of an individual who finds himself in trouble, the "public good" is a kind of abstraction. Yet journalists are expected to keep sight of that abstraction—and quite often they do, to the point that they sometimes may be suspected of allowing some vague notion of public welfare to justify excess and abusiveness. But the journalist who cares too much is a dangerously susceptible figure—one who has lost his professional armor. Nathanael West's *Miss Lonelyhearts* was a young columnist assigned by a cynical managing editor to reply to the miserable supplicants who asked the newspaper for personal advice. He cared too much and was overwhelmed by misery. The greatest of all the lonelyhearts columnists, Dorothy Dix, had survived misfortune as Floyd Gibbons survived the icy sea. Her advice was molded by hard-won understanding:

I have had what people call a hard life. I have been through the depths of poverty and sickness. I have known want and struggle and anxiety and despair. I have always had to work beyond the limit of my strength.

As I look back upon my life, I see it as a battlefield strewn with the wrecks of dead dreams and broken hopes and shattered illusions—a battle in which I always fought with the odds tremendously against me, and which has left me scarred and bruised and old before my time.

Yet I have no pity for myself; no tears to shed over the past and gone sorrows; no envy for the women who have spared all that I have gone through.

For I have lived. They have only existed. I have drunk the cup of life down to the very dregs. They have only sipped at the bubbles on the top of it. . . . It is only the women whose eyes have been washed clear with tears who get the broad vision that makes them little sisters to all the world [Dix, 1926].

Dorothy Dix started her career as a "sob sister," which is what women reporters were called if they could be relied upon by their editors to go into a highly charged situation, such as a scandalous murder trial, and elicit from the grieving family revealing information that would be refused an out-wardly hard-boiled reporter. Every reporter has done some handholding, but as a figure the sob sister belongs to another era. That blending of honest sympathy and cynical journalistic attention in the service of an impatient editor nevertheless should serve to remind us of the complexity of the jour-nalistic enterprise and of the emotional burdens it places on reporters and editors. The philosophy teachers' paragon of skill and virtue sometimes appears in American journalism—perhaps slightly more frequently than the philosopher king appears in world politics—and we should be grateful for the company of Bill Bolitho, George Orwell, A.J. Liebling, Janet Flanner, Dorothy Thompson, Jonathan Schell, and the others. But since we are inter-ested in journalistic competence and not journalistic genius, it might be more practical for us to construe the advice of the three teachers as an invita-tion to devise a *process* that encourages the development of a higher compe-tence in journalism. To outline this process, we must pay some attention to the measure of performance that journalists apply to themselves and to one another, and then we must try to describe the complicated organizational and institutional setting in which journalism is carried on.

Journalists have trouble defining the word "journalism." They also have trouble deciding what is good and what is bad in journalism. Utter incompe-tence is easy enough to define. It is characterized by inaccuracy, careless-ness, stridency, sensationalizing, and a variety of other offenses. Deliberate deception by reporters is not tolerated; neither is dishonesty nor serious vio-lation of ethical standards. The public will not see much of this incompe-tence because the offender will be fired from his or her job. But on the other hand, the combination of skills that sometimes is called "mere competence" earns only lukewarm praise. The commendations that appear in house organs such as the *Scripps-Howard News* describe the sort of consistent per-formance that is rewarded by news organizations. The press thrives on rou-tine, and when you consider how much information in how many tiny bits is handled each day by any newspaper or television or radio news operation, you will begin to see why competence in the successful completing of the daily routine is so highly prized. And the performance of this routine requires a committment that goes beyond what the Baltimore journalist Gerald Johnson once called "mere job-holding."

In a speech made in 1958 at the University of Minnesota, Johnson divided "the occupation of collecting and disseminating news" into three categories: job-holding, newspaper work, and journalism. Admitting that his classification was "extremely fluid," he suggested that devotion and not skill—not skill alone—was the crucial factor:

"Find a man who says of his connection with any of the media of publicity, 'It's a living,' and you have mere job-holder; but find one who says, 'It's life,' and you certainly have a reporter, perhaps a star."

Johnson's reporter is a dedicated and proficient performer of the art of "newspaper work." His star, however, practices "journalism." Journalism, he said, is

> a sort of emanation from reporting but it is not reporting, for it conforms to no style-book. It is literature, but a very special form of literature, one that baffles the most astute professors of English. And it is an activity so intensely personal that I set above it in that respect only Solomon's great mystery of life, the way of a man with a maid.

His examples are not from the Associated Press wire. He mentions Caesar's *Commentaries,* John Hersey's *Hiroshima* and William Hazlitt's famous report of a prize fight. Hazlitt, who wrote his report in 1822, "violates every rule known to a self-respecting copy-desk," Johnson said.

> He has no lead, he ambles. He dashes off after every fugitive idea that crosses his path, now to this side, now to that. He is sublimely indifferent to personal names, place names and dates. He actually lost count of the number of rounds, and it is from other sources that we learn that the bout went seventeen. I cannot recall a piece of writing that, judged by the accepted standards of news reporting would better justify firing the cub reporter who turned it in.

But, Johnson said, this incompetent piece remains an inspiration to journalists because it provides the crucial details and the description which tells the reader

> what happened, how it happened and, to a very great extent, why it happened. . . . It presents the event as a whole—the fighters, the crowd, the tension, even the weather. All those extraneous circumstances that at first seemed

inexcusable padding contribute to the total effect, and not one could be omitted without some loss [Johnson, 1976].

The elevation of content over form, of discernment and wholeness over the accepted stylistic ordering of facts, provide some sense of why it is so hard for journalists to define competence. They are always admiring and imitating the rule-breakers, whose violations—however diluted—then become the new rules of competence. This is explained partly by the fact that journalism in many ways is the "intensely personal" activity that Johnson describes. When journalists talk or write about one another, as they do candidly in obituaries or tributes or admiring profiles, they quite often praise the way that personal qualities find expression in journalistic work. Journalists rarely are praised for displaying learned skills; they are praised for showing the best of themselves—in a word, for having integrity and for insisting that personal integrity shape their work. This may seem peculiar, for the code of objectivity requires that the universal standards of impartiality and factuality should dictate performance. But it seems a strong if not a consensus viewpoint within journalism that good people will meet that standard and do so in an admirably competent way if they are allowed or encouraged to carry into their work the qualities that make them likeable or interesting or useful or stimulating people. Tom Wolfe became a journalistic "star" of the 1960s and 1970s because he found a way to express in his reporting his own verve and his eclectic intellectual curiosity, and the "new journalism" he generated became an inspiration and set a new standard of competence for feature writers in newsrooms across the country. The personal qualities that find expression in journalism may not always be pleasant (Westbrook Pegler and H.L. Mencken were not pleasant) and to succeed they must find a congenial setting. There are, for example, all kinds of newspaper editors—editors who are avuncular or scathing, inspiring, managerial, visionary, or technical. The success of any editor depends on the character of the publication that employs him or her. When publications change, editors leave, their previously admired competencies now irrelevant.

Roger Piantadosi wrote a profile of Meg Greenfield, columnist and editorial page editor of the *Washington Post,* which suggests the way that idiosyncracy may be transmuted into a standard of competence in a congenial setting. Reporting what he had learned of Greenfield through conversations with her colleagues at the *Post,* Piantadosi said she sometimes is described as

intense and preoccupied, curt, abrupt, even downright imperious—a perfectionist who drives her staff as hard as she drives herself. References are com-

mon to a high turnover on the editorial page, although her defenders say it is
no higher than elsewhere at the 'creatively tense' *Washington Post.* In some
quarters, she has a reputation as a trimly packaged holy terror. . . . Meg
Greenfield has been getting paid to pick fights for some time now. She is a
fearsome, five-foot-one prospect here in her office backed by a wall full of
well-scarred classics [Piantadosi, 1982].

Other sources told Piantadosi that she was "the brightest person on the
fifth floor," that she owned the "most intelligent mind of anyone I know,"
and that her "steel-trappish mind" allowed her to "seize and elicit the point,
the simple point." Former editorial writer Roger Rosenblatt said,

> [she] never edits heavily, but what she edits is essential. In a way I don't know
> how she does it—it's this combination of egotism and diffidence and I don't
> understand how it works in the same person. Maybe it isn't diffidence. Maybe
> it's two professionals working so separately that they really don't interfere
> with each other [Piantadosi, 1982].

An even trickier puzzle and a journalistic success of magnitude equal to
Greenfield is Gene Roberts, editor of the *Philadelphia Inquirier*, described
by reporter Paul Taylor:

> The intriguing thing about Roberts' success is that it is grounded on the traits
> he advertises least. There is an urge to credit all to the Roberts persona, which
> makes for irresistible copy: a mix of country bumpkin, crafty fox, and Orien-
> tal mystic. Roberts can be the spellbinder who holds court in his office deep
> into the night telling vivid, journalistic war stories; he can be the cajoler who
> persuades reporters who had something else in mind that their taking over the
> Mount Holly bureau is somehow crucial to the survival of the free world. He
> can be the mystic who is prone in midconversation to lapse into bizarre black
> holes of silence, for which the only known (and widely practiced) response is
> to inanely pour out your innermost secrets; he can be the good ole boy who,
> as either perpetrator or target, has presided over practical jokes that have
> brought camels, frogs, chickens, bedouins, belly dancers and motorcycles
> into the newsroom, and once, in a retaliatory strike, an elephant to the home
> of an unsuspecting editor; and he can be the absentminded bungler who gave
> up smoking to stave off not cancers but immolation. He put himself on fire
> once, his desk several times [Taylor, 1983].

Beneath his eccentricities Roberts is "surprisingly conventional," Taylor
writes—a careful planner and a close student of the details of newspapering,
an editor bursting with ideas for stories, but his air of unpredictability and

whimsy seems to be the ether which carries his ideas, or a means for accentuating their importance (Taylor, 1983).

All this is not meant to suggest that the American press thrives on eccentricity or that journalists are incapable of recognizing excellence unbolstered or unconcealed by the workings of a powerful personality. It does suggest how important personality may be as an emblem of accomplishment in a craft, business, or profession (nobody yet knows what to call journalism) in which decisions are made and examples are set speedily, intuitively, and imitatively. In journalism, success defines competence. The ingredients of success are not always clearly understood. Ron Rosenbaum reported in *Esquire* how Van Gordon Sauter, Vice-President of CBS News, introduced the "Theory of Moments" at CBS. The idea is to identify and seize the moment that reveals the essence of a story: "It's not a State Department briefing on Lebanon, not a picture of artillery fire destroying a house in Beirut; it's a Lebanese woman screaming in the rubble of her kitchen. It's the deserted railway spur rusting away in the desert of Alamogordo, where once the first atomic bomb was exploded." Rosenbaum's glimpse of CBS anchor Dan Rather in his office implies that "moment-think" was swiftly arriving at "the status of a doctrine" as an approach to the news that deserved enthused and uncritical acceptance.

> You can hear it in Rather's office, for instance. He's talking about his penchant for doing stories that "touch off tiny sunbursts of thought. Van keeps saying we need stories that reach out and touch people. Moments. Every broadcast needs moments. . . . When somebody watches something and *feels* it, *smells* it, and *knows* it. . . . If a broadcast does not have at least two or three of those moments, it does not have it."

Having completed his observation of the production of *CBS Nightly News,* Rosenbaum offered this conclusion. He said he felt that he was

> witnessing a heroic but doomed battle. . . . What was going on in that tiny arena was a last-ditch struggle of the forces of human reason against the runaway engine of instant information that electronic news-gathering has created. Here in the fishbowl, a small band of the best and brightest brains around are each day struggling to prove that it's still possible to know everything and make sense of things as they happen, that it's still possible to stay on top of things. . . . But I also feel, since you asked, that they run into trouble when they shift from the application of reason to moment-by-moment developments and turn to the evocation of feelings Moment by Moment [Rosenbaum, 1982].

Competence, then, involves the recognition of a successful formula or practice, and it doesn't hurt if that formula or practice is advanced by a persuasive and colorful personality.

Reporters or journalistic writers quite often recognize in the work of their
outstanding colleagues similar combinations of qualities that go beyond skill
or proficiency. The assumption is that practice does not make perfect; good
journalists are good because they are concerned and interested individuals—
witnesses—and it doesn't hurt if they are heretical in their dismissal of conventional, established journalism.

One expression of competence is the reporter's ability to recognize the
journalistic value of some incident, situation, or personality. News-gatherers
call this "news judgment"; it sometimes is argued, particularly with regard
to events that are so unusual or momentous that they defy conventional
description, that a journalistic maverick may understand them while a
routine-ridden professional will not. So in his introduction to a new collection of reporting by A.J. Liebling, *New York Times* critic Herbert Mitgang
quotes Liebling's disdainful remarks about the School of Journalism at
Columbia University. There he found "all the intellectual status of a training
school for future employes of the A & P" and turned instead to French literature which offered a truer preparation for the journalism he would write.
Liebling has been a model for generations of reporters. He was so highly
thought of that when the editors of *More* started their journalism review
(defunct) they seriously considered calling the magazine *Liebling.* His fame
rests with the fluency and wit of his style, but this style is the expression of
an unorthodox man:

> He was a scholar who could be spotted in newspaper morgues and libraries;
> he was a reporter who was unafraid to write elegantly if the subject required
> elegance; he could empathize with so-called unimportant men and women on
> the fringes of society and he could be acerbic about hypocrites and temporiz-
> ers—especially in the American press. Whether on the fields of war or on the
> attack against pompous assess in the suites of the high and high-handed, he
> was courageous.

> One of the main reasons why Liebling is so admired by younger journalists
> today is precisely because he practiced in print that old-fashioned virtue, cour-
> age. Few major newspapers or newsmagazines, and none of the television
> networks, allow their reporters the freedom to expose the venality of powerful
> corporations and conglomerates and commanding individuals, in and out of
> government, who direct or fail to regulate their fortunes and our lives. The
> watchword among modern news executives is "objectivity," which in their

cowardly signal language means "cool it." Thank God Liebling was not "objective" [Liebling, 1982].

Idiosyncracy seems inescapable as a model for competence. Certainly, every newsroom offers examples of proficiency—professionals of undoubted capability—and they are watched by younger staff members who are learning journalism. They set an example, too. But those who set new standards for competence quite often possess basic mastery of the recog-'nized qualities required for good work—and something more, the "emanation" that Gerald W. Johnson could not explain. William Shawn, editor of *The New Yorker,* knew that Janet Flanner had that quality. Flanner, who for five decades wrote from Europe under the pen name Genet, was "a stranger to fatigue, boredom, and cynicism." In this passage Shawn managed to explain something of Flanner's value by detecting in her seemingly random reporting technique the inevitable expression of the pilgrimage of that "exquisite mechanism"—her mind. He also tells us something of the creative nature of reporting:

> New information resides nowhere until it has been identified, objectified, assembled, and communicated by one or another kind of reporter; and every reporter sets out on every quest more or less in the dark. At first, there is little to go on except instinct; but at last, as fragment after fragment falls into place, the information materializes and some light, with luck, is cast. What distinguished Janet Flanner from her colleagues was the sureness of her instinct, the individual mind in which her reports took shape. Her mind was an exquisite mechanism, awhir with wit, warmed by reserves of passion. Her reporting methods were eccentric—seemingly haphazard. Facts came to her out of the air, and turned out to be the facts that she needed and that counted. As if by inadvertence, she wrote political, social, and cultural history of the first order. She looked beyond what the ordinary eye could see, and she heard vibrations too delicate for the ordinary ear. She picked up signals, intimations, atmospheres, dim forms, ambiguous voices, and out of all this she constructed as accurate a representation as we have had of what was going on in Europe between 1925 and 1975 [Drutman, 1979].

It is interesting how often the word "empathy" appears in tributes and testimonials to journalists of outstanding reputation. We are accustomed to the notion that journalists are hard-boiled, skeptical if not cynical, watchful, probing, inquisitorial, emotionally insulated. Yet Flanner was a fine reporter because she was avidly alive and deeply involved in life. Liebling cared for those who lived on the fringes of society; in an introduction to her work, *Life Magazine* photographer Margaret Bourke-White was described as a witness whose pictures "will remain as silent testimony to the richness, tur-moil, and quality of life on earth during the second quarter of the twentieth century" because she possessed "a child's sense of wonder, an adult's under-standing of tragedy and a strong impulse to share experience." Beyond these "excellent credentials for photojournalism," Theodore M. Brown observed, "her empathy, discerning eye, and agile mind created a body of work which establishes her as one of the great visual artists of our time" (Callahan, 1972).

This respect for the photographer as deeply discerning witness is expressed in other accounts of the careers of eminent photojournalists. Henry R. Luce said that only after he saw Alfred Eisenstaedt's photographs of Mississippi sharecroppers in 1935 was he certain that

> our ideas for the picture magazine [*Life*] would work. For Eisie showed that the camera could do more than take a striking picture here and there. It could do more than record "the instant moment." Eisie showed that the camera could deal with an entire subject—whether the subject was a man, a maker of history, or whether it was a social phenomenon. That is what is meant by pho-tojournalism. . . . It has often been remarked that Eisenstaedt takes little interest in the techniques of photography—or at any rate he doesn't seem to. . . . When I visualize Eisie on an assignment, I do not see a man with a camera; I simply see a man looking, a man unobtrusively, quietly, but intently looking . . . Essentially, Eisenstaedt is a man looking, with a camera as a magical adjunct more or less automatically recording what he sees.

And that is not all. Eisenstaedt was as positively curious about the world as Bourke-White and Flanner. To him, "the world, and especially the world of people, is a serious proposition. It is also amusing, wondrous, shocking, and infinitely various." And he shared Liebling's concern about "all manner of 'ordinary people' of all races" (Eisenstaedt, 1980).

In the writings of the photographers themselves, the act of witnessing may be recounted in terms that approach the mystical. "My photographs at best hold only a small strength, but through them I would suggest and criti-cize and illuminate and try to give compassionate understanding," wrote W. Eugene Smith (1969), another *Life* staff member, a distinguished photojour-nalists and a pioneer photoessayist.

> And through the passion given into my photographs (no matter how quiet) I would call out for a spiritualization that would create strength and healing and purpose, as teacher and surgeon and entertainer, and would give comment

upon man's place and preservation within this new age—a terrible and exciting age [Smith, 1969].

The ability to witness is the sign and essence of the human competence behind the box that records the images; when the photographer's humanity is shocked or offended, the camera is reduced to device alone, nothing more than that. Then, confronted with unbearable horror, as some have been— perhaps particularly those who photographed in the Nazi death camps at the end of World War II—the photographer must put down the camera, or call upon some other resolve. Carl Mydans said that Bourke-White

was often asked—and she felt the question implied criticism—how she, as a sensitive person, could photograph the stark and ghastly scenes at Buchenwald at the end of the war. "Sometimes I have to work with a veil over my mind," she answered. "When I photographed the murder camps the veil was so tightly drawn that I hardly knew what I had taken until I saw the prints of my own photographs."

"And sometimes," she once said to me, "I come away from what I have been photographing sick at heart, with the faces of people in pain etched as sharply in my mind as on my negatives. But I go back because I feel it is my place to make such pictures. Utter truth is essential, and that is what stirs me when I look through the camera" [Callahan, 1972].

These reflections may appear to carry our discussion of competence far— very far—from the toilings of the reporter who covers the court house (or the White House), the photographer doing a feature on the roller derby or the sports editor checking box scores. But perhaps not so far as we might suppose. The first half of the twentieth century was a glorious period for American journalism: Lincoln Steffens, Ida Tarbell, and Ray Stannard Baker revived and to some degree invented muckraking at *McClure's Magazine*; John Reed galloped off in the vanguard of Pancho Villa's cavalry; Floyd Gibbons had an eye shot out by a German machine gunner and, undaunted, joined Seldes, Walter Duranty, Vincent Sheean, Bolitho, and Anna Louise Strong for a gloriously romantic era of reporting from Europe, Africa, and Asia in the 1920s; broadcast news emerged; great magazines were introduced; and World War II was characterized by the daring and by the deeply sympathetic reporting of a legion of fine journalists, some of whom were wounded (W. Eugene Smith was one) and some martyred— notably, Ernie Pyle.

If the culture of a profession, craft, or calling consists of its greatest achievement, if achievement sets standards and standards indicate the range of competence, if the best is what we look to for guidance, then the sort of work that is discussed in this chapter provides the framework of competence. Journalism in this century—and perhaps for all time in that crisis is its arena—is a row of crucibles from which pours the accomplishment which, cooled, sets standards. These accomplishments may have an undesirable warping effect (Walter Lippmann noticed the "cloud of accusation," the unhealthy suspicions, produced by the muckrakers), and the emphasis in this chapter on high journalistic drama may appear to minimize the value of competent routine in journalism. But in many ways the continual recharging of that routine, its maintenance at a high level, depends on innovation and example. Many of these examples appear first outside the mainstream and then work their way inward as alert journalists adapt them as technique. There is a tendency—particularly in journalism schools—to define the craft (profession, whatever) too closely, thereby ruling out influences actually useful to working journalists. Thucydides, Xenophon, and Caesar's *Commentaries* are not taught in schools of journalism, yet they are models for the reporting of a good many journalists, including the group of new "literary journalists" of whom Tracy Kidder is one. As they were drawn into the twinings of Vietnam, American reporters found ever greater value in Graham Greene's 1956 novel of Vietnam, *The Quiet American*, and a few journalistic pilgrims sought him out for interviews after the war was over. Michael Herr, whose *Dispatches* was considered by many to include some of the best reporting on Vietnam, conveyed in those pages a dazed and drifting ambiance that owes something both to Greene and to that brilliant prowler of moral sewers, William Burroughs, who also is not read in journalism schools. The journalistic mind, at its best, is eclectic and reaching and is not confined to narrow tradition, if only because the intrusions of reality shatter formulas. So competence is drawn together from the challenge of observing an indefinite, surprising, alarming world.

The press is the hemophiliac of institutions—"chronically ill-tempered," Federal Trade Commission Chairman Michael Pertschuk once observed, "at any form of external scrutiny" and not readily given to internal scrutiny. One of its purposes is to provide criticism and forums for criticism; yet, when its own practices are challenged, it shows itself as the prickliest of prey, defending its privileges self-righteously and at times sullenly, institutionalizing new prerogatives with impressive speed and defending these as though John Milton had demanded them in *Areopagitica*. In practice, because it is so various, the American press manages to operate with some vitality but, as the experience of dying newspapers has shown again and again, the press does not innovate willingly. It does not search out challenges and opportunities with any great energy; newspapers and magazines and broadcast news operations typically engage the world outside the newsroom only in regular and prescribed fashion; the press does not throw itself joyously into the community it serves (local, regional or national); its community services quite often have ingratiating intent. The press, as Pertschuk learned when he tried to hold a symposium on corporate ownership of the press in 1979, does not invite criticism; it does not (by and large the press did not show up for the symposium) like pressure (Kirkhorn, 1979).

There is no purpose feeding this defensiveness by suggesting that the press operates in a very complex atmosphere—and that the complexity of the opportunities and challenges that surrounds press organizations contributes to the way they define competence. Most agencies of the American press follow the understandable corporate strategy of simplifying challenges from outside the organization and meeting them individually, if they must be met at all. Nevertheless, there is no denying some degree of complexity and, undeniably, there exists an assortment of factors that affect the process that produces competence.

Every journalist knows that the most important competency a journalistic organization can have is the ability to remain solvent—better yet, to prosper. There are magazines that cannot support themselves without subsidies, contributions from their readers or grants from benefactors—for example, *The Nation, The Progressive,* and *The National Review.* These magazines make valuable and sometimes invaluable contributions, but they are not in a position to offer a large staff of highly paid journalists the security, mobility, and professional opportunity available to writers, reporters, and editors employed by the television networks or by wealthy newspapers such as the *Los Angeles Times,* the *Chicago Tribune,* and the *New York Times.* But prosperity may bring problems. Ben Bagdikian's documenting of the increase in corporate ownership of the press raises the ominous prospect of control of public discourse by a few rich corporations. Prosperity in itself does not ensure a high level of competent journalism. Wealthy local press monopolies—one newspaper towns—may find their news staffs lapsing into complacency or, in a well-meaning effort to imitate the conditions that would exist with competition, they may become too responsible. "When there was more competition," said Sig Gissler, editorial page editor of *The Milwaukee Journal,* "you spoke rather shrilly for your position. While we do state what we believe, we also present the arguments of others in our editorials." *The Journal,* independently owned by the same local company that owns the competing *Sentinel,* manages to be forthright, but it is possible to envision a local situation where the over-balancing of opinion would dilute all strongly stated opinions—as a fear of libel judgments and editorial caution already have in many localities (Kirkhorn, 1982).

Corporate group or monopoly ownership also undermines credibility. Executives of press organizations feel that they dealing with a much more skeptical public than the rather docile and apparently unified public of a generation ago. A lot of people seem to disbelieve much of what they find in the press, and the press has been trying to counter this threat to "credibility" or "accountability" by becoming (or by appearing to become) more believable and trustworthy. Corrections of factual errors now are featured rather than hidden in many newspapers—emblems of contrition and sincerity. More than 30 newspapers across the country employ ombudsmen to investigate and reply to complaints about articles. Van Gordon Sauter of CBS News told the National Press Club that even with 57 lawsuits outstanding, he felt that CBS's credibility was high and that "sustaining that credibility is the most important thing we do" (C-Span, 1983). The institutional competence attached to credibility—truthfulness, accuracy, thoroughness—is reinforced also by internal press critics, a few of which are working for news organizations in the United States; by journals of press criticism such as *Columbia Journalism Review, WJR,* and *The Quill;* by independent press critics such as Bagdikian and Michael Arlen; and by codes of ethics, widely adopted or revised during the crisis of public confidence which brought about considerable self-scrutiny by the press in the early- to mid-1970s.

Quite often the most provoking criticism comes from outspoken former insiders. Bagdikian was a *Washington Post* editor; and in a speech delivered at the 1982 convention of the American Newspaper Publishers Association, Kurt M. Luedtke (former executive editor of the *Detroit Free Press* and scriptwriter for "Absence of Malice") attacked the newspapers for claiming "special privilege" without displaying any true sense of responsibility toward the society that entrusts the press with that privilege.

"Now you are forever inventing new rights and privileges for yourselves, the assertion of which is so insolent that you apparently feel compelled—as I certainly would—to wrap them in the robes of some imaginary public duty and claim that you are acting on my behalf," Luedtke told the publishers.

> Meantime, we have bred a whole generation of newspaper people who without apparent difficulty hold simultaneously in their heads the notions that they are armed with a mandate from the public and are accountable to no one save you. You ride whichever horse suits you in the situation until eventually you are persuaded that whatever you choose to do with your newspaper is somehow done in the service of the Republic. . . .

The publication of a newspaper is in itself a pretentious act: It should come with a daily apology. We are met instead with your firm insistence that you must be uncontrolled so that you can perform—unbidden—an essential public service which is so essential that the people for whom it is being performed must not be allowed to control it. That is wonderfully circular but not very endearing. Such thinking must inevitably lead to arrogance, and it has [Luedtke, 1982].

"By a reasonable standard," Luedtke said, "the American daily print press turns in a performance that is simply competent." But it tends to dismiss or ignore its critics and it produces newspapers "for people as you think they ought to be, not as they are." Americans, Luedtke said, "are hungry for information, material that they can put to use in their immediate lives," but instead of providing it, the newspapers devote attention to goings on in governmental buildings where "Monday through Friday, some tax-supported something or other is staging an event for you to cover with whoever happens to be available. It looks like news, it feels like news and nobody reads it. Creating detailed information which the reader can actually use is substantially more costly in both time and newsprint" (Luedtke, 1982).

Many of Luedtke's fellow journalists would consider his scolding of the publishers to be unnecessarily harsh, but other featured speakers at the convention seemed to agree that the organizational competence of the press was flawed by an unwillingness or inability on the part of journalists to truly understand who the readers are and what they need from journalism. Ruth Clark, vice president of Yankelovich, Skelly, and White Inc. which has conducted research of newspaper audiences, said the papers should offer readers "Facts. Relevance. Information. Help and direction, and then the goodies."

Your readers are grown-up—matured and changed a lot since the '70s. Those who found you irrelevant in the '70s—the dashing, live it up, 'me' generation—are older, not your main market, and many are in deep and serious trouble. They need and want your help. They want to read you because you are essential, not peripheral. Yes, they will love your special sections, but the new love affair will be built on a more solid and meaningful relationship—that is, if you get to know them and edit your papers with their needs in mind [Clark, 1982].

Seriously considered, the advice and the chidings that journalists are hearing—which, to some degree, they are inviting—may bring change, if only because they call attention to new zones of incompetence. Or perhaps it should be called noncompetence: the passive disregard by journalists for possible new opportunities to serve the people. There are some dangers. The old journalistic creed which held that people should be told not what they want to hear but what they need, as citizens, to know had its own nobility and its own utility. But the defining of noncompetence could inspire a journalistic renaissance (thereby, a redefining of competence in broad and potent terms) if it led journalists to fully understand (beneath the loftiness of some of the rhetoric) the true value of the work of Bourke-White, Smith, Liebling, Ernie Pyle—and, yes, the daring and colorful Gibbons. We need not recreate the catastrophes that these journalists recorded because the value of their work was not in the magnitude of events but in the depth of sensitivity they brought to reporting. Of Ernie Pyle, Randall Jarrell wrote, "His writing, like his life, is a victory of the deepest moral feeling, of sympathy and understanding and affection, over circumstances as terrible as any men have created or endured" (Jarrell, 1945).

It is easier for specialized journalistic publications to define their purposes and focus sympathetic attention on questions of interest to readers than it is for publications of general readership. In an obituary essay for Ronald R. Parent, editor of *Notre Dame Magazine*, James Winters recalled Parent's insistence that the magazine "reflect the standards, aspirations and diversity of the University it represented." In the first issue of the magazine, one of the very best of its kind, Parent wrote the following:

> We want to stimulate thought, to make this magazine a challenging intellectual experience to all who take the time to read it." The magazine should, he said, express "those values and insights, those spiritual and intellectual concerns, that are so much a part of the life and substance of Notre Dame. We wanted to deal squarely and honestly with the issues of our time, to address all those subjects that would interest people who feel strongly, even passionately, about Christian values and ethics [Notre Dame Magazine, 1982].

When *Newsweek* set out to express its higher aspirations in its fiftieth anniversary issue, editor-in-chief William Broyles, Jr.'s, statement of purpose sounded as though the magazine was being rededicated to its readers but in a way that would offer them relief from *Newsweek's* weekliness—its routine competence. Broyles said the magazine has "made sense of wars and depressions, presidents and popes, great achievements in science and the arts, rapid changes in culture and life-styles," but in this "extraordinary saga of five heartland families" the magazine would observe those "whose lives testify to what our country has been and is becoming. We are a nation of dreams becoming reality; this issue brings to life generations of people who dreamed very American dreams, and who found that many of them came true." It was praiseworthy for *Newsweek* to cut beneath transience and find virtue in the ordinary lives of "heartland" (a touching journalistic fiction) families. But it required an expedition from New York of reporters, photographers and of the new editor-in-chief himself, and its purpose was incantatory as well as informational: Parent could be confident of the unity of his audience however many internal differences of opinion might arise; Broyles, less certain of common interest, was summoning his audience of readers to witness itself in mythological costume, as the enduring stuff of North America (Newsweek, 1982).

One audience of the press that is unlikely to be impressed by aspirations or sentimentality consists of corporations who feel that their activities have been distorted through television and newspaper coverage. These corporations, especially those that have been willing to express objections outspokenly, have urged news executives and reporters to more carefully exercise basic competence by accurately and evenhandedly reporting facts.

Under the direction of Herbert Schmertz, its vice president for public affairs, Mobil Corporation published and distributed a booklet examining ten cases in which, the corporation felt, it had been unfairly treated by the press. The range of criticism of journalistic competence is revealing. Mobil accused the press of reporting rumors that created the impression that during the energy crisis of 1973-1974 loaded oil tankers were waiting offshore for oil prices to rise; of "inaccurately, shoddily," and one-widely reporting on the oil industry in ways that were "damaging to the industry;" of—and here the target is network news—oversimplifying reporting on oil and preventing the oil companies from replying to charges; and of doing "hatchet jobs" in which oil executives are characterized as "hoodlums." The essence of Mobil's accusation is that the press, particularly the network press, assumes a critical, hard news stance, delivers incomplete or inaccurate reports, then prevents reply. Statements by corporations replying to charges are not deliberately suppressed; more often they are ruled out because they do not conform to news policy. They are too long or too complicated to be presented in a news broadcast or they violate network rules:

> The three networks have two barriers which prevent free flow of information and ideas: the structure of network news shows, and the denial of access to non-network groups. All three networks have essentially the same policy regarding controversial issues: Namely, that the public will best be served if controversial issues of public importance are presented in formats determined by broadcast journalists—almost invariably in the employ of the networks.

The result of this policy is that the networks decide what issues to present, the format, the spokesmen, the depth, and the duration.

The report goes on to say that at best, news programs provide "a headline service," eliminating the possibility of

accurate and complete coverage of complex issues. . . . The result of these structural defects is not necessarily bias. The major point is not that TV news is biased, but rather that complex issues cannot be adequately presented within these limits. Thus, television is failing to present to the American people the widest spectrum of views, opinions, and facts. It denies the American people the tools to decide the great issues they face [Mobil Corporation, 1983].

From the standpoint of competence, what is interesting about this statement is that it construes journalistic incompetence as the outcome of policies intended to ensure fairness. It criticizes the networks for retaining control over information by keeping it in the hands of salaried professional journalists. This practice, seen by journalists as one of the best guarantees of professional objectivity, is seen by the corporation as a sort of device for the silencing of embarrassing or (for network news) unmanageable criticism. So journalists are criticized for exercising competence which, in effect, restricts the competence of the people, their ability to obtain necessary information.

For quite a long time, journalism was seen as a refuge for the otherwise incompetent—for the drunk, the dissolute, the disillusioned, for those who were waiting for careers (quite often literary) and for those who had waited too long. "One profession alone seemed possible—the Press," wrote Henry Adams. The press was

still the last resource of the educated poor who could not be artists and would not be tutors. Any man who was fit for nothing else could write an editorial or a criticism. The enormous mass of information accumulated in ten years of nomad life could always be worked off on a helpless public, in diluted doses, if one could but secure a table in the corner of a newspaper office. The press was an inferior pulpit; an anonymous schoolmaster; a cheap boarding-school; but it was still the nearest approach to a career for the literary survivor of a wrecked education [Adams, 1974].

Of course, Adams was no ordinary derelict, and the American press never has been the habitation only of derelicts. They were a minority even in the 1920s, a period in which journalism was notoriously and unfairly characterized (and not alone in *The Front Page*) as a nest of losers practicing vicarious dissatisfaction. "Essentially, he is an actor," the humorist Irvin S. Cobb said of the newspaper reporter of the 1920s:

> He can mingle with millionaires and talk about billion-dollar deals when he doesn't have the rent money in his pocket. He can sleep in a stuffy hall bedroom and write knowingly about the revels of the rich. He's living the life of the people he writes about, and his own life is altogether out of the picture. That seems to me to be the lure of the game [American Press, 1929].

Seymour Krim (1971) said the reporter of the 1950s looked like this:

> Traditionally, the average cityside newspaperman was a machine, a phone-bully, a sidewalk-buttonholer, a privacy-invader, a freebie-collector and not a writer at all—he had a formula for processing his information. . . . Newspaper offices were known in the trade as being comfortable, in-the-know flophouses where losers came to trickle out their lives.

Sometimes, the assumption of a higher competence cancels out the lower. Max Lerner, columnist for the *Los Angeles Times* Syndicate, said that as a "true reporter," confined to the facts, "I have generally laid an egg." But from the "hunger for frame and structure and meaning" that he detected in the public, he was led to a pursuit beyond factuality: "not only to know but to know the meaning." And it is from this quest that it became clear to him that "journalism is a discipline, like all other human sciences—a very demanding discipline" (The Quill, 1983).

Otherwise incompetence reaches all the way down to the present. Benjamin C. Bradlee, executive editor of the *Washington Post*, said this of newspapering: "It's still the most exciting business there is. I mean, what the hell would you do if you weren't in the newspaper business? I don't know what I'd do. I don't know who'd hire me, either. And I don't know what I'd be good at except maybe chopping wood" (Gartner, 1983).

None of this should be taken too seriously. Amiable self-depreciation is the journalist's avocation; banter is the parlance of the newsroom; earnestness is suspect and so is ambition, (except perhaps among the breathless television reporters who are always one step behind their audition tapes). The journalist's identity is a paradoxical one. Reporters and editors like to believe that they survive the flux: Senators, pop singers and con-men will come and go but, as one Chicago reporter used to say, "we will be here."

Yet, reporters are constantly reminded by their editors that they are dispensable (the demoralizing effect of these reminders is one reason editors are being taught to think about motivation), and there are other frustrations. Accumulated wisdom, for example, is virtually useless for most reporters. The uniform level of expression in broadcast journalism and in the newspapers dictates style so a reporter with 5 years of experience sounds in print the same as a reporter with 25 years of experience. And while journalists speak disdainfully among themselves about the powerful, they are helplessly drawn to power—the backhandedly admiring jokes about Henry Kissinger that persist with the Washington press attest to this.

But, unbound, as it is in the work of journalists who set the standards of the higher competence, the journalistic character will reveal a tough and likable integrity. By and large journalists are intelligent people, and sympathy was part of their professional identity long before it became fashionable to talk about "caring." It would be helpful to journalism if this integrity could be more confidently inserted into discussions of journalistic competence. But that is not easy for members of an occupation not much given to introspection, whose prohibitory codes of ethics may leave an outsider with the impression that all journalists are potential petty thieves and scandalmongers in need of restraint.

The critics of the press who have emerged in the 1980s seem to be aware of the difficulty of encouraging serious scrutiny within a press which operates more and more by reflex as the pace of news-gathering accelerates. "The press acts instinctively in times of crisis," Jeff Greenfield has said, describing that reaction as a "tropism: . . . As plants grope toward light and amoebae move toward food the press responds instinctively to crisis." "Consider it," Lerner has said: "There is nothing now which can escape us. Nothing which leaves a spoor eludes us. For decades we have been pursuing all the ascertainable facts—scorching the earth, fiercely, for facts" (The Quill, 1983). The process begins to seem automatic; mechnical proficiency becomes identical with competence. How can the press move beyond proficiency, beyond reflex, and find ways to include in its own competence an appreciation for the richness of its tradition?

I have suggested that individual competence in journalism commonly is established through the imitation of success, and that success often is dramatized for the learning journalist through the play of personality of the example. So a profile of the reporter Murray Kempton begins with a scene in which competence is being learned:

At the Democratic National Convention in 1980, a small brigade of young reporters dogged the footsteps of a man in a dark green suit. The man picked his way through the crush on the floor of the convention hall, pausing now and then to glance up at the podium. When he paused, the young reporters paused too. Then the man moved on again, puffing on his pipe and cradling a spiral notebook in his arm. None of the young reporters has a pipe to puff on, but most of them had notebooks cradled in their arms, and when the man in the green suit stopped to scribble an observation, the young reporters scribbled too. They looked like obedient goslings.

Yet, was Kempton imitable?

He is an old-fashioned reporter who knocks himself out in his search for stories and then writes them up in an elegant style that combines the pithy wickedness of Martial's epigrams with the restrained excess of late Augustun prose. He is an eloquent champion of the lowly and a tireless persecutor of the corrupt and unjust. A dramatist at heart, he plies his trade wherever circumstances have contrived to build a stage [Owen, 1982].

In his industry and his respect for the poor, Kempton is an example to be followed. His style, however, is personal and highly refined—less imitable. But that is not important. His attitude toward society, his desire to portray it exactly and with wit—these are things that can be learned and that will enhance the competence of the learner. And largely, these are the moral attitudes of one who has decided to spend his life witnessing, and portray, society.

Journalistic organizations can provide environments for the development of a higher competence by emphasizing in positive and enlarging ways the responsibility of journalists to act as witnesses and to admit that journalism is—has become—an occupation in which imagination and a morality beyond ethical proscription are factors. Gibbons three colleagues had "imagination enough" not to report from a scene of death and misery. They allowed moral qualms to shut down, for a time, their mechanical competencies. But here, too, as with responsibility, a larger view of imagination is required.

There are different kinds of journalistic imagination. Gibbons was one of those journalists whose competence was expanded by an anticipatory imagination—before he boarded the *Laconia* he could envision the ship under attack, himself in a lifeboat and, rescued, cabling a story. W. Eugene Smith said he could anticipate the nature of events and suffered no traumas from his experience because "few of them were beyond the realm of my imagination." The founders of publications quite often project an imaginative vision that defies tampering. In the fiftieth anniversary issue of *Esquire*, editor Phillip Moffitt said that founder Arnold Gingrich has intended to "create a magazine whose name stood for quality in thinking, in living, and in writing." This "simple and brilliant idea" had been so successful that "we have invented solutions to problems, only to discover that he had come up with them 45 years earlier; and we have found ourselves commissioning pieces similar to those he sought decades ago." (Moffitt, 1983).

The foreign correspondent Georgie Anne Geyer (of another generation than Gibbons, but, like him, having her roots in Chicago journalism) said in one of her autobiographical pieces that her reporting had led her through different levels of proficiency at different levels of reality:

> What we are talking about—in all of this—is a basic way of looking at societies, and then of analyzing them, and finally of writing about them. It is a process that proceeds on several levels, until it goes from your usual surface "reporting" of a society to a deep and mysterious and totally penetrating psychological portraying of it. It is a new kind of "reporting" and, to my mind and soul, an absolutely crucial one [Geyer, 1982].

If readers and viewers are to experience anything through journalism that is not transient and superficial, reporters and editors must allow themselves, and one another, to experience depths of reality. This is as important in local as in international reporting. The departure from formula journalism (more than a feeble departure, therefore encouraging); a press criticism that moves beyond worrying over transgressions to positive engagement with the responsibilities of journalists in a perilous and wonderful world; a greater understanding by journalists of the richness of their moral tradition and of their occupational identity—all of these promise a more comprehensive and more serviceable sense of competence for journalists.

REFERENCES

Adams, H. *The education of Henry Adams*. Boston: Houghton Mifflin, 1974.

C-Span, *Broadcast of National Press Club proceedings*, Warner-Amex Cable Service, June 21, 1983.

Callahan, S. *The photographs of Margaret Bourke-White*, Boston: New York Graphic Society, 1972.

Clark, R. Newspapers in the 1980's. *Presstime*, June 1982, pp. A2-A4.

Dix, D. *Dorothy Dix: Her book*. New York: Funk and Wagnalls, 1926.

Drutman, I. *Janet Flanner's world*. New York: Harcourt Brace Jovanovich, 1979.

Eisenstaedt, A. *Eisenstaedt: Witness to our time*. New York: Viking Press, 1980.

Gartner, M. The first rough draft of history. *American Heritage*, June 1983, p. 14.

Geyer, A.G. The reporter beneath the chador. *Washington Journalism Review*, 1982, pp. 42-43.

Jarrell, R. Ernie Pyle. *The Nation*, May 19, 1945, p. 120.

Johnson, G.W. *America watching.* MD: Stemmer House, 1976.

Kirkhorn, M. Media Monotony. *The Progressive,* March 1979, pp. 10-11.

Kirkhorn, M. The virtuous journalist. *The Quill,* February 1982, p. 8.(a)

Kirkhorn, M. The view from Fourth & State. *The Quill,* November 1982, p. 24.(a)

Kirkhorn, M. Barefoot on the Sahara. *The Quill,* January, 1983, pp. 21-23.

Krim, S. *Shake it for the world, smartass.* New York: Dell, 1971.

Liebling, A.J. *Liebling at home,* New York: PEI Books, 1982.

Lippmann, W. *The phantom public.* New York: Macmillan, 1927.

Luedtke, K.M. The twin perils: Arrogance and irrelevance. *Presstime,* June 1982, pp. A4-A7.

Mobil Corporation, *The energy crisis and the media: Ten case histories.* Mobil Corporation, 1983.

Moffitt, P. Esquire from the beginning. *Esquire,* June 1983, p. 14.

Newsweek, Spring 1982.

Notre Dame Magazine, October 1982, p. 3.

Owen, D. The best kept secret in American journalism is Murray Kempton. *Esquire,* March 1982, p. 49.

Piantodosi, R. Meg Greenfield. *Washington Journalism Review,* April 1982, pp. 32-35.

Rosenbaum, R. The man who married Dan Rather. *Esquire,* November 1982, pp. 53-64.

Scripps-Howard News, 1983, pp. 15-20.

Seldes, G. *Tell the truth and run.* New York: Greenberg, 1953.

Smith, E. W. *W. Eugene Smith.* New York: An Aperture Monograph, 1969.

Taylor, P. Gene Roberts: Down-home editor of the Philadelphia Enquirer. *Washington Journalism Review,* April 1983, pp. 35-41.

The Quill, January 1983, p. 23.

5

The Importance of Social Cognitive Abilities in Organizations

BEVERLY DAVENPORT SYPHER

An understanding of communication is indispensible in understanding organizations. In almost every phase of organizational functioning, individual communication abilities affect the ways in which people go about getting their work done. Communication is both a product of organization members and the process by which social action and structure are coordinated through emergent situational meanings. Social structure provides a framework for interaction, and it is also the product of interaction.

Admittedly organizations achieve goals through the interdependence of various subsystems within the larger the system (Katz & Kahn, 1978); and while the individual is only one subsystem, he or she is an extremely important one. It has become increasingly apparent that organizations will not be effective in what they set out to accomplish unless a sufficient number of members have the ability to communicate effectively. Without adequate communication skills, appropriate new members may not join or be recruited for the organization, new members may have difficulties in assimilating, present members may have difficulties in coordinating activities, superiors or those with higher status may misunderstand those who, for one reason or another, have less status, and vice versa. Role, values, norms, organizational and individual identities all are developed, changed, accepted and rejected through communication. The level of communication competence among organization members is likely to affect each of these activities.

The focus on individuals in the organization is not new. Likert (1967) suggested several years ago that organizations are coordinated through "linking pins," and the individual is the pin that provides such linkages. More recently, Mehan (1978) pointed out that it is the activity at the micro-level that produces the systematic pattern of macro-organizational structure. But even though the importance of the individual in the organization is widely acknowledged, communication at the individual level—or the skills and abilities necessary for processing information and linking organizational units—has received little attention. Despite Argyris's (1962) and others' longstanding suggestion that interpersonal competence is a key to organizational effectiveness, only in the last few years have efforts been made to investigate the various features of individual competence in the organization.

Recently Boyatzis (1982) provided sound empirical evidence concerning the individual competencies necessary for effective managerial functioning. Boyatzis found that communication related factors such as social development, interpersonal skills, and effective public speaking were important in differentiating between poor, average, and superior managers. Other discriminant factors included in his list were self-control, spontaneity, perceptual objectivity, diagnostic use of concepts, concern with impact, and use of unilateral and socialized power. Other research, including results from recent leadership studies, points to the importance of communication skills among organization members. In one such study, investigators specifically highlighted individual perspective-taking skills as the crucial variable separating successful leaders from those whose careers had been derailed (McCall & Lombardo, 1983).

Unfortunately, these recent findings, like most traditional organizational communication research, tend to focus exclusively on managers and their communicative and job performance. As a result, the communication skills and abilities needed for effective performance by the majority of organizational members have gone unaddressed. Although the literature reviewed in this chapter shows that similar communication skills are likely to influence the job performance of all organizational members, few studies have been conducted focusing on the communication skills of nonmanagers.

The lack of attention focused on individual communication abilities among organization members may be a result of the divergent research traditions in the organizational communication area. Perhaps because of the multifaceted role communication plays in explaining organizational functioning, there is little consensus regarding the appropriateness of a particular approach to research. Philosophical and theoretical differences have resulted in divergent research foci. For example, traditional organizational communication research has been criticized because of its focus on concrete, observable communication phenomena, its preoccupation with perceptions of communication climates, its management bias, and its overreliance on self-report measures. This functionalist based research (Putnam, 1982) falls victim to all the general criticism leveled at previous variable analytic research (B. Sypher & Applegate, 1982; Putnam, 1982). Network research, on the other hand, is anchored in sociological foundations and reliant on sociometric methods to understand an organization's structure. The quantity of information, the direction of information flow, and members' roles are emphasized over the individual (for a review, see Jablin, 1980).

More recent approaches to organizational communication have highlighted the interpretive nature of humans in creating and maintaining organizational realities (Pacanowsky & O'Donnell-Trujillo, 1982; Deetz, 1982; Martin, 1980; Hirsch, 1980, Pettigrew, 1979; B. Sypher & Applegate, 1982; and Putnam, 1982). This interpretive orientation, identified as an organizational culture approach, places individual communication behavior at the focus of attention. Moreover, cultural approaches to organizational studies point to the importance of shared understanding about such things as values, heroes, goals, and ideologies in predicting strong organizational cultures (Martin, 1981; Deal & Kennedy, 1982). Because social cognitive skills contribute to shared understanding and shared understandings are unique features of organizational cultures that are proposed to affect performance, an interpretive orientation to organizational communication that focuses on individual social cognitive abilities seems most appropriate for the analysis of organizational "cultures."

The purpose of this chapter therefore is to offer an individual abilities approach for understanding communication in organizational contexts. The choice of this approach is firmly grounded in interpretive orientations. As such, individuals are considered the primary focus of attention as they create and sustain organizational realities in which members function to achieve organizational goals. Realizing that the interdependence of organization members makes goals accomplishment possible, this approach directs our focus to the requisite skills and abilities individuals utilize in reaching shared interpretations and clarifying expectations about organizational situations.

Based on these assumptions, such an approach points toward a program of research designed to investigate individual communication behavior and its relation to selected organizational outcomes and human performance. The ends to which communication behavior is directed (i.e. motivation, manipulation, participation, etc.) are not necessarily the concern of this approach; the skills necessary to accomplish these ends are of primary concern. This is not to say, however, that interactional goals do not impact on individual communication performance or that they are unimportant in and of themselves. But for now the question is, "What kinds of skills are important in helping organization members understand self and other role expectations and thus perform successfully in organizational situations?

A focus on the individual in the organization guides us to more general research findings regarding effective or competent communication behavior. There is an abundance of literature that focuses on communication competence; however, many of these findings are equivocal and philosophical differences separate much of this research. For the purposes of this chapter, competence is reviewed in terms of trait, behavioral, and social cognitive approaches. Following the competence review, the remainder of this chapter offers a social cognitive explanation for individual performance in the organization. Findings from recent research suggest that differences in communication related abilities are strong predictors of an individual's success in an organization.

COMMUNICATION COMPETENCE REVIEWED

Communication competence has been examined from a variety of perspectives. Relevant research questions to date have focused on differences between interactants' styles of communicating and characteristics or skills which contribute to effective interpersonal functioning (see Table 1 for a listing). Early attempts to conceptualize competence as both knowledge and skill have influenced subsequent attempts to define it in terms of a variety of cognitive, behavioral and contextual perspectives. Several categorical schemes have been employed to review and discuss this work (Hecht 1978; Kely, Chase and Wiemann 1979; Wiemann 1980), however this review categorizes the competence literature in terms of trait, behavioral and general social cognitive approaches.

THE TRAIT APPROACH

A number of researchers have equated competence with certain personality traits or abilities. In these studies, competence is viewed as a cognitive as opposed to a behavioral construct. From this perspective, Kelly, Chase and Wiemann (1979) described communication competence "as a mental or psychological phenomenon distinct and separate from behavior" (p. 4). Competence in this respect is anchored in evaluators' perceptions of traits which constitute effectiveness, thus self reports measures are most often utilized to measure these traits. A large number of studies embrace this perspective and can be described as an attempt to isolate general traits or characteristics of competent communicators.

Seigburg and Larson (1971), for example, operationalized communication competence in terms of an observation-based category system composed of traits of most and least enjoyable communicators. In this study, "experts" rated the degree to which each category was typical of a person with whom they least enjoyed conversing. Seiburg and Larson isolated five characteristics of enjoyable communicators: direct acknowledgement,

TABLE 5.1
Communication Competence: Related Studies and Reviews

Important Characteristics	Sieburg Larson (1971)	Bienvenu (1971)	Hart & Burks (1972)	Miller & Steinburg (1975)	Delia & Clark (1975)	Allen & Brown (1976)	Bochner & Kelly (1976)	Cushman & Craig (1976)	Feingold (1976)	Delia (1976)	Parks (1976)	Ruben (1976)	Weimann (1977)	Norton (1978)	Kelly, Chase & Wiemann (1979)	O'Keefe & Delia (1979)	Delia, O'Keefe O'Keefe (1982)
Commitment to others/attentive	X								X			X	X	X			
Expression of positive feelings/support	X	X				X								X			
Clarification/descriptiveness	X	X					X	X						X			
Agreement/similarity	X								X								
Listening		X			X				X								
Self-disclosure							X		X								
Self-concept/self-role behavior		X										X					
Coping with feelings		X				X	X	X									
Impression leaving														X			
Relaxed													X	X			
Open							X							X			
Dominant														X			
Goal attainment/control				X	X	X					X				X		X
Nonverbal cueing								X									
Interaction management								X				X	X		X		X
Adapting/flexibility			X		X		X	X	X			X	X		X	X	X
Empathy/perspective-taking					X		X	X	X	X		X	X		X	X	X
Appropriate language			X						X								

expression of positive feelings, clarification, agreement, and support. Characteristics of unenjoyable communicators included responses which are tangential, irrelevant, interrupting, impervious, incoherent, and impersonal. In a similar study, Bienvenu (1971) developed the Interpersonal Communication Inventory for measuring communication effectiveness. This inventory is composed of items intended to measure patterns, characteristic, and styles of communication. Bienvenu reported the results of a content analysis that revealed four dimensions of an effective communication style: a strong self-concept, listening abilities, clarity of expression, and the ability to cope with angry feelings. Hecht (1978c) was critical of both these studies and argued that "since Bienvenu constructed the items fit a priori notions of communication competence, the content analysis reveals nothing more than the item construction procedures" (p. 354).

In yet another effort to measure varying degrees of communication traits or characteristics, Norton (1978) developed the Communicator Style Inventory. This measure requires subjects to rate themselves on ten different dimensions, one of which Norton labeled "communicator image." Included in this dimension are items concerning how effective a communicator the rater perceives himself or herself to be. The other nine dimensions are dominant, dramatic, animated, open, contentious, relaxed, friendly, attentive, and impression-leaving.

Norton (1978) reported the more positive communicator image was characterized as impression leaving, open, attentive, relaxed, friendly, and dominant. The three best predictors of communicator image were impression leaving, open, and dominant. Other research by Norton and Pettegrew (1976) revealed similar findings. In particular, they found a dominant, open communicative style was judged to be significantly more attractive than dominant and nonopen, nondominant and relaxed, and nondominant and nonrelaxed styles. Berger (1977) concluded, "The general thrust of research on communicator style is to isolate various facets of self-presentation which influence such factors as attractiveness and effectiveness in interaction" (pp. 219-220). Communication competence and communicator style, thus, are conceptually linked in that judgments of competence are the consequences of variations in communication style (Kelly et al., 1979; Wiemann, 1978; and Berger, 1977).

Brandt used Norton's (1978) "communicator image" dimension of the Communicator Style Inventory and found a significant positive relationship between perceived communicative effectiveness and task attractiveness (r = .74). The latter construct was developed to examine how subjects' preferences to work with one another were influenced by their respective communication abilities. In Brandt's study, participants expressed preferences to work with other persons after having observed them interacting. However, judgments about tasks attractiveness were based on speculation as to how the two would work together as the observers had never interacted with the subjects.

Norton's measure has been received with mixed reviews. While many attempts have been made to replicate and expand Norton's initial work (Norton and Warnick, 1976; Norton and Miller, 1977; Norton and Pettegrew, 1976; and Norton, 1978), some researchers have been critical of this approach. For example, H. Sypher (1980) warned of the methodological entanglements associated with self-report measures in general. Specifically, Sypher (1980) suggested that Norton's (1978) correlations between his dimensions of communicator style may be illusory in that they reflect respondents' implicit perceptions of related communication behaviors instead of reports of actual behavior (see also Sypher and Sypher, forthcoming for other problems associated with self-reports).

COMPETENCE AS BEHAVIORAL SKILLS

While many researchers have focused on the trait approach, a number of others have emphasized the performance aspect of communication competence. Competence in this respect is anchored in the behavior of the communicator. From this perspective, competence is both a function of social skills and social outcomes—not merely a reflection of one's perceptions of competence. Parks (1976), for example, emphasized the control aspect of competence when he described the competent communicator as "one who maximizes his or her goal-achievement through communication" (p. 1). Kelly et al. (1979) explained as follows:

> The fundamental assumption underlying this definition is that individuals who are competent are those who are able to influence their environment in such a way as to reduce uncertainty through understanding of and adaptation to the environment [p. 10].

This perspective is consistent with Miller's and Steinberg's (1975) assumption that "the basic function of communication is to control the environment so as to realize certain physical, economic, and social rewards from it" (p. 62). Such a perspective suggests that communication competence is dependent on certain skills that allow persons to achieve rewards and goals.

From this perspective, Cushman and Craig (1976) defined communication competence in terms of one's listening, cueing, and negotiation skills. They suggested that the effective communicator is one who is able to strategically negotiate with others to clarify expectations toward situations. Bochner and Kelly (1976) similarly defined communication competence as one's ability to formulate and achieve objectives by effectively collaborating with others and appropriately adapting to situational or environmental variations. They suggested the competent communicator has five skills: empathy, descriptiveness, ownership of feelings, self-disclosure, and flexibility. According to Brandt (1979), such an "other-oriented" perspective suggests that "goal achievement, communication skills, and sensitivity to both situations and other persons are equally stressed" (p. 225).

Allen and Brown (1976) isolated five performance dimensions of communication competence: controlling, feeling, informing, ritualizing, and imagining. In a similar review, Ruben (1976) proposed seven dimensions of communication competence: display of respect, interaction posture, orientation to knowledge, empathy, self role-oriented behavior, interaction management, and tolerance for ambiguity. He claimed these characteristics are important to "successful" cross-cultural training and cross-cultural adaptation. Feinghold (1976), on the other hand, posited "other-orientedness" as the primary descriptor of competence; while Wiemann (1977) proposed a five-component model that included interaction management, empathy, affiliation/support, behavioral flexibility, and social relaxation.

Despite the numerous communication competence studies, several dimensions repeatedly appear among researchers' descriptions. These are empathy or other-orientedness, interaction management, and behavioral flexibility. Following an extensive review, Kelly, Chase, and Wiemann (1979) concluded that these appear to be the preeminent characteristics of an effective communicator. Empathy which is generally considered the "other-oriented" dimension of competence, has been described as "the imaginative transporting of oneself into the thinking, feeling and acting of another and so structuring the world as he does" (Dymond, 1950, p. 343). In this respect, empathy stripped of affect is the same as social perspective-taking and role-taking (for a review see Burleson, 1982; Delia, 1976). Empathetic abilities allow one to make assessments of another's intentions, inferences and views of a situation, and subsequently this knowledge provides a basis for communicative choices.

Behavioral flexibility, on the other hand, is one's ability to adapt to the situation by making appropriate communication choices. Delia, O'Keefe, and O'Keefe (1982) pointed out that a speaker's knowledge of the listener serves as a base for selecting appropriate messages tailored to the listener. However, Wiemann (1977) suggested that "knowledge of appropriate behavior is of little use to an interactant if he cannot implement that knowledge when called upon to do so" (p. 211). In essence, behavior flexibility is adaptability. Individuals who have behavioral flexibility are able to adapt to the situational demands of the interaction because of their knowledge of what is appropriate. This may include using appropriate language, providing support if needed, meeting cultural and/or social demands, and so on.

Of the three central characteristics of a competent communicators, interaction management is probably the most important as it encompasses both perspective-taking and behavioral flexibility. As Delia and O'Keefe (1978) argued, interaction management is necessary for generating or reaffirming shared interpretations. Interaction management would include such skills as appropriate turn-taking for speaking, appropriate control over topics initiated and discussed, nonverbal cueing, listening, and other similar skills relevant to specific interactional goals. According to Wiemann (1977), competent communicators are capable of managing the "procedural" aspects of the interaction so that if flows smoothly.

The preceeding review points to a broad array of communication competence components; and surprisingly, there is a large degree of empirical consensus concerning the constituent characteristics of a competent communicator. However, the theoretical and methodological components of each position vary enormously. The trait approach suffers from methodological difficulties associated with self-report measures including illusory correlations, the halo effect, and other memory biases. And for the most part, the focus on behavioral variables appears to lack a substantive theoretical analysis of how communication competence is instrumental in the development of other communication outcomes. From the literature just reviewed, we find ourselves with the problematic task of choosing between competing explanations and equivocal findings about communication competence.

As discussed earlier, this state of affairs is not dissimilar from that facing organizational communication researchers. Isolated and unrelated accumulations of findings often present more questions than they answer. Since empirical results only make sense within the conceptual system of the original inquiry, a choice between competing explanations must be made and the scope of the substantive theory underpinning one's choice must be elaborated. In keeping with these demands, the remainder of this chapter is devoted to explaining how a more general social cognitive approach can fruitfully guide research on communication competence in organizational settings. Findings from recent studies help explain the relationship between social cognitive functioning and individual performance in organizations.

A SOCIAL COGNITIVE APPROACH TO COMPETENCE

Social cognition is the process of representing knowledge about people and their relationships. This knowledge is generally believed to be acquired through participation in ongoing, dynamic interactions. Much of the research on social cognition has been concerned with the influence of stored social categories, expectations, beliefs, and the like on the process of new social information (Higgins et al., 1981).

In the communication field, social cognition is defined as thought directed toward interaction (Roloff & Berger, 1982). One program of research within this social cognition framework is that of constructivism (Delia et al., 1982). Constructivism avoids a number of the previously reviewed shortcomings in communication research in that it offers a contextually defined analysis of individual social cognitive abilities and related interactional skills. In their early work, Delia and Clark (1975) described the competent communicator as one who "utilizes knowledge of a shared code (language and rules) to express meanings in a form calculated to control another's interpretations so as to control the other's beliefs or actions toward some particular issue, event or policy" (p. 2). The constructivist conception of control is based on Kelly's (1955) theory of personal constructs. Kelly argued that individuals rely on personal judgmental dimensions or constructs to understand social situations and thus predict and control events. More recently, O'Keefe and Delia (1979) have argued that interpersonal constructs form the basis of communicative choices as constructs are the dimensions along which communication relevant listener characteristics are judged.

Two of the constituent aspects of the constructivist approach to communication are social construal processes and the development of a differentiated strategic behavioral repertoire (Delia et al., 1982). The development of such characteristics is considered to undergird one's ability to produce listener-adapted messages, and adaptation in this respect seems to be a general requirement for effectiveness. This reasoning supports the need to investigate communication competence across situations as one might have cognitive and behavioral skills that lead to effectiveness in one context and not in another.

Within their constructivist-developmental framework, Delia et al., have pursued research that seeks to identify the constituent processes involved in the development of communication competence. Early in the development of this program of research at the University of Illinois, Delia and Clark (1975) argued that

the principal focus of research on communicative competence should be upon further probing the interrelations among the broad array of factors participating in communicative competence: language, knowledge of the social rules and norms governing situated language, analytic skills, social-cognitive abilities, listening and information processing strategies, and strategic behavioral control at increasingly complex levels [p. 7].

In general, constructivists argue that as communicators develop the capacity to more effectively conceptualize the subjective perspectives and psychological characteristics of their listeners (become more cognitively differentiated), they should be better able to produce listener-adapted messages.

The constructivist position has several advantages over the trait and behavioral approaches. First, this type of research overcomes the methodological problems associated with self-report measures by relying on free-response measures of communication-relevant abilities. Second, constructivists view the situational and/or contextual nature of communication as a preeminent characteristic of competence. More importantly, the constructivist position offers a thorough analysis of the philosophical and theoretical underpinning of communication, specifically, and of effectiveness, more generally (Delia et al., 1982). Moreover, this approach seems to be more efficacious in explaining communication behavior in general because it is grounded in theory, reflective in nature, and interpretive in orientation. Couched in a more general social cognitive framework, the following analysis draws from constructivist concepts to explain the role of individual communication abilities in the organization.

SOCIAL COGNITIVE ABILITIES AND COMMUNICATION BEHAVIOR IN ORGANIZATIONS

At the outset, it was suggested that communication is both the outcome of human performance and the process by which social action and structure are coordinated. From a social cognitive or constructivist framework, communication is viewed as the process by which organization members reach shared understandings through emergent situated meanings. Characteristics relevant to these achievements become the focus of inquiry from an interpretive orientation to communication and organizations. Among those skills are social construal processes and related interactional behavior.

In an effort to investigate the relative importance of some of these characteristics to other organizational activities, several recent studies have been conducted. While a host of research questions warrant investigation (and some of these will be reviewed later), the initial studies reported here were designed to investigative individual differences among organization members' social cognitive abilities, including cognitive differentiation, perspective-taking, self-monitoring, and listening. From a social cognitive viewpoint, these are considered among the constituent characteristics of a competent communicator.

The investigation of communication abilities in organizational contexts is important for a number of reasons. First, the research enterprise is being carried out in a naturally occurring environment where the phenomena under investigation are important. Second, the results of parallel inquiries strengthen confidence in similar findings and potentially broaden the scope of the substantive theory of which the study was a part.

THE CONSTRUCT OF COGNITIVE DIFFERENTIATION

As suggested earlier, Delia et al. have contended that cognitive differentiation undergirds social construal processes and related communicative behaviors (for a review, see O'Keefe & Sypher, 1982). Even though cognitive differentiation or complexity (as it is sometimes called) is conceptualized in varying ways, the general notion is that highly differentiated individuals are those who cognitive systems contain relatively large numbers of hierarchically integrated interpersonal constructs.

A variety of methods have been proposed to measure cognitive differentiation, and a host of competing measurement problems have arisen. However, in their review, O'Keefe and H. Sypher (1981) singled out Crockett's (1965) Role Category Questionnaire (RCQ) as evidencing the most reliability and validity of the competing measures. This measure usually requires respondents to provide descriptions of two persons—one they like and one they dislike. Although most research using the RCQ has asked for two-peer descriptions, the differentiation scores utilized in the organizational studies reported in this chapter are based on descriptions of liked and disliked coworkers. Since these studies were designed to investigate the relationship between social cognitive abilities and individual member performance in organizations, the coworker descriptions were considered more contextually relevant.

The RCQ is not without its critics (Powers et al., 1981) and potential problems. However, there appear to be clear evidence to dispel the notion that cognitive differentiation as measured by the RCQ is merely a measure of intelligence (H. Sypher & Applegate, 1982) or loquacity (Burleson et al., 1981). Independent investigations provided sound evidence that differentiation is a distinct and separate construct. More recent problems with the RCQ center around interpretations of the measurement scores. O'Keefe and Delia (1979) suggested that the RCQ may be tapping the organization of impressions as opposed to abstract or dispositional differentiation. Some persons, they argued, may be able to access large numbers of constructs because the constructs form general impressions or sets of beliefs which are more schematized and thus easier to retrieve. As O'Keefe and Delia (1979) pointed out, "performance on the RCQ might be primarily a function of the degree of organization among a person's beliefs and unrelated to actual numbers of constructs" (p. 64).

Despite these potential problems and interpretive difficulties the RCQ measure of cognitive differentiation appears to be the best predictor of respondents' behavior on communication related tasks. And regardless of recent reinterpretations of the RCQ, it is apparent that cognitive differentiation is related to the impressions we make about others and the resultant strategies we employ to communicate.

Indeed there is significant evidence to conclude that cognitive differentiation is positively related to a number of communication relevant abilities (Clark & Delia, 1977; Delia & Clark, 1977; Applegate, 1978; Delia et al., 1978; O'Keefe & Delia, 1979; and O'Keefe & Sypher, 1981). Specifically, past research has shown that highly differentiated individuals generated a greater number of persuasive arguments (O'Keefe & Delia, 1979), were better perspective-takers (Hale & Delia, 1976), were less reliant on simplifying schemas for understanding social relations (Delia & Crockett, 1973), were less likely to get cognitively overloaded (Mower White, 1977), and were more effective communicators (Hale, 1980) than their less differentiated peers. While there certainly is not unequivocal support for maintaining that cognitively differentiated persons are necessarily more effective communicators, evidence for such a claim is building. This variable's relationship to various communication related abilities suggests its importance in understanding communication competence.

The RCQ in Organizational Studies

Several recent investigations have sought to determine the relationship between organizational members' degree of cognitive differentiation and their performance in the organization (Sypher, 1981; Sypher & Sypher, 1981; Sypher et al., 1983). This research has shown that the more highly differentiated individuals are likely to be situated in higher levels in the organization ($r = .57$). Although the correlations were weak to moderate, the results of these studies have also shown that cognitively differentiated respondents (as measured by the RCQ) judged themselves to be more effective communicators, and supervisors and peers judged them to be more persuasive than their less differentiated peers (Sypher, 1981). The strongest of these relationships were found in an organization that implicitly and explicitly values communication.

What is clear from these data is the relative importance of cognitive differentiation as a correlate of individual success in organizations. As cognitive differentiation is considered a critical ability related to one's communicative performance and communication is considered crucial for effective organizational functioning, these findings are not surprising. Differences in cognitive differentiation are likely to affect the way people are assimilated into organizations and resultant interpretations about self and other role expectations. The degree to which such interpretations can be allowed to differ while organizations can still function adequately is a question of theoretical as well as applied interest.

On the other hand, findings concerning the RCQ's relationship to organizational level and coworkers' perceptions raise more questions than they answer. First, we must explore the ways in which cognitive differentiation affects job level. For example, were highly differentiated persons promoted more often or hired into higher positions more often than their less differentiated peers? Or, are highly differentiated individuals in higher organizational levels because they developed these skills and abilities as they move upward in the organizational hierarchy? Perhaps more differentiated persons understand others' psychological perspectives and subjective characteristics in a way that helps them develop better relationships, interpret the organizational realities of others more accurately, and thus accommodate better or easier than their less differentiated peers. Another unanswered questions concerns the relationship between cognitive differentiation and self-impressions and their combined impact on individuals' behavior in organizations. These albeit tentative findings provide support for a continued focus on cognitive differentiation and its relationships to competent organizational behavior and interpersonal success.

PERSPECTIVE-TAKING ABILITY

Athay and Darley (1981) called perspective-taking an instrumentally relevant factor of competence. They contended that actors vary enormously in their capabilities for understanding the perspective of others. Perspective-taking ability, in this view, is dependent upon cognitive skills in detecting and accurately interpreting behavioral cues and verbal communication (Athay & Darley, 1981).

The bulk of research linking perspective-taking to differences in communicative behavior has focused on children's development. Such studies have generally found a positive correlation between tests of role-taking ability and measures of more general social competence. In reviewing some of these findings, Burleson (1982) pointed to the crucial function of role-taking in such diverse communicative activities as effectively adapting the form and content of a message to an audience; managing the topic of the conversation; selecting the proper titles, honorifics, and forms of address; choosing the appropriate speech registers and sociolinguistic codes; and maintaining coherence in discourse (for a review, see Delia & O'Keefe, 1979).

Burleson (1982) reported that construct system differentiation, and to a lesser degree construct abstractness, contributed significantly to the prediction of affective perspective-taking ability in children and adolescents. While differentiation and perspective-taking are closely tied, they are not the same. Differentiation is a measure of the schemas persons have available to create perceptions. Thus, differences, in perspective-taking abilities are a function of how differentially elaborated individuals cognitive structures are with respect to various domains of activity and involvement. Burleson (1982) concluded that qualitative developments in the underlying cognitive structures are responsible for variations in perspective-taking abilities.

Perspective-Taking in Organizations

The domain specific view of cognitive development points to the increased need for investigating perspective-taking in various interpersonal contexts. The research findings reported in this section were part of a larger effort to investigate social cognitive functioning among adult members of a specific organizational population. The relative importance of cognitive differentiation to perspective-taking in the organization provided the focus for this part of the research.

For this study (Sypher, 1981), employees in various levels of a large East Coast insurance organization (e.g., levels ranged from 1 to 24) responded to questions about their descriptive and affective perspectives regarding a hypothetical situation involving a superior and subordinate. This measure requires respondents to answer questions regarding the hypothetical actors' likely attitudes and feelings about a specific work situation. Responses are scored in accordance with the respondents' ability to take increasingly complex perspectives of the actors. This measure was adopted from earlier measures designed to investigate perspective-taking in other situations (Hale & Delia, 1976; Pelias, 1978).

Employees whose construct systems contained relatively large numbers of constructs from which to form impressions of others demonstrated more developed perspective-taking skills ($r = .51$). Better perspective-takers were located in higher levels in the organization, and evaluated themselves as better perspective-takers. In addition, supervisors scored significantly better than nonsupervisors on the perspective-taking abilities task.

These findings suggest that perspective-taking is also an important factor in achieving individual success in organizations. Yet, perspective-taking ability undoubtedly has a number of important characteristics, possibly including listening behavior and nonverbal cueing. Perspective-taking has already been found to relate to other communicative behaviors including conversation management and message production (Delia & O'Keefe,

1979), thus the apparent interrelatedness of various communication skills needs to be more fully explored across various contexts.

One may suggest, for example, that better perspective-takers also tend to be more competent in monitoring their own behavior in such a way as to suggest that they understand the perspective of another. Other evidence generated in the program of research reported here, in fact, revealed strong positive correlations between self-monitoring behavior (Snyder, 1974) and perspective-taking abilities. This latter finding (which is reviewed in more detail in the next section) provided some empirical support for Athay and Darley's (1981) notion about the interrelatedness of the constituent characteristics of competence. They suggested this:

> In order to act effectively, people must define situations perceive other persons, plan strategically, construct performance patterns, monitor their own self-presentations and interpret those of others, satisfy role demands and enforce them on others [p. 282].

The importance of perspective-taking abilities for individual behavior in organizational contexts is twofold: This feature may provide a new way of looking at organizational relationships from an interpretive orientation, and/ or it may provide a new framework for explaining organizational communication issues previously researched. First, we may find the ability of organizational members' to understand the psychological characteristics and subjective realities of those with whom they work may influence the level of difficulty they have in assimilating to the organization, developing good relationships with their coworkers and supervisors (which according to many is a significant predictor of communication and job satisfaction), understanding role expectations necessary for effective organizational functioning, being able to interpret the realities within an organizational culture and thus take part in creating and sustaining them, among other things.

Second, perspective-taking skills among organizational members may help to explain past findings about such things as semantic information distance (Tompkins, 1962), superior-subordinate relationships (Jablin, 1979), work group functioning, leadership effectiveness, promotion, and conflict resolution. Differences in perspective-taking ability appear to be a plausible explanation for many of the organizational communication problems grabbing researchers' attention in the past.

SELF-MONITORING

Within a social cognitive, framework, a number of researchers are focusing on the role of the self in explaining communication performance. Snyder

(1974), for example, posited that the ability to monitor one's self presentation is a key characteristic of interpersonal competence. He differentiated between persons who are more and less able to attend to social contexts when planning behavior and added (Snyder, 1979) that high self-monitoring individuals are more sensitive and responsive to situationally appropriate interpersonal cues than low self-monitors:

> The prototypic *High Self-Monitoring Individual* is one who, out of concern for the situational and interpersonal appropriateness of his or her social behavior, is particularly sensitive to the expression and self-presentation of relevant others in social situations and uses these cues as guidelines for monitoring (that is regulating and controlling) his or her own verbal and nonverbal self-presentation. By contrast, the prototypic *Low Self-Monitoring Individual* is not so vigilant to social information about situationally appropriate self-presentation [p. 89].

Research on self-monitoring has shown that high self-monitors are more accurate in recalling information about another (Berscheid et al., 1976) and pay closer attention in inferring anothers' intentions (Jones & Baumeister, 1976). In a more recent investigation, Dabbs, Evans, Hopper, and Purvis (1980) found that high self-monitors were better at influencing than at accommodating others and that they were more verbal than their low self-monitoring peers. In yet another study, Turner (1980) found that high self-monitors constructed a greater number of humorous remarks, humorously labeled more cartoon captions, rated themselves as more humorous, and were rated by others as more humorous in group discussions.

Roloff and Berger (1982) distinguished between the external focus of the high self-monitor and the internal focus of the low self-monitor. For example, Sampson (1982) found that high self-monitors define themselves in terms of the external environment, and low self-monitors defined themselves in terms of personal traits. Moreover, Snyder and Cantor (1980) found that high self-monitors gave more vivid descriptions of prototypic individuals than low self-monitors, but low self-monitors provided more vivid descriptions of themselves than did high self-monitoring individuals. Most recently, Sypher and Sypher (1983) reported significant positive relationships between self-monitoring and perceived communication effectiveness. Athay and Darley (1981) concluded that "a picture emerges of the high self-monitor as an individual who has grasped the central social fact that achieving one's purposes requires accurate perceptions of the signals sent by others, as well as well-developed signaling capacities of one's own and has therefore developed the skills necessary to do both these tasks" (p. 305).

Self-Monitoring in the Organization

More recent work has revealed significant positive relations between self-monitoring, self-reports of communication effectiveness (Sypher & Sypher, 1983; Sypher et al., 1983) and cognitive differentiation among organizational members. More specifically, our data revealed that upper-level employees in a large insurance corporation tended to be more cognitively differentiated, higher self-monitors than lower-level employees (Sypher & Sypher, 1981). In addition, research in several organizations found supervisors to be more cognitively differentiated than nonsupervisors; however, no significant differences were found between the self-monitoring behavior of supervisors and nonsupervisors (Sypher et al., 1983). This research also showed that three subscales of the self-monitoring inventory (as identified by Briggs et al., 1980) were differentially related to cognitive differentiation. The extraversion subscale was the only factor to correlate significantly and positively with the RCQ measure. In the same study, supervisors scored significantly higher on the extraversion subscale than nonsupervisors (Sypher et al., 1983). The results of these investigations suggested that cognitively differentiated and perhaps high self-monitors tended to be more successful in organizations than less differentiated, low self-monitoring individuals.

These findings further our understanding of what theorists have contended for sometime and Boyatiz (1982) has recently confirmed. That is, the ability to get along with others is a requirement for competent organizational performance. And as effectiveness in "getting along" with others is related to interpersonal and communication competence, one can argue that the interpersonally competent organizational members probably have an advantage over their less competent peers in achieving individual advancement.

A great deal of evidence exists to demonstrate the important role self-monitoring plays in interpersonal and communicative competence. The ability to get along with others is dependent upon presenting oneself in situationally appropriate ways. Not surprisingly, the research also shows that individuals with relatively developed self-monitoring abilities also evidenced advanced communicative skills and demonstrated sophisticated social cognitive functioning.

LISTENING

Listening is also considered to figure prominently in the understanding of communication competence. Indeed, a number of communication researchers have pointed to the importance of listening in the communication process (Hart & Burks, 1972; Delia & Clark, 1975; and Cushman & Craig, 1976). The importance of listening also has been recognized by corporate organizations who continue to sponsor programs designed to improved their employees' listening abilities. We are all probably aware of this emphasis if for no other reason than from having watched the national advertising campaign on listening adopted by a leading manufacturer of data processing machines. This organization touts its superiority by claiming that their employees are better listeners and thus more pleasing and more efficient to work with. They attempt to give their campaign—and to some extent their organization—credibility by offering listening workshops for their personnel.

However, despite previous theoretical and current applied interest in listening behavior, few efforts had been made to explore the various aspects of the listening process until very recently. Findings from recently reported research revealed that listening was indeed a unique characteristic separate from standard characteristics of memory (Bostrom & Bryant, 1980) and, for the most part, appeared unrelated to intelligence as measured by ACT socres (Bostrom & Waldhart, 1980). In addition, these researchers have concluded that listening is a multidimensional construct.

In an effort to address the multidimensionality of the listening construct, Bostrom and others developed the Kentucky Comprehensive Listening Test based on the various components of listening highlighted in memory and communication research. This test was designed to investigate a complex set of suggested listening-related skills including short-term memory (usually described as attention), intermediate-term memory with rehearsal, lecture or long-term listening (usually defined as memory or the "crucial process" involved in listening), interpretive listening (sometimes called "vocalic listening), and listening with distraction (Bostrom, 1983).

In early work with this measure, Bostrom and Waldhart (1980) found that individuals differed considerably in their performance on the various listening-related tasks. For example, some individuals performed well on the short-term memory task but not so well on the lecture listening task (Bostrom & Waldhart, 1980). They concluded that the various subscales were indeed tapping individual characteristics of listening, and that listening and its relation to other communications abilities needs to be more fully explored.

Measuring Listening Abilities in the Organization

Findings from recent research (Bostrom & Bryant, 1980; Sypher & Bostrom, 1983), provided further evidence for the validity of the various subscales of the Kentucky Comprehensive Listening Test; individuals differed in their abilities on each part of the test. More importantly, findings from research utilizing this measure in an organizational setting (Sypher & Bostrom, 1983) point to relationship between various social cognitive abilities and individual aspects of listening. In their recent work, Sypher and Bostrom (1983) found that the total scores on the listening test positively correlated with Crockett's (1965) measure of cognitive differentiation ($r = .32$), B. Sypher's (1981) version of the perspective-taking task ($r = .48$), Snyder's (1974) self-monitoring scale ($r = .47$), and O'Keefe & Delia's (1979) persuasive arguments task ($r = .53$).

However, findings regarding the relationship between listening and individual success in the organization are somewhat mixed. Only the short-term memory and rehearsal subscales correlated positively with one's level in the organization; however, other correlations, while nonsignificant, were in the predicted direction (Sypher & Bostrom, 1983). Interestingly, these authors also reported that the data suggest a positive relationship between the long-term memory subscale of listening and organizational communication satisfaction ($r = .36$). For some reason, it appears that those who could store more information for later retrieval reported more satisfaction with the communication that exists in their organization. The reasons for this finding, however, are not entirely clear. Even though the data reported by Sypher and Bostrom (1983) regarding individual organizational performance and listening behavior is tentative, there appears to be some evidence to suggest a relationship between other measures of communication competence characteristics and listening ability among organizational members.

The findings from the Sypher and Bostrom (1983) study suggest a number of possible directions for future research. First, listening research should be done in settings where listening is important. The organizational context especially meets this demand as a relationship between listening behavior and successful job performance seems likely. Caldwell and O'Reilly (1982) suggested that the unsuccessful search for correlates of successful job performance is the result, at least in part, of assessing individual differences "without a clear appreciation for why these should directly affect job performance" (p. 124). The reasons why listening should directly affect job performance seem evident, yet investigations have consistently avoided this aspect of communication and have even avoided looking at individual communication more generally. Because of its possible relationship to motivation, job expectations, superior-subordinate relationships, interpretations of organizational reality and the like, listening investigations should be included in the search to understand more fully individual job performance.

Second, investigations of the interrelationships among various social cognitive abilities should no longer exclude listening, as Sypher and Bostrom's (1983) preliminary findings pointed to a number of interesting relationships between listening and social cognitive development. However, further refinement of the Kentucky Comprehensive Listening Test might require a change in the content of the lecture task to include information about people and interpersonal relationships. As social cognition is generally considered thought directed toward interaction (Roloff & Berger, 1982), the relationship between listening and other social cognitive skills might be strengthened if the listening tasks were person related.

SUMMARY

One way to conceptualize competent communicative performance is through the understanding of social cognitive functioning. The purpose of this chapter has been to point out the efficacy of a social cognitive approach to communication competence in the organization. A review of previous competence research reveals some conceptual but little theoretical or methodological similarity. Among the key competence characteristic identified by communication researchers are perspective-taking or empathy, interaction management, and behavioral flexibility.

In this chapter, variables related to these dimensions of competence were recast in social cognitive terms. In addition, a review of some recent research conducted in organizational settings highlighted specific social cognitive abilities related to individual organizational success (e.g., cognitive differentiation, perspective-taking, self-monitoring, and listening). This research showed that higher-level organizational members and supervisors evidenced superior social cognitive functionings.

It is hoped that further efforts aimed at investigating communication from an interpretive orientation will increase our understanding of the role of communication in organizational settings. The social cognitive approach outlined here is philosophically similar and methodologically accommodating to the cultural approach to organizational communication; and because of the interpretive orientation, researchers will no doubt continue to explore the ways in which individuals create and sustain organizational cultures. Hence, further explorations of the role of social cognition in culture development promises to be a fruitful area of research. However, the success of further research rests on researchers' efforts to design programs of study that are philosophically, theoretically, and methodologically consistent. We must keep in mind that an understanding of organizational communication is dependent upon an understanding of communication in general.

REFERENCES

Allen, R. & Brown, K. *Developing communication competence in children.* Skokie, IL: National Textbook Co., 1976.

Applegate, J.L. The impact of construct system development on communication and impression formation in persuasive contexts. *Communication Monographs,* 1982, *49,* 277-290.

Argyris, C. *Interpersonal competence and organizational effectiveness.* Homewood, IL: Dorsey Press, 1962.

Athay, M. & Darley, J. Toward an interaction-centered theory of personality. In N. Cantor & J. Kihlstrom (Eds.) *Personality, cognition and social interaction.* Hillsdale, NJ: Erlbaum, 1981.

Berger, C. Interpersonal communication theory and research: An overview. In B. Ruben (Ed.) *Communication yearbook 1.* New Brunswick: Transaction Books, 1977.

Berscheid, E., Graziana, W., Monson, T., & Dermer, M. Outcome dependency: Attention, attribution and attraction. *Journal of Personality and Social Psychology,* 1976, *34,* 978-989.

Bienvenu, M. An interpersonal communication inventory. *Journal of Communication,* 1971, *21,* 381-388.

Bochner, A. & Kelly, C. Interpersonal competence: Rationale, philosophy and implementation of a conceptual framework. *Speech Teacher,* 1974, *23,* 279-301.

Bostrom, R. Measuring listening behavior: The Kentucky Comprehensive Listening Test. Unpublished manuscript, Department of Communications, University of Kentucky, 1983.

Bostrom, R. & Bryant, C. Factors in the retention of information presented orally: The role of short-term listening. *Western Journal of Speech Communication,* 1980, *44,* 137-145.

Bostrom, R. & Waldhart, E. Components of listening behavior: The role of short-term memory. *Human Communication Research,* 1980, *6,* 211-227.

Boyatzis, R. *The competent manager: A model for effective performance.* New York: John Wiley, 1982.

Brandt, D. On linking social performance with social competence: Some relations between communicative style and attributions of interpersonal attractiveness and effectiveness. *Human Communication Research,* 1979, *5,* 223-238.

Burleson, B. The affective perspective-taking process: A test of Turiel's role-taking model. In M. Burgoon (Ed.) *Communication yearbook 6.* Beverly Hills: Sage, 1982.

Burleson, B., Applegate, J., & Neuwirth, C. Is cognitive complexity loquacity? A reply to Powers, Jordan, and Street. *Human Communication Research,* 1981, *7,* 212-225.

Caldwell, D. & O'Reilly, C. Boundary spanning and individual performance: The impact of self-monitoring. *Journal of Applied Psychology,* 1982, *67,* 124-127.

Clark, R.A. The impact of self interest and desire for liking on the selection of communicative strategies. *Communication Monographs,* 1979, *46,* 257-273.

Clark, R.A. & Delia, J. Cognitive complexity, social perspective-taking, and functional persuasive skills in second-to-ninth-grade children. *Human Communication Research,* 1977, *3,* 128-134.

Clark, R.A. & Delia, J. Topoi and rhetorical competence. *Quarterly Journal of Speech,* 1979, *65,* 121-136.

Crockett, W.H. Cognitive complexity and impression formation. In B. Maher (Ed.) *Progress in experimental research* (vol. 2). New York: Academic Press, 1965.

Cushman, D. & Craig, R. Communication systems. Interpersonal implications. In G. Miller (Ed.) *Exploration in interpersonal communication.* Beverly Hills: Sage, 1976.

Dabbs, J., Evans, M., Hopper, C., & Purvis, J. Self-monitor in conversations: What do they monitor? *Journal of Personality and Social Psychology,* 1980, *39,* 278-284.

Deal, T. & Kennedy, A. *Corporate cultures: The rites and rituals of corporate life.* Reading, MA: Addison-Wesley, 1982.

Deetz, S. Critical interpretive research in organizational communication. *Western Journal of Speech Communication,* 1982, *46,* 131-150

Delia, J. & Clark, R.A. A constructivist approach to the development of rhetorical competence. Presented at the annual meeting of the Speech Communication Association, Houston, 1975.

Delia, J. & Clark, R.A. Cognitive complexity, social perception, and listener-adapted communication in six-, eight-, ten-, and twelve-year-old boys. *Communication Monographs,* 1977, *44,* 545-376.

Delia, J. & Crockett, W. Social schemas, cognitive complexity, and the learning of social structures. *Journal of Personality,* 1973, *41,* 413-429.

Delia, J., Kline, S., & Burleson, B. The development of persuasive communication strategies in kindergarteners through twelfth-graders. *Communication Monographs,* 1979, *46,* 241-256.

Delia, J., O'Keefe, B., & O'Keefe, D. The constructivist approach to communication. In F.X. Dance (Ed.) *Communication theory.* New York: Harper & Row, 1982.

Dymond, R. Personality and empathy. *Journal of Consulting Psychology,* 1950, *14,* 343-350.

Feingold, P. *Toward a paradigm of effective communication: An empirical study of perceived communicative effectiveness.* Doctoral dissertation, Purdue University, 1976.

Hale, C. Cognitive complexity-simplicity as a determinant of communication effectiveness. *Communication Monographs,* 1980, *47,* 304-311.

Hale, C. & Delia J. Cognitive complexity and social perspective-taking. *Communication Monographs,* 1976, *43,* 195-203.

Hart, R. & Burks, D. Rhetorical sensitivity and social interaction. *Speech Monographs,* 1972, *39,* 75-91.

Hecht, M. Measures of communication satisfaction. *Human Communication Research,* 1978, *4,* 350-368.

Hecht, M. Toward a conceptualization of communication satisfaction. *Quarterly Journal of Speech,* 1974,*64,* 47-62.

Higgins, E.T., Herman, C., & Zanna, M. *Social cognition: The Ontario symposium* (vol. 1). Hillsdale, NJ: Lawrence Erlbaum Associates, 1981.

Hirsch, P. Ambushes, shootouts, and knights of the roundtable: The language of corporate takeovers. Presented at the annual meeting of the Academy of Management, Detroit, 1980.

Jablin, F. Superior-subordinate communication: The state of the art. *Psychological Bulletin,* 1979, *86,* 1201-1222.

Jablin, F. Organizational communication theory and research: An overview of communication climate and network research. In D. Nimmo (Ed.) *Communication yearbook 4.* New Brunswick, NJ: Transaction-International Communication Association, 1980.

Katz, D. & Kahn, R. *The social psychology of organization* (2nd ed.). New York: John Wiley, 1978.

Kelly, G. *A theory of personality* (2 vols.). New York: Norton: 1955.

Kelly C., Chase, J., & Weimann, J. Interpersonal competence: Conceptualization, measurement and future considerations. Presented at the annual meeting of the Speech Communication Association, San Antonio, 1979.

Likert, R. *The human organization.* New York: McGraw-Hill, 1967.

Martin, J. Stories and scripts in organizational settings. In A. Hastorf & A. Isen (Eds.) *Cognitive social psychology.* New York: Elsevier, 1982.

McCall, M. & Lombardo, S. What makes a top executive? *Psychology Today*, 1983, *47*, 118-119.

Mehan, H. Structuring school structuring. *Harvard Educational Review*, 1978, *48*, 32-64.

Miller, G. & Steinberg, M. *Between people: A new analysis of interpersonal communication*. Chicago: Science Research Associates, 1975.

Mower White, C. Cognitive complexity and the completion of social structures. *Social Behavior and Personality*, 1977, *5*, 305-310.

Norton, R. Foundation of a communicator style construct. *Human Communication Research*, 1978, *4*, 99-113.

Norton, R. & Miller, L. Dyadic perceptions of communicator style. In B. Ruben (Ed.) *Communication yearbook 1*. New Brunswick: Transaction Books, 1977.

Norton, R. & Pettegrew, L. Attentiveness as a style of communication: A structural analysis. *Communication Monographs*, 1979, *46*, 13-27.

O'Keefe, B. Delia, J. Construct comprehensiveness and cognitive complexity as predictors of the number and strategic adaptation of arguments and appeals in a persuasive message. *Communication Monographs*, 1979, *46*, 231-241.

O'Keefe, D. & Sypher, H. Cognitive complexity measures and the relationship of cognitive complexity to communication: A critical review. *Human Communication Research*, 1981, *8*, 72-92.

Pacanowsky, M. & O'Donnell-Trujillo, N. Communication and organizational cultures. *Western Journal of Speech Communication*, 1982, *46*, 115-131.

Parks, M. *Communication competency*. Presented at the annual meeting of the Speech Communication Association, San Francisco, 1976.

Pelias, R. *An experimental investigation of the effect of a psychologically-centered literary interpretation course on college students' level of social perspective-taking*. Doctoral dissertation, University of Illinois at Urbana-Champaign, 1979.

Pettigrew, A. On studying organizational cultures. *Administrative Science Quarterly*, 1979, *24*, 570-581.

Powers, W., Jordon, W. & Street, R. Language indices in the measurement of cognitive complexity: Is complexity loquacity? *Human Communication Research*, 1979, *6*, 69-73.

Putnam, L. Paradigms for organizational communication research: An overview and synthesis. *Western Journal of Speech Communication*, 1982, *46*, 192-206.

Roloff, M. & Berger, C. Social cognition and communication: An introduction. In M. Roloff & C. Berger (Eds.) *Social cognition and communication*. Beverly Hills: Sage, 1982.

Ruben, B.D. Assessing communication competence for intercultural adaptation. *Group and Organization Studies*, 1976, *1*, 334-354.

Sampson, E. Personality and the location of identity. *Journal of Personality*, 1978, *46*, 552-568.

Sieburg, E. & Larson, C. Dimensions of interpersonal response. Presented at the annual meeting of the International Communication Association, Phoenix, 1971.

Synder, M. The self-monitoring of expressive behavior. *Journal of Personality and Social Psychology*, 1974, *30*, 526-537.

Snyder, M. Self-monitoring processes. In L. Berkowitz (Ed.) *Advances in experimental social psychology* (vol. 12). New York: Academic Press, 1979.

Snyder, M. & Cantor, N. Thinking about ourselves and others: Self-monitoring and social knowledge. *Journal of Personality and Social Psychology*, 1980, *39*, 222-234.

Sypher, B.D. *A multimethod investigation of employee communication abilities, communication satisfaction and job satisfaction*. Doctoral dissertation, University of Michigan, 1981.

Sypher, B.D. & Applegate, J. *The organization of culture and the culture of organizations: A review and elaboration of interpretive approaches to organizational communication research*. Presented at the annual meeting of the Speech Communication Association, Louisville, 1982.

Sypher, B.D. & Bostrom, R. *The relationship of various social cognitive abilities and listening behavior among organizational members*. Unpublished manuscript, Department of Communication, University of Kentucky, 1983.

Sypher, B.D. & Sypher, H.E. *Individual differences and perceived communication abilities in an organizational setting*. Paper presented at the annual meeting of the International Communication Association, Minneapolis, 1981.

Sypher, B.D. & Sypher, H.E. On seeing ourselves as others see us: Convergence and divergence in assessments of communication behavior. *Communication Research*, forthcoming.

Sypher, B.D., & Sypher, H.E. Perceptions of communication ability: Self-monitoring in an organizational setting. *Personality and Social Psychology Bulletin*, 1983, *9*, 297-304.

Sypher, B.D., Sypher, H.E., & Leichty, G.B. Cognitive differentiation, self-monitoring and individual success in organizations. In Landfield, A. & Epting, F.R. (Eds.) *Anticipating personal construct psychology*. Lincoln: University of Nebraska Press, 1983.

Sypher, H.E. Illusory correlation in communication research. *Human Communication Research*, 1980, *7*, 83-88.

Sypher, H.E. & Applegate, J.L. Cognitive complexity and verbal intelligence: Clarifying relationships. *Educational and Psychological Measurement*, 1982, *51*, 537-543.

Turner, R. Self-consciousness and memory of trait terms. *Personality and Social Psychology Bulletin*, 1980, *6*, 273-277.

Wiemann, J. Explication and test of a model communication competence. *Human Communication Research*, 1977, *3*, 195-213.

Wiemann, J. & Backlund, P. Current theory and research in communication competence. *Review of Educational Research*, 1980, *50*, 185-199.

6

Children's Understanding of Television Commercials

The Acquisition of Competence

THOMAS R. DONOHUE
TIMOTHY P. MEYER

Communication competence in television is primarily a function of understanding: the medium, its syntactical conventions, (production and narrative) expectations dictated by social and normative influences and values, the level of sophistication required of viewers by the content; and, lastly, familiarity with the medium and content nurtured by repetition and development in both cognitive and social senses. TV commercials, however, are notably different from other television content in two ways. First, commercials' primary purpose is to sell—to facilitate the movement of goods and services throughout the American economy. While the persuasive approach may be quite subtle or implicit, the basic intent of commercials is not: Quite simply, viewers are being entreated to exchange money for the product or service advertised. Second, television commercials compress so much information into 10-, 20-, and 30-second packages that a different set of technological and narrative conventions are used, necessitating that the viewer become a "quick study" in order to grasp the meaning of the message.

Consequently, this chapter examines the acquisition of competency in understanding television commercials. A considerable body of evidence has accumulated during the past twenty years that points out the unique nature of television's most criticized, pervasive, and (some would argue) its most creative content form.

Critics and practitioners both tend to agree that TV commercials are an ingenious, inventive American innovation. The very thought that someone would attempt to sell everything from cereal to automobiles in 10-second messages and spend hundreds of thousands of dollars to do it is mind boggling.

In the 1950s and throughout most of the 1960s, 60 seconds was the accepted and conventional length for a TV commercial. The dramatic annual rise in rates charged for time, brought on in part by the fact that there were more people who wanted to advertise than time slots available, led networks and stations to divide the pie into increasingly smaller units until 30-second commercials became the norm. The net result is that even more pressure has been placed on creative people to "tell the product's story"—and make the commercial memorable—in the time it takes a telephone to ring only five times. Such pressure has led to the use of more and more audiovisual and technological "pyrotechnics." At any given time, the American television commercial is representative of the limits of imagination in the overlaying of brief narratives with gimmicks, the net result of which (as advertisers fervently hope) are messages that ultimately lead to increased sales.

To get a grasp of how advertisers believe commercials work to persuade viewers, a short discussion of principles accepted by the advertising industry, is helpful. Most marketers subscribe to the notion that advertising affects people in stages, and that ordinarily by only moving viewers sequentially through all stages will the desired behavior occur. The most widely accepted sequence describing how one is eventually persuaded to buy includes attention, awareness, knowledge, likability, conviction, purchase, and evaluation.

Attention

It is not enough to create a TV commercial, pay to have it aired, and simply assume people will attend to that message. In fact, more attention is difficult to achieve in our fiercely competitive message milieu. For example, estimates have shown that the average consumer may be exposed to as many as 1200 commercial messages a day (via all media). Americans are literally awash in advertisements and commercials. Consequently, in order to get our attention, an ad must stand out from the thousands of others with which we come in contact. An audio and visual "feast," surprise, the use of celebrities, compelling or catchy music and/or a unique opening or closing are just a few of the ways in which creative people attempt to "grab" an audience.

Awareness

The next stage in the sequence is characterized by the viewer's ability to identify the product or service being advertised. While that may seem to be an easy task, when one considers how many soaps, soft drinks, automobiles, and paper products are perpetually advertised, awareness is hardly a given. In fact, regular misidentification or inaccurate attributions of commercials and products is not unusual. One of the more famous examples occurred in the middle 1970s when a highly entertaining and recognizable Alka Seltzer commercial caused those surveyed to be able to describe, almost the entire commercial with great accuracy, except they were unable to recall the name of the product in sufficient numbers for the ad to be considered "effective." More recently, a survey of viewers who watched the ABC miniseries "Winds of War" recalled many products that were advertised during the various episodes. Unfortunately, none of the product ads recalled with any minimal frequency were actually advertised in the many commercials accompanying the series. Awareness, therefore, is the ability to differentiate one's product from the others in the marketplace. Normally, it is accomplished by using a *unique selling proposition* (USP). A USP is a physical or psychological benefit that purports to set the product apart from its competition and in doing so makes the viewer aware of the product's uniqueness.

Knowledge

The cognitive dimensions of the process focus on relative merits of a product within its competitive milieu. Included in this category are price, applications or uses, cost per unit, availability and physical characteristics. All one knows about a class of products and the relative advantages of various products within a product class comprise the cognitive dimension. It is a dispassionate amalgam of alleged facts, figures, performance data, and so on.

Likability

The affective dimension may or may not be related to knowledge of a product. Brand loyalty—the propensity to buy a product simply because it has always been a family favorite or because one simply likes it and considers no others—is one example of how the affective dimension operates. Creating likability, however, is quite a different matter. Where the person has no history with a product, making it likable entails convincing the viewer that the USP is sufficient reason to be attracted to the product, or for instance, that a celebrity spokesman would not be associated with an inferior product. Likability may have little or nothing to do with what one knows about the product's actual performance. Clothing fads and beer preferences on college campuses have very little to do with value for dollar or controlled, scientific taste-tests. However, it is generally accepted that people like and use products for myriad reasons, none of which is necessarily related to the cognitive dimension.

Conviction

Conviction is the threshold at which the viewer is determined to try the product. It is characterized by a decision that is often the result of having moved through the preceding four stages. The decision may be subject to change, but it is a definite (whether conscious or not) inclination to try the product. It is conviction that most often moves people to visit one automobile showroom over another. Conviction may be seen as a fairly stable inclination for the short run because the filtering process has reduced thousands of bits of information, hundred of messages, tens of alternatives to a fairly readable schema that allows for a small number of plans of action with accompanying contingencies (e.g., What will I do next if my first choice car has its wheels fall off during a test drive? Try another model or go to another dealer to look at a second choice?).

Purchase/Evaluation

Normally, purchase and evaluation are discussed separately. For the purposes of this chapter we will consider them together because we are concerned with the acquisition of competence in the understanding of how television commercials work. Purchase/evaluation serves as a reinforcement mechanism and is a postcommunication function—albeit an extremely important one—in future responses to commercials and evaluation of claims and products. Consumers believe they make wise decisions. It follows, therefore, that people are reported to be highly attentive to ads for products they have recently purchased. But, actual experience with a product is a valuable tool in the evaluation of subsequent products and claims made for them in commercials. For example, children learn very quickly that cereals that promise cosmic taste explosions and toys that appear to be the most exciting thing since ice cream rarely match these expectations. Experience teachers us that a certain amount of exaggeration is part of the communication process—in both interpersonal and mediated communication. A certain amount of benign cynicism subsequently becomes part of the evaluation process. This is called an "adult discount" or "puffery," which will be discussed in detail later in the chapter.

The steps listed above represent the marketer/advertiser's conceptualization of the process that describes how consumers behave. And, as is the case with all process models, it suffers from exceptions that can be seen by nearly everyone with little difficulty. The value in describing the model lies in gaining insight into how professional electronic media communicators approach their craft. By knowing what they attempt to achieve, the task of grasping how consumers process the contest they create becomes easier.

The differences between television commercials and regular dramatic programming, thus, are pronounced enough to warrant a separate analysis, especially because they contain a plethora of implicit and explicit values that have caused concern among governmental legislators, regulators, and policymakers as well as teachers and parents. During the late 1970s the Federal Trade Commission held hearings to determine whether television commercials should be eliminated from children's television programs. It is not our purpose here to go into the details of those hearings but, succinctly stated, the major questions addressed by the opposing sides were (1) Do children under the age of eight understand the purpose and intent of commercials designed for them? Specifically, as the intent of commercials is to persuade and to cause consumption, are television commercials inherently deceiving children? (2) Do TV commercials warp the social values of children and adults alike? Other questions dealt with consumption as a social value and considered whether it is necessarily a negative attribute—if so, under what circumstances?

Advertisers and pressure groups, whose stated purpose was to have TV commercials severely restricted if not banned on children's television, spent millions of dollars parading academics and other experts before representatives of the FTC. Nevertheless, the result was that there was "no conclusive evidence" that would justify any new legislation. The fact is, it remains impossible to specify which television commercials—if any—are harmful to which children under what circumstances. The byproduct of the hearings, however, was that researchers began to address the questions of how children come to understand that TV commercials are substantively different from programming and how and when they realize they must take product claims—whether exaggerated or not—with a grain of salt. Greater understanding of how competency occurs in children's understanding of television commercials was a useful result of the hearings despite the cost (a cost to taxpayers of millions of dollars which ended in an impotent, inconclusive whimper). Before a detailed discussion of how commercial competency is acquired, a definition of what advertising communication competency is would be helpful. Quite simply, one is a successful critic/consumer of television commercials when he or she can understand the following:

(1) Products are always shown in the best possible light, appearing to contribute to the increased happiness of the user.
(2) Product claims often describe most products within the same class (10 milligram aspirin).
(3) Many USPs are fanciful attempts to differentiate products (bottled waters, gasolines) that defy differentiation.
(4) Competitive claims often focus on a small, unimportant product feature because there are no differences among competitors regarding major features (functional characteristics).
(5) Fulfillment/happiness can seldom be purchased, especially at such a low price.
(6) Exaggeration is a basic human characteristic.
(7) American media are supported by advertisers who are in business to make a profit.
(8) Advertising can contain valuable information that helps a person make a better informed purchase.

A person who comprehends these statements is sufficiently innoculated to be able to enjoy the artistry, humor, and cleverness that make American television commercials so enjoyable without suffering adverse psychological or financial side effects.

To understand how we learn to place TV commercials in a "proper" perspective, one needs to look at how children come to understand their environment. The same principles of child development that explain how a brain matures, thereby facilitating qualitative leaps in cognitive functioning, also help explain how a child learns to make subtle distinctions between TV commercials and program content (Piaget, 1969). And while there is a great deal of controversy over when and how these qualitative leaps occur, it is not our purpose to argue for a static model in which we specify at what age children come to understand various ascending degrees of subtlety. Rather, we merely wish to describe the dynamics of the process.

Infants—roughly 1-18 months—react to extremes and contrast. Their eyes follow sudden movements, they are attracted to bright colors and loud or animated noises and above all their attention span is extremely short—a matter of seconds. Everyone has seen a child playing in the presence of a television, seemingly oblivious to the program, suddenly shift his attention to the television when the commercial comes on. While the child has no understanding of the words or perhaps even the pictures, he is attracted by the quick shifts in color, movement, music, and pacing. It is the rapid change that initially attracts attention and then the compressed action, dialogue, and music that holds attention for as long as the child is inclined. Initially, form—the production conventions and the technology itself—creates interest in television commercials. Infants gradually become conditioned to expect and even anticipate the interruptions. Because their mental capacities seem to generally allow concentrations of no more than 20 to 30 seconds, they may even attempt—at a superficial level—to make primitive sense of what they see. This inference is only speculation. Some research has shown, however, that children as young as two years old describe commercials as a punctuation device—"it divides the programs"—or perceive an even more sophisticated function—"they [commercials] tell you about things." It is well accepted that commercials are the most attractive feature of television in the case of very young children.

Young children, approximately ages two to eight are generally described by developmental psychologists (à la Piaget) as being in the concrete operational stage because they can understand narrative content at its most basic or "concrete" level. They can report, for example, the narrative accurately including what a product does, how it is used, and what happened (factually) in the commercial. It is precisely the apparent acceptance of the commercial at face value that concerns those worried about the effects of TV commercials on children. Their argument of course is that because children accept content as "fact," they are being deceived and consequently commercials are inherently unfair. Extending that argument, one could argue further that because television programs stereotype people, situations, and human emotion, all television content is inherently deceptive and, ergo, unfair. However, those concerned about consumer values are motivated by the desire to keep children from becoming "consummate consuming minions."

A simile often used in describing concrete operational children is that their minds are like clean slates waiting to be written upon. That which can be written during this period are basic categorizing, storing facts and differentiating on the basis of shape, color, size, and form. Thus, product distinctions would be made essentially on a physical basis. The trouble to which cereal manufacturers go to create novel shapes and colors in the product is testimony to the tactile and visual orientation of two- to eight-year-olds.

Abstract notions of the chain of events that created the concept of sponsorship or profit motive are generally beyond these children's youngest comprehension levels. They report that the purpose of commercials is "to show you things you can buy," "to tell you about the thing," or "to show you how to use it."

However, lest we leave you with the impression that older children (eight years or older) are as guideless, naive, and wide-eyed as the youngest in the group, our experience and research indicate that the seeds of understanding are sewn quite easily early on. Children between six and eight have repeatedly told us that sometimes toys "don't do what they show on television," a comment which is the result of simple, classical learning—the integration of expectations vicariously created with real life experiences (a concept discussed in greater detail later in this chapter).

Between the ages of eight and twelve, children acquire the mental agility that enables them to complete the most complex thought patterns, and most in this age group are capable of understanding the sophisticated nuances in most commercial messages. (Rossiter & Robertson, 1974). During this stage adult discount usually develops. Adult discount is the ability to be benignly cynical, to understand that there are multiple perspectives to any "story," and that exaggeration is not necessarily a form of lying with destructive consequences. Moreover, they learn that people are prone to exaggerate, leave out details in a narrative, and otherwise add material to the teller's best advantage. One of the reasons children come to acquire the adult discount early is perhaps because most children quickly learn through experience how to manipulate facts themselves and then become increasingly aware of such techniques in others.

An important aspect of adult discount is that apparently it seldom causes the development of generalized, large-scale distrust of societal institutions, as some critics would have us believe. Normally, children understand that some advertising claims are exaggerated and learn through experience when those exaggerations are important enough to warrant avoidance of the product. Such skepticism is seldom generalized or abstracted in such a way that it causes distrust of all products and advertisers; rather, it tends to be neatly compartmentalized, a process that characterizes concert operational stage children.

By the age of twelve, when children begin to challenge many of the institutions in their lives, they have become adept critics of television commercials. Preadolescents are often openly critical of commercials, pointing out exaggerations while watching with their friends or siblings. They're savvy, quick to recognize questionable claims, and generally "streetwise" where commercials are concerned (Ward et al., 1977).

Clearly, competence in learning how to sort the levels of "truth" in the thousands of messages to which children are exposed is largely attributable to increased maturity of the brain. Few would argue that within various age groups there exists a wide disparity in the ability to exercise critical thinking ability because people differ in native intellectual ability, social skills, adeptness with language and its subleties, and critical past experiences. Such differences account in a large part for much of the differences we observe among people. There are social and psychological variables, however, not necessarily related to the innate character of a person that seem to account for differing levels of competence. Each is discussed below.

EXPERIENCE

While simple exposure to commercials does not an expert make, it certainly helps—especially as cognitive development proceeds. People become more adept at videogames through practice, and they learn to anticipate which obstacles and situations will occur in sequence. So do television viewers learn over time how various scenarios will be scripted. Television commercials follow tightly scripted patterns and formulas that lead to predicted conclusions. Whether the formula consists of slice of life vignettes, demonstrations of effectiveness, or humorous counterpoint (to mention only a few), the 10- to 60-second scripts are highly redundant. There are only so many claims one can make for soaps, cars, cereals, toys, or pet food, and only so many strategies for leading consumer through the five steps mentioned in the beginning of the chapter. The main consequence of all this is that the viewer becomes quickly attuned to and can predict the possibilities (Atkins, 1976). In addition, whereas interpersonal communication has the possibility for endless innuendo from each unique communication experience, the same commercial may routinely be seen 50 or more times by an individual viewer. Seldom do we get that many exposures to the same exact message elsewhere in our communication environment. In fact, rare is the person who has not found himself or herself humming or singing a commercial jingle or theme song. The extreme redundancy that is prevalent within TV commercials themselves and through their repetition in exposure leads to the ability to remember (often in minute detail), the content of those 10- or 20- and 30-second "stories."

Another form of redundance which facilitates the understanding of the TV commercial idiom is found in the types of situations and stories used. The basic formats—with slight variations—include a demonstration in which the product is used, slice-of-life discovery of the product, blind or contrived testimonials, humorous characters as spokesmen, the use of celebrities, and so on. The conventions of good taste necessitated by the need to appeal to a broad audience assure that commercials will be fairly uncomplex and obvious in their formats to even the least sophisticated viewer. Thus, each viewer quickly builds a lengthy repertoire of commercial possibilities for a finite number of products, types, treatments, and situations, and predictable applications allow one to become an "expert" in a relatively short amount of time. Certain product categories tend to use the same type of advertising formats. For example, soap and detergent advertisers favor slice of life; soft drinks use experiential and/or taste tests; automobile manufacturers favor demonstrations. Even the very young viewers quickly learn that when the commercial begins with two women chatting in a kitchen about washday blues, the range of products that will be touted in the coming seconds is quite narrow. Except where the element of surprise or humor is a major aspect of the commercial, advertisers count heavily on immediate recognition, as after five seconds up to 50 percent of the commercial may have already elapsed.

Because the stakes are so high—a 30-second commercial in prime time television routinely costs over 125 thousand dollars—advertisers are reluctant to experiment or alter the formula with which they have grown comfortable during television's 45 year history. The consequence of predictability, redundancy, and a lack of new formats in television commercials is that viewers gain extensive experience with the syntax of commercials very early even if no one formally introduces or discusses the topic. Advertisers consequently rely on viewer familiarity and take advantage of it in shaping commercial content.

Attempts to be innovative and partially disguise commercials as programming has met with much criticism (Bever et al., 1975) and has been banned for children's television programs. Examples include using animated characters (Fred Flintstone) to sell vitamins on his own cartoon program with virtually no separation between program and commercial. Such tactics as host selling and insufficient delineation or demarcation of commercial and program were among the many practices found unacceptable for preadolescents by industry watchdogs. The assumption of course was that those most vulnerable would be even more deceived and motivated when favorite hosts spoke for a product or when it was believed that the commercial was simply an extension of an entertaining cartoon. Along similar lines, there has even been some controversy surrounding commercials obviously designed for adults. Political campaign specialists have hypothesized that when candidates' commercials appear to be news—designed to look like an impartial interview by a newsman with the candidate—voters would find the commercial more credible than a traditional ad and would be more inclined to vote for him. "Make news not commercials" was a headline of a TV Guide article in which political media specialists extolled the virtues and effectiveness of "infomercials." Subsequently, many corporate advertisers have attempted to blur the distinction between institutionalized information dissemination and persuasion. So far such attempts have yet to demonstrate an appreciable difference in perceptions of candidates, corporations or causes. Viewers are not easily influenced. However, the net results of such commercials may be in the desired direction because the information they contain may be just what a consumer wants.

SYNTAX OF FORM

As was mentioned earlier in this chapter, commercials are one of the most creative forms of television content. In fact, many of the syntactical devices that form the basis of the technological foundation of the video narrative were either developed or perfected by TV commercial makers. Examples of such devices include a split-screen with parallel action occurring in each, the extensive use of highly original sound tracks and music, the use of animated and live characters in the same sequence, camera movement on still frame pictures, and "high energy" rapid editing—hundreds of edits per minute. Such creativity was born of necessity. With so little time to tell a story and to make a point, creative people sought to develop means of executing faster transitions and devices to indicate simultaneous action and accelerating time. Devices that work well quickly become convention and are eventually incorporated into other forms of film and videotape. It must be emphasized here that it is not simply technological wizardry that defines video syntax any more than the ability to make strange or obscure sounds defines the evolution of language. Rather, it is the ability of a communicator to convey a message to a large number of people in a parsimonious yet appealing way. As esthetics play a role in spoken language—some words are more pleasing to the ear and seem to convey the essence of intended meaning more succinctly than others—particular visual techniques do the same for the eye. A fine example of a visual technique that found its way into the language was developed during the student unrest of the 1960s and through the Vietnam war. The technique was slow movement or zooming in on a still photograph—usually one of people experiencing pain or anguish. The technique became popular in political commercials during the 1968 and 1972 presidential elections where the camera slowly zooms in on the pathetic face of a burned Vietnamese child, on an American student's screaming face during the Kent State disaster, or on countless other distorted faces during deplorable situations. Because still photographs can capture the height of an emotion they allow the viewer to read even more into the picture; the simple movement of the camera on the still picture supplemented with voice over commentary can be extremely riveting and dramatic. Repetition of the use of movement on stills is a technique that has become a convention, understood by creative people and viewers alike.

One may legitimately ask how creative people and television critics know viewers really understand the thousands of conventions, especially as grammar lessons are seldom given or even discussed with regard to video syntax. The answer is that visual conventions are learned in much the same way language is learned—assimilated through practice, repetition, and by inquiry into what the technique means in the context of what is being viewed. Generalization then occurs when the convention appears repeatedly in an attempt to convey—broadly speaking—time-, space-, and people-relational similarities. Sound tracks and dialogue fit the same mold. Orchestrated sound tracks as well as jingles have been used to heighten the full range of human emotions, and even the most unsophisticated viewer can identify what kind of music should accompany a given mood or situation. Again, that is because the range of alternatives is relatively narrow and portrayals are broadly defined. Dialogue in the visual media is highly truncated, stilted, and repetitious so that a minimum of understanding of specifics is necessary to grasp the literal, intended meaning of the message. Television commercial dialogue is even more simplistic and obvious so that even people who speak a minimum of English can grasp the essence of the message.

The best way to describe how easily viewers learn the syntactical conventions of television commercials is through a report of how first-time viewers of a film in 1905 were expected to react to Edwin S. Porter's *The Great Train Robbery*. The film, which contained the first parallel edit (a cut to action occurring simultaneously elsewhere) was ridiculed by critics as going beyond viewers' capacity to understand picture sequences that were not in strict chronological order. Not only did viewers understand the technique without any explanation, but it seemed somehow natural to them, at least according to film historians. The same is true of new techniques. A contextual milieu helps provide meaning for a visual technique much in the same way a sentence can help determine the definition of an unfamiliar word.

Lastly, as commercial makers are in the business of promoting understanding among the widest number of viewers, the widely varying levels of sophistication found in literature are generally absent in television scripts. Writers can choose a segment of a market for which the style their prose including complexity of sentence structure, difficulty of words, and level of abstraction. In visual media, such latitude seldom exists. Of course some magazines and even some television programs attract highly sophisticated audiences. And over the last four decades, there have been some fairly sophisticated, clever, and erudite commercials. However, the varying levels of complexity found in printed media are not easily attained in visual media where time and absolute numbers of viewers are the most valued commodities. True, there have been attempts at some longer and more in-depth commercials in the form of five-minute political spots. Research has shown, however, that such messages are not particularly effective if one measures increased recall and understanding against the increased cost compared to a one minute or less commercial.

EXPERIENCE WITH ADVERTISED PRODUCTS

Perhaps the best instruction in the art of understanding television comes in the crucible of experience. The advertising literature is rife with studies in which product expectations—nurtured by TV commercials—were not realized, as evidenced by an initial surge in sales followed by a precipitous drop. Who would not be lured by such slogans as "blondes have more fun," "put sex appeal into your smile," "I'm Cindy, fly me," and "guaranteed 24-hour protection." Most such enticements are simplistic solutions to more complex problems. A person who wants sex appeal in his smile is not thinking of his teeth. Rather, it is the state of his social life that is the center of his concern in much the same way the woman who decides to dye her hair blonde to have fun is not thinking about the color of her hair. However, many people are looking for quick fixes and easy answers. Consequently, they are willing to try a plethora of advertised products to remedy a perceived problem or enhance themselves. In an overwhelming number of cases their lot is not noticeably improved as had been suggested, and they either quit using the product or most often switch to another brand. It is disappointment that makes a consumer street-smart and helps imbue competency in understanding television commercials. Simple learning through direct experience forms the basis for such expertise.

For children, the lessons are even more dramatic because children are especially attracted to promises of performance. Commercials that depict toys that travel twenty feet in the air and then parachute, land upright, and continue on are quickly discounted as children learn that the toy does not perform nearly as well at home as it was shown on television. Through editing and other technological devices, toys can appear to offer much more than is possible in actuality. The same people who fought for heavy restriction of advertising on children's television argued that technological enhancement of products' performances was another argument for prima facie evidence that TV commercials were deceptive and unfair. In response to those criticisms, the three television networks imposed a voluntary ban in 1975 on commercials that employed special effects to enhance a product's visual performance. With regard to other products, children and adolescents gradually learn which of the cereals and candy that look terrific taste terrific, and which products designed to increase athletic prowess, enhance appearance and prevent bad breath don't fulfill expectations (Ward et al., 1977). When expectations are balanced against performance, consumers gradually learn not to expect the best possible outcome from a given product. The learning process is gradual and not unflattering because in our desire to solve problems instantly, we are always willing to try a medicine man's elixir just on the chance that it might work or help this one time. The key, however, is that most consumers are willing to be persuaded because the costs are not high. If a cereal tastes like sawdust or a deodorant fails, one is out only a relatively small amount of money so that the risk of psychological investment is minimal. Word of mouth is the most widely used and respected means of evaluating products. People learn vicariously what works and what doesn't through friends and acquaintances.

The net result is that television commercials are only one means of discovering about products. If one brand of "plastic" hollandaise sauce tastes terrible and friends report that they have had similar experiences with other brands, then all simulated and artificial hollandaise—perhaps all plastic sauces—should and will be avoided. In addition, much of people's daily conversations revolve around consumer issues. Discussions focusing on where the best bargains can be found and of who's producing "lemons" in a given product category and what's new help form the basis of a great deal of competency in advertising evaluation. Thus, people bring a great deal of experience and expertise to advertising in general and television commercials specifically. They usually have a history with most generic product lines and perhaps they have tested several in a line. They talk to friends and relatives and they know—if only implicit—that attempts to deal with large problems and issues by using products are going to be largely unsuccessful. The wealth of experience and knowledge consumers bring to commercials should not be viewed as an impenetrable armor that causes consumers to be doubtful, even of the most extravagant claims. In each of us resides an optimist who wants products to perform miracles. Operationalized, such hopes translate into rationalizations the likes of which would allow us to admit that while we understand that a particular brand of toothpaste is not going to dramatically increase our sex appeal we say to ourselves, "Well, it couldn't hurt." It is a "just-in-case" mentality that moves us to understand that while the chances a product will be a panacea are infinitesimally small, so is the investment on our part. As the prisoners of our expectations, which in turn help color future perceptions, we tend to want products to perform as we hope they will and are likely to give them ample opportunity to meet those expectations.

PARENTAL INTERVENTION

Perhaps the most effective tool in the management of television's influence on children and young people is parental intervention. As with other forms of media content, the easiest way to gain competence in consuming the medium is the centuries old tutorial method. Nothing helps a child learn to read like adult instruction one-to-one. Similarly, appreciation of music and art is best achieved through intimate discussions in the presence of the form being discussed. Art history as well as classical and popular forms of music can be analyzed most effectively when a person can see a painting while its unique nature or style is being discussed or when examples of music can be heard to illustrate that which is the focus of attention. Television commercials are essentially no different. In gaining competency in understanding the various levels upon which commercials operate, nothing works so well as parental/adult discussion of commercials during the message or just after it appears. Such discussions work best in a question-answer format in which general and specific topics are intertwined. Television commercials are somewhat easier to discuss than television programs because while values and appropriate and inappropriate behaviors are discussed, the range is much more narrow and less abstract and complex than in some television programs. For example, a commercial for a diet soft drink that features slim attractive people enjoying themselves is not difficult to conceptually analyze. That our society values slim, attractive people and that one should aspire to be that is a manageable topic for discussion for even fairly young people. On the other hand, moral and ethical dilemmas faced by people within the context of a dramatic program require more cognitive sophistication on the part of the child. Consequently, the discussion of commercials is an excellent place to begin in imparting viewing skills in children. And since few school systems provide formal instruction in television viewing skills, the importance of such instruction is more critical than if the information and expertise were available elsewhere. We teach our children how to read books as a high priority, but neglect to teach them to "read" television and film (Anderson, forthcoming).

Experience and research indicate that there are several approaches to teaching children under eight years of age television commercial viewing skills, each of which has its particular benefits. The first is the traditional classroom instructional method in which the topic is introduced in a general way and children are encouraged to help construct or list ways in which television commercials are different from other forms. The instructor leads the class through form and content distinctions gradually moving on to notions of purpose, function and strategies for making a product attractive and desirable. Children demonstrate the ability to accept such instruction quite easily, and the results indicate that it is a successful approach. This method makes liberal use of examples from TV commercials the children in all probability have already seen. It is most efficient both in terms of time and the range of topics covered, because the instructor is in charge of pacing, length of time spent on a topic and other pedagogical variables. Of course, the weakness of such an approach is that an instructor proceeds at his or her pace which may or may not conform to the children's ability to understand. But such is the daily plight of the classroom teacher on all subjects.

Another approach used successfully in teaching television commercial consumer skills is a role playing exercise based on an accepted form of creative dramatics used in many school systems (Donohue et al., 1983). The role playing approach is designed to involve children in discovery through creating messages and commercials. It can be used with one or a number of children. Typically, a leader/teacher/parent creates a game in which children are given the task of creating a commercial for a fictitious brand of generically familiar product—Flakos Corn Flakes, for example. When possible, children can be divided into groups of three or more and left to their imaginations. They are given the task of dramatizing a commercial for the product that they have created. When more than one group is involved it can be turned into a competitive process in which the winning group gets a prize (a new Mercedes, for example). The advantage of this approach is that the children are totally involved in recalling how commercials attempt to make products desirable and in selecting one which they choose to imitate and use based on their assessments of what seems to be the most appealing persuasive strategy for their peers. Occasionally, some children are sufficiently ingenious that their persuasive strategies are actually novel and enchanting—a clear indication that they are possessors of substantial insight into how we attempt to motivate others to do what we want them to do. Role playing is an extremely enjoyable method of learning but is most effective when similarities of appeals—form and content—are discussed at the end of the presentations.

The only problem with a participatory discovery process is that not all aspects necessarily are self-discovered and it is a time-consuming process. Children with whom we have explored creative dramatic role playing have responded with great enthusiasm. Another benefit of employing this approach to imparting TV commercial viewing skills is than an adult or instructor gets a great deal of insight into what aspects of TV commercials make the greatest impression on children. Similarly, the appeals used, the type of presentation made, and the interactions employed within their skits affords an adult viewer the opportunity to see how children interpret various persuasive and commercial genres. In one of our field experiments, one first-grade group decided that the best way to market cereal was to put a toy that was worth twice as much as the price marked on the box in with the cereal, while another group opted to try an approach that would be easy to convince "your mom to get it for you"—regardless of the high sugar content. Anecdotes related to children's theatrical antics abound.

The third approach involves the integration of videotaped material and live presentation. Our experience indicates that a general orientation period of approximately ten to fifteen minutes during which the general purpose and function of television commercials is discussed is needed. Children are encouraged to ask questions and participate in a discussion pertaining to the topic. Next a videotape with a number of commercials for adults and children's products using a wide variety of formats and appeals is played. After each commercial, the machine is stopped and a series of questions is asked regarding motive, intent, persuasive behavioral strategies, and rationale for the particular format used. Children are prompted and encouraged to participate in a free-flowing discussion. Participants are helped to proceed inductively to generalizations and conclusions about television commercials, the usual result of which is a pretty fair grasp of some principles of video persuasion. Ideally, all three and perhaps other approaches should be used in school systems as well as the home to get the greatest possible benefit. The long-term results of such instruction is that an accurate perception of the role of TV commercials in context of American broadcasting can be nurtured, thereby facilitating the development of the adult discount and helping to minimize the possibility of the occurrence of a generalized distrust of societal institutions. The purpose of understanding, which occurs anyway, can be appreciably speeded up for younger children.

As is the case of all human endeavors, intervening variables determine the extent to which people are affected by mass media messages or any other stimuli. These intervening variables or other factors are personal and environmental influences that are important determinants of how much—if at all—television commercials will affect a given individual. A brief discussion of these variables follows.

INTELLIGENCE

Research has indicated that intelligence plays a major role in how people are affected by TV commercials. Intelligence is related to perceptual acuity and the ability to intuit motive, intent, and strategy. Perspective talking is a higher order function, and more intelligent people (when age is controlled) are more adept at putting themselves in someone else's place. Consequently, more intelligent people are less likely to take commercials at face value or believe exaggerated claims for far-fetched comparisons. Also, subtle humor tends to be more readily understood by those who can grasp the subtlety and innuendo contained in ironic manipulations of situations and language.

FAMILY REARING AND MANAGEMENT STYLES

The interaction and communication style of a family can also play a large role in how commercials are consumed. Families that emphasize and encourage a great deal of talk about media and the institutions and values they portray are likely to produce children who are quite knowledgeable about goods and services as well as the commercials designed to promote them. Families where consensus decisions are made or at least where input is solicited from family members in the decision-making process are going to produce people who can articulate rank-ordered priorities for a wide range of consumer items. On the other hand, in an authoritarian family where a decision is presented as a fait accompli and where little or no discussion of how consumer decisions are made are not likely to imbue family members with a clear set of criteria with which to proceed in learning how to become an intelligent consumer of goods and persuasive media messages.

In addition, most families have normative policies about how television is to be used. Some have strict rules and regulate exposure, while others have a more laissez-faire attitude. A family's viewing style is likely to carry over into consumer issues as well. Some parents tend to yield easily to requests for advertised products while others steadfastly avoid most advertised products. Children learn the extent to which television may serve as a catalogue for goods, and their perceptions of the utility of TV commercials in their own lives will vary greatly. Parents who yield easily can expect to hear a litany of requests for advertised toys and foods.

The extent to which a family is oriented toward trying new products is also an important managerial variable. The diffusion of innovations literature is full of examples of innovators—people willing to try new products immediately after their introduction—who rely heavily on mass media advertisements to find out about the innovation. Similarly, families who could be classified as innovative consumers would be expected to attend to and value TV commercials more than their more conservative counterparts.

There are many other aspects of the influence family communication style has on the potential effect of and competence in understanding persuasive mass media messages. However, for the purposes of this chapter it is sufficient to point out that the differences in the way in which families conduct the business of daily living has a telling impact on how they respond to persuasive messages. Far more research in this area is needed, however, to document the range of differences produced and styles used and their relevant contexts.

SELF-CONCEPT

Research over the last 30 years has demonstrated that persuasibility varies inversely with perceptions of self-worth. People with high self-concepts tend to be less persuasible than those whose self-concepts are low. Given that assurance and confidence can vary by product category, one needs to consider role of self-concept when attempting to conceptualize how people learn to use and process TV commercials. Some people rely heavily on advertisements to provide information on appropriate ways to dress, travel, interact with others, entertain—the list is extensive. It is important to note that the extent to which people rely on commercials is partly a function of their confidence in their own ability to arrive at solutions and to select appropriate courses of action.

Finally, competence in processing persuasive mass media messages varies significantly from individual to individual based on a myriad of environmental and personal needs. The extent to which a person uses the information will depend on its perceived utility. It may be that for some, TV commercials are processed at levels at which they are perceived to be no more than a nuisance. For others they may be categorized primarily as entertainment, while a third group may be interested in the information value. Different commercials may be processed at deeper levels by the same person.

As television's most innovative form of content, commercials, uniqueness and appeal lie in the drama, excitement, music, visual pyrotechnics and humor they are able to communicate in just a few seconds. Competence in processing TV commercials ultimately rests on the use to which they are put and to the individual's ability to assimilate their form and content into their own particular framework and environment.

REFERENCES

Anderson, J. Television literacy and the critical viewer. In Bryant and Anderson (Eds.) *Watching TV, understanding TV*: Research on children's attention and comprehension. New York: Academic Press, forthcoming.

Anderson, J. et al. An ethnological approach to a study of televiewing in family settings. Presented at WSCA Convention, 1979.

Atkin, C. Television advertising and children's observational modeling. Presented ICA Convention, 1976.

Bever, T. et al. Young viewers' troubling response to TV ads. *Harvard Business Review*, 1975, *53* (November-December), 109-120.

Donohue, T., Henke, L., & Meyer, T. Learning about television commercials: The impact of instructional units on children's perceptions of motive and intent. *Journal of Broadcasting*, 1983, *27*, (3), 251-261.

Donohue, W., Donohue, T., & Henke L. *Parental childrearing practices and the impact of conflict from product request denials*. Unpublished manuscript.

Piaget, J., & Inhelder, B. *The psychology of the child*. New York: Basic Books, 1969.

Rossiter, J. & Robertson, T. Children's TV commercials: Testing the defenses. *Journal of Communications*, 1974, *24* (Autumn), 137-144.

Runyon, K. *Consumer behavior* (2nd ed.). Columbus: Merrill, 1980.

Sprinthall, N. & Collins, W.A. *Adolescent psychology: A developmental view*. Reading, MA: Addison-Wesley, forthcoming.

Ward, S., Wackman D., & Wartella, E. *How children learn to buy*. Beverly Hills: Sage, 1977.

7

Communication Competence for Teachers

Avoiding Aporia

H. THOMAS HURT

America is rapidly becoming a nation peopled by educated illiterates. The report by the National Commission on Excellence in Education (1983) has served to dramatically underscore the reality of this assertion. And this assertion represents a real and very dramatic American tragedy: Students have become unwilling and unprepared to learn.

The responsibility for this tragedy is easy to assign to a variety of ephemeral and undefined variables (e.g., home, economy, social environment, or what have you) or to students, who are rendered intellectually impotent by these conveniently "uncontrollable" conditions. After all, poverty does breed an intellectual vacuum. And who can control parents? Besides, if the social system refuses to support education, what can be done to change those conditions? And if these questions cannot be answered (let alone clearly defined), then humans cannot be blamed for the problems; one can blame only the human systems, in which we exist and which, for some mysterious reason, can be created by humans but cannot be controlled.

As a communication professional and a professional educator, I find those assumptions offensive and absurd. After devoting a substantial portion of my career to studying the effects of communication on human learning, I was not terribly surprised to discover that many of the issues discussed by the National Commission point directly to the importance of the role of

AUTHOR'S NOTE: This chapter is dedicated to Ev Rogers, who gave me direct and indirect hope in the future; and especially to Bud Wheeless, my friend, brother, colleague, and fellow Texan, who provided close support through good and bad times, who signed the matchbook, and who's close enough to come looking after two weeks.

communication in the process of education and, more importantly, to the consequences of the improper use and understanding of communication in the classroom. Having taken that point of view, let me express for you the philosophy I am going to use to direct the writing of this chapter: Because teaching is a communicative act, the primary responsibility for students' failure to learn rests with the teacher.

Obviously my philosophy implies that teachers communicate ineffectively. This should not be taken to mean that I believe that teachers do not speak well; rather, it means that I believe that teachers do not know what communication is and have received inadequate training in its use. In fact, many professional educators with whom I have worked believe that communication is the study of English, and talking is something most everyone can do. A colleague of mine in the English Department at North Texas State University once loudly argued against an oral communication core requirement by stating that, "if people were to see a picture of a North Texas State student, I would rather have the student seen with his head in a book than with his mouth open" (the sexist language was his). To help you to understand this perception of communication as commonplace and simple, let's examine two aphorisms about education and the role of communication in the learning and teaching process.

Aphorism 1: There really aren't many bad teachers.

This aphorism is patently untrue. There are many bad teachers and the number of bad teachers is increasing far too rapidly. The report of the National Commission support this unfortunate judgment. In that report, the commission stated that "too many teachers are being drawn from the bottom quarter of graduating high school and college students." But those of us who are professional educators don't need the commission's report to confirm our own anecdotal experiences. And we also know that it is not even an absence of subject matter which makes a teacher bad. It is also the inability to transmit subject matter effectively. All of the subject matter in the world will not make a teacher competent unless that information can be accurately and appropriately moved to students. You need only to examine written university course evaluations to get an idea of the impact of this deficiency. Numerous student complaints contain words such as "boring," "dull," "unclear," "cold," "distant," and the like. Rarely does a student complain of knowledge incompetence. All of the words reflect communication problems and point to a lack of training and communication competencies for educators.

Aphorism 2: The teacher who speaks well publicly, teaches well.

This aphorism is subtly dangerous because it "feels" as if it must be correct. Teaching looks like a public speaking event. A teacher (at the front of the room) talks to a group of students (rest of the room). It is the basic linear speaker and audience model. As a consequence, the closest many teachers come to so-called "communication" training is a public speaking course and maybe a course in oral reading. (The remaining "communication" training, if any, is often divided between English composition and theater courses.) As a result, teachers' instruction in human communication, when given this public presentation focus, is analogous to a chocolate sundae without the ice cream—a bit sticky and not very satisfying (McCroskey & Wheeless, 1976; Hurt et al., 1978).

Not only is such a training focus free of substance about human communication processes, it results in a set of unfortunate biases about the classroom communication process. Rogers and Kincaid (1981) defined the biases as the psychological bias and the bias of mechanistic causation.

The Psychological Bias. The psychological bias is reflected in two focuses taken in the research: (1) the individual as the unit of analysis (e.g., Berlo, 1960); and (2) the individual as the object of "blame" (e.g., Woolfolk & Woolfolk, 1979).[1] In the first case, the impact of communication on the individual student is examined externally to the social context in which the student is imbedded. Barton (1968) argued that this bias resulted in research which was analogous to "a biologist putting his or her experimental animals through a hamburger machine and looking at every hundredth cell through a microscope; anatomy and physiology get lost; structure and function disappear and one is left with cell biology." Thus, for the teacher trained in the linear public presentational "philosophy" of human communication, students are perceived as static receivers who respond to the teacher independent of the classroom and social environments which likewise shape and alter their ability to learn.

In the second case, having removed students from the context in which they learn, it becomes easier to "blame" them individually for the failure to learn. After all, when the student (in the linear model) is perceived as an individual receiver, then he or she must have the responsibility to receive. Yet recent research by Bostrom and Waldhart (1980) identified the complexity of receptive (listening) processes which are differentially affected by the communication mode employed by the source (e.g., lecture or dyadic interaction). Thus, even using a linear approach to studying communication, "blame" must be (at least) equitably distributed between students and teachers for learning failures. Unfortunately, training in public speaking and English composition does not adequately deal with this point of view.

The Bias of Mechanistic Causation. An extension of the linear concept of individual blame is the imposition of the notion of causality on the communication process. In other words, communication is perceived as functioning mechanically. When the teacher speaks, the students are "caused" to learn, *all other things being equal.* Rogers and Kincaid (1981) pointed out that although the causal analytic method has worked well in the physical sciences (e.g., the physics of billiards), it has worked less well in the communication sciences. They argued that the

> greatest difference between the explanation of physical phenomena and human communication, however, is that the "objects" of communication (unlike billiard balls) have purposes of their own. Human beings do not always use information in the way that is intended by its 'source,' nor in the way it is necessarily interpreted by the observer/researcher [p. 42].

Implicit in this assumption is the insight that teachers may not always "cause" students to learn by speaking to them; rather, in many cases, evidence for student learning best occurs when students are talking, not when teachers are talking (Hurt et al., 1978). Again, unfortunately, public speaking and English composition training result in teachers making the *post hoc ergo propter hoc* fallacy about the relationship between communication and human learning, particularly in those cases where the teacher may be a reasonably accomplished public speaker.

In effect, then, these two aphorisms seriously delude us about both the role and affect of communication on human learning. Such delusions have resulted in a failure to defined seriously teacher competency in terms of communication proficiency and to substitute training courses in public speaking, English composition, and the like for communication instruction. In the following sections I will define instructional communication, examine what I believe to be the most appropriate model of communication for use in instructional settings, compare it to the models currently in use, and finally define two generic types of teacher communication competencies that *must* be instituted prior to solving the series of other interrelated problems confronting the education professions.

DEFINING INSTRUCTIONAL COMMUNICATION

At the onset, it should be made clear that there is a distinct difference between instructional communication and speech education. I have alluded above to the former as the study of effects of communication on human learning, whereas the latter deals with training professionals to teach speech (Wheeless & Hurt, 1979). Clearly, the remainder of this chapter deals with instructional communication and should not be treated as a series of rules for teaching speech.

Defining instructional communication is a complex task. One approach is to define it in terms of contemporary learning theory. In an outstanding review of the literature relating learning theory and instructional communication, Lashbrook and Wheeless (1978) defined the latter as "the study of communication variables, technologies, and/or systems as they relate to formal instruction and the acquisition and modification of learning outcomes." Such a definition, while operationally useful, does not define instructional communication. Rather, it defines what instructional communication researchers *do*.[2] As instructional communication is a subset of the larger field of human communication, what is needed is a definition of instructional communication that links it directly to human communication processes so that teacher communication competencies can be clearly specified; in effect, a definition that states what instructional communication *is*.

INSTRUCTIONAL COMMUNICATION DEFINED

Hurt, Scott, and McCroskey (1978), in a text presenting direct applications of communication theory to classroom instruction and learning, defined human communication as "the stimulation of meaning in the mind of another by means of verbal and non-verbal message codes." We then diagrammed this definition as the instructional communication model shows in Figure 7.1

As even a cursory examination of this model indicates, it appears to contain all of the information necessary to understand what is meant by instructional communication, yet in spite of the presence of a feedback loop and the apparent shared source/receiver roles, this model (and definition) nonetheless leads into a cul-de-sac of psychological bias. The individual remains the unit of analysis (and ultimately, blame). Fundamentally, the problem rests with the constituent definition relating to the "stimulation of meaning." that simple phrase implies not only a psychological bias, but also the bias of mechanistic causation. We remain trapped by the false cause fallacy.

At a recent conference of the International Communication Association, Scott and Elliot (1983) presented a unified model for instructional communication research, interestingly allied to an earlier diffusion model proposed by Rogers and Shoemaker (1971). Scott and Elliot's model is diagrammed in Figure 7.2

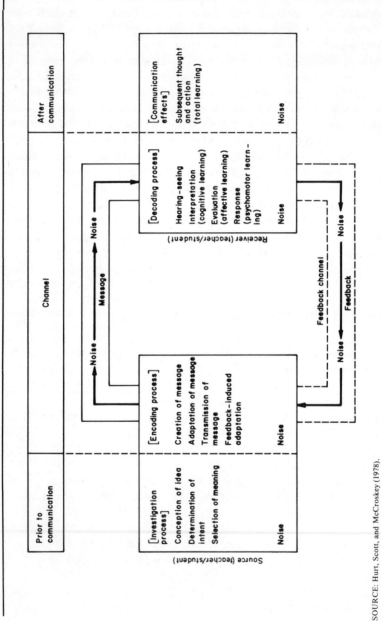

SOURCE: Hurt, Scott, and McCroskey (1978).

Figure 7.1 Hurt, Scott, and McCroskey's Model of the Classroom Communication Process

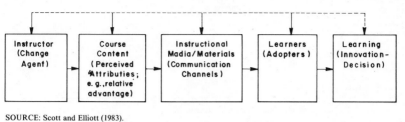

SOURCE: Scott and Elliott (1983).

Figure 7.2   An Innovation-Decision Model of the Classroom Communication Process

Scott and Elliot argued additionally that the "learning process is essentially a function of the first three stages of the innovation-decision process." They expressed this analogy as follows:

> The first function of the innovation-decision process, knowledge, is represented by cognitive learning . . . Persuasion, the second function discussed by Rogers and Shoemaker (1971), involves the formation of favorable or unfavorable attitudes toward the innovation. As such, it bears more than casual relationship to the definition of affective learning. The third function of the innovation-decision process, decision, is closely aligned with behavioral learning . . . Conceptual similarity between the two processes clearly indicate(s) that learning can be considered to be a unique case of the communication of innovation.

This conceptual similarity has been diagrammed in Figure 7.3.

Scott and Elliot have offered us intriguing analogies for use when studying communication and human learning. But as analogies, they do not tell us what instructional communication is nor do they free us from the restrictions of the psychological and mechanistic causation biases. Consider Figure 7.2. It is based upon earlier work by Rogers and Shoemaker and is called the "optional decision" model (1971: 101-118). It was intended to describe *individual* decision behavior. Figure 7.3 is a micro representation of the intellectual processes that are alleged to govern the individual's decision to innovate. Thus, both analogies remove the individual from a social matrix and the failure to innovate (or learn) still resides with the individual. In a more recent work, Rogers (1983) has criticized these models for those reasons in particular. Even more troublesome from an educational perspective is the removal of the onus of failure from the teacher, a problem I have discussed above.

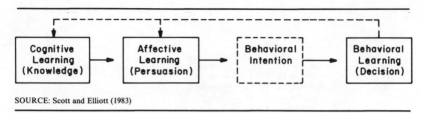

SOURCE: Scott and Elliott (1983)

Figure 7.3   Stages in the Innovation-Decision Model

Although the models discussed above are so linear as to leave us plagued by the two biases, they do provide a comparative baseline against which to judge the model I am offering as a way out of this current linear entrapment. The model of human communication processes that I am going to present was first developed by Larry Kincaid (1979) and recently utilized by Rogers and Kincaid (1981). It is called the "convergence" model of human communication, and my own research (also to be discussed below) has demonstrated its power as a concept for use in instructional communication. The covergence model as represented by Rogers and Kincaid is illustrated in Figure 7.4

In order to facilitate your interpretation of Figure 7.4, I will simply reproduce for you below the original description and explanation offered by Rogers and Kincaid (1981):

> When information is shared by two or more participants, information-processing may lead to mutual understanding, mutual agreement, and collective action. The components of the convergence model are organized at three levels of "reality," or levels of abstraction: (1) the physical level, (2) the psychological level, and (3) the social level.
>
> Once the interpretation and understanding of information is raised to the level of shared interpretations and mutual understanding, *what once could be considered as individual information-processing becomes human communication among two or more persons who hold the common purpose (if only for a brief moment) of understanding one another* [italics added]. Whether or not the participants actually do converge (or diverge) to reach a mutual understanding is a question for empirical research. Collective action requires the actions of two or more individuals, built upon a foundation of mutual agreement and understanding. When two or more individuals believe that the same statement is valid, it becomes true by consensus or mutual agreement with some degree of mutual understanding . . .
>
> Four possible combinations of mutual understanding and agreement are possible: (1) mutual understanding with agreement, (2) mutual understanding with disagreement, (3) mutual misunderstanding with agreement, and (4) mutual misunderstanding with disagreement [p. 56].

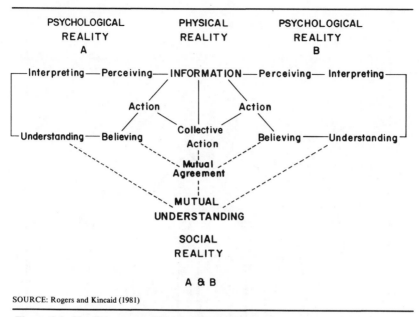

SOURCE: Rogers and Kincaid (1981)

Figure 7.4   The Convergence Model of Communication

To further assist your interpretive skills, a more dynamic picture of the convergence model shown in Figure 7.5.

Clearly, information and mutual understanding are the dominant variables of the convergence model. As such, if has a direct and immediate bearing upon instructional issues. First, the acquisition and storage of information is a teacher responsibility, as discussed by the report of the commission. Second, the powerful concept of mutual understanding extracts us from the linear biases and distributes responsibility (for learning) more equitably across all communication parties.

Thus, I am going to define instructional communication as follows:

> Instructional communication is the process whereby participants create and share information with one another in order to reach mutual understanding for purposes of cognitive and psychomotor learning.

Although it must be pointed out that much of human communication is instructional, instructional communication (although not limited to the classroom) is *purposively* directed to the production of cognitive and psychomotor learning. Learning will be defined as the process of the acquisition of communicated concepts that enable the learner to generalize appropriate

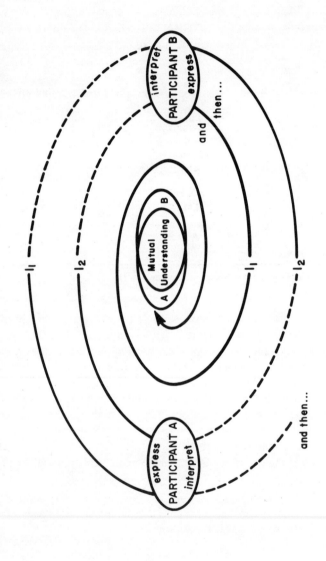

SOURCE: Rogers and Kincaid (1981)

Figure 7.5   The Dynamics of the Convergence Model

intellectual and psychomotor skills to new and unique instances of the communicated concepts. Ergo, instructional communication implies cognitive and psychomotor change.

Again, let me point out that instructional communication differs from other forms of communication (e.g., interpersonal, organizational, mass communication) organizational, by virtue of its purposive direction. For example, much of interpersonal communication is nonpurposive (phatic and nonverbal) or results in no change (Kin, 1975); and when it is purposive many of its functions are reinforcing of extant concepts and skills which results in no meaningful learning outcomes (McCroskey & Wheeless, 1976).

COGNITIVE COMMUNICATION COMPETENCIES

The list of cognitive communication competencies about which teachers should be aware can be overwhelming. In fact, in 1978 I chaired a communication competencies committee for the Instructional Communication Division of the International Communication Association. The committee generated a list of over 100 hierarchically ordered competencies for public school teachers (and I'll make the list available upon request)! So it seems rather pointless to simply regurgitate that list within the confines of this chapter. Instead, I'd like to return to the definition of instructional communication I proposed above and focus upon the concept of "mutual understanding."

From an instructional perspective, the classroom must be treated as an organized, dynamic human system (including the teacher) where a system is defined as a set of interrelated parts coordinated to accomplish a set of goals (Rogers & Kincaid, 1981). Recently, Cook (1983) and Cook and Hurt (1983) adapted Hurt's (1978) model of organizational communication systems for classroom use. This model is shown in Figure 7.6

In Figure 7.6, the arrows represent the directionality of the effects of the three subsystems upon each other. The result of this interaction is instructional communication, which purposively (and hopefully) results in cognitive and psychomotor learning.

The subsystems of this triadic structure are defined as follows. The physical structure is the material components and the spatial location of elements within human systems (Hurt, 1978). The social structure is the formal and informal composition of subgroups or units within human systems that govern horizontal and vertical communication flow (Hurt, 1978). Finally, the psychological structure is comprised of consistent patterns of perceptions among individuals and subunits of human systems that mediate individual responses to and productivity within the system (Hurt, 1978; Inkson et al.,

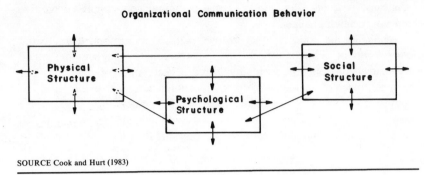

SOURCE Cook and Hurt (1983)

Figure 7.6   The Organizational Communication Structure in Classrooms

1968; Hurt & Tergen, 1977; Hall, 1963). In instructional terms, the physical structure refers to the physical arrangement and material characteristics of a classroom; the social structure refers to the patterns of formal and informal relationships that develop and evolve dynamically within classrooms;[3] and the psychological structure refers to the the the extra-classroom experiences and languages that students bring with them to the classroom.

The utility of this model vis-à-vis classroom outcomes was recently reported by John Cook and me (Cook & Hurt, 1983). In essence, Cook and I were attempting to determine how well the model (with physical structure held constant) could predict to very real classroom learning outcomes; student satisfaction with the utility of the material learned, and final grades. The students studied were enrolled in five sections of a large basic course (N = 81). The psychological structural variables were students' reported communication apprehension and their judgments of instructors credibility as information sources. Social structure was assessed using the network analytic procedure developed by Bernard and Killworth (1973) called CATIJ. From the network output, metric estimates of students' social integration (the degree to which individuals are linked to other members of a system, DSI) were derived.[4] In addition the raw communication apprehension scores were adjusted by the degree of social integration, working on the assumption that although communication apprehensives experienced anxieties abut interacting they nonetheless had the same desires to interact as did nonapprehensive students (cf. McCroskey, 1978). This variable—adjusted communication apprehensive (AOC)—and an affective measure of general liking of the course were treated as structural interaction variables which were produced by the interaction of the three substructures and were assumed to also be predictive of the classroom consequences. The data was analyzed using a canonical correlation procedure in order to preserve the systemic nature of the two data sets. The results were sufficiently impressive ($Rc = .77$, $Rc^2 = .59$) to justify considering classrooms as intact human systems. The major predictor variables were DSI and AOC, a particularly important finding supporting the perspective taken in this chapter. DSI was positively related to the learning outcome (.726) and AOC was negatively related (-.801). These and the remaining structural variables accounted for all but 41 percent of the variance in learning outcomes in a naturalistic classroom setting.

These arguments and data lead to the first cognitive communication competency (CC) of teachers.

> CC1: Teachers must be thoroughly trained in principles of human communication systems as they function in all classrooms.

Lest you be deceived into believing that these data apply only to college sophomores, Ray Preiss and I (Hurt & Preiss, 1978) studied the effects of social integration and communication apprehension of middle-school students on two similar classroom outcomes (attitudes toward school and final grades). We found that less well-integrated students had significantly lower grades and more negative attitudes toward school than did their better-integrated peers. Similar effects of human systems on learning outcomes for younger and older students have also been reported in the literature (cf. Coleman, 1961; Davis, 1961). So, teachers should understand that CC1 applies to a wide range of student ages and levels of development.

Even more importantly, as social integration in a classroom is dependent upon human communication, teachers must allow adequate opportunity for functional interaction to occur. Thus, I have led us to our second CC:

> CC2: Teachers must understand that the act of communication should never be punished or negatively reinforced.

Although it's tempting to scream "shut up" at random, inappropriate talking, only the substance or rule-violation should be criticized—never the act itself.

The concept of a human system is complex and sometimes overwhelming. Thus it might be helpful at this point to discuss some of communication roles—or functions—that teachers and students perform in classroom communication systems.

Greg Sawyer and I (1983) examined the effects over time of opinion leadership (the informal ability to control the attitudes and behavior of individuals in a human system) and social integration on human learning. Learning was defined as a score on a 100-point objective test based upon cognitive objectives whose reliability was known (alpha $= .91$). We collected system network data over three equal time periods in two lab sections of a large lecture class ($N = 55$). We took the time-series data because we knew that communication roles and relationships do not remain static. The result of the regression analysis predicting test scores was most impressive ($R = .81$, $R^2 = .66$). We then examined the relationships of two predictor variables to the criterion variable.

Two measures of social integration were used—desired social integration (number of links desired with others), and obtained social integration (number of links received from others). In the case of the former, students who did better on the examination began the semester with few links with the instructors but increased the number as the semester progressed (and received more from the instructors), while less successful students started with few instructor links and ended with little change (and fewer links from instructors). In addition, we also found that system "stars" (students seeking and obtaining a large number of links to and from other students) did significantly less well on the final than did "non-stars." We concluded that these students were functioning as social and not task facilitators, and post-hoc interviews with them and other students confirmed this. Likewise, students who were task opinion leaders (students initiated interactions with them about task-related problems) did significantly better on the exam than did social opinion leaders.

The consequences of this research lead to the third and fourth CCs:

CC3: Teachers must be aware that communication system roles cannot be generalized from one interactive issue or classroom to another. Classrooms are dynamic systems.

CC4: Teachers must understand the communication roles played by individuals within classroom communication systems so that they can manipulate those roles to more effectively manage the classroom communication system.

As promised, in this section I have attempted to identify those generic cognitive competencies about which teachers must be trained in order to serve as effective communication managers in order to facilitate learning. Again, these are intentionally general. Volumes have been written about these subjects. Nonetheless, instruction for teachers in these areas has largely been ignored. Thus, these CCs represent areas of focus that should be known by all professional educators. In the section that follows, however, I'm going to specify more specific communication-related psychomotor competencies.

PSYCHOMOTOR COMMUNICATION COMPETENCIES

When I refer to psychomotor communication competencies I am referring to communication acts or, more accurately, skills that teachers must effectively perform. And I purposively refer to teachers only because teachers must transmit information effectively to help reach mutual understanding in classrooms. Thus, these skills competencies (PMs) will be written such that they describe effective communication skills. It must be remembered, as I pointed out above, that these skills occur in the context of communication principles. As such, I'm going to open this section with one final CC:

CC5: Teachers must understand those communication principles which govern the effective processing of transmitted information (e.g., verbal, nonverbal, dyadic, and small group communication; cf. Hurt et al., 1978).

When dealing with the following communication skills, I'm going to deal only with the command component, or the ability to communicate so the message may be interpreted correctly (Norton, 1977). Because subject matter is so variable I'm not going to deal with the report or content component.

While the impact of general teacher communication skills on student learning seems obvious, they also have a direct and pragmatic effect on teachers; they are predictive of course evaluations.

Chermesh and Tzelgov (1979) examined the effects of teacher leadership behaviors on university students' teacher evaluations. Because leadership was considered, certain communication acts were included in the causal model. They sampled 4367 students enrolled in 55 courses with 77 instructors. Chermesh and Tzelgov found that different communication skills were causally related to two intervening variables (course structure and consideration of students), which in turn were causally related to course evaluations.

Thus, using the data from the Chermesh and Tzelgov study, the following very pragmatic PMs can be generated:

PM1: Effective teachers communicate in such a way as to provide a well-structured class.

PM1a: Effective teachers clearly explain course objectives and work expectations of students.

PM1b: Effective teachers clearly and concisely answer questions.

PM1c: Effective teachers clearly explain relationships between course content and course objectives.

PM1d: Effective teachers skillfully clarify relationships among various course topics.

PM1e: Effective teachers clarify materials requiring elaboration.

PM1f: Effective teachers explain objectives for each learning activity.

PM2: Effective teachers communicate in such a way as to provide consideration for students' needs.

PM2a: Effective teachers communicate in such a way as to arouse student interest in a topic of instruction.

PM2b: Effective teachers communicate in such a way as to maintain an atmosphere that encourages learning.

PM2c: Effective teachers communicate in such a way as to inspire interest or excitement in the content of the course.

It is, of course, obvious that good teaching evaluations have a very real and significant impact on the quality of professional life, particularly with the recent discussions regarding merit pay increases for public school teachers. But beyond this pragmatic concern, it is possible to extrapolate backwards to these PMs and infer that better teachers are better communicators. And while dealing with this topic of pragmatic career concerns, it is interesting to note that Chapman and Lowther (1982) in investigating variables that were predictive of teachers' career satisfaction found that the ability to communicate effectively and persuade others to accept one's ideas (e.g., mutual sharing and collective action) were positively related to job satisfaction. Ergo, it is not unreasonable to conclude that more effective communication can result in better course evaluations and greater job satisfaction for teachers.

But how should these skills be more specifically defined? An examination of PM1 through PM1f indicates that communication clarity is a substantive predictor of the control of classroom structure. In a recent study, Kennedy, Cruickshank, Bush, and Meyer (1978) defined the communication characteristics of clear teachers as judged by students. The researchers asked 1263 middle-school children in Ohio, Tennessee, and Australia to respond to sets of behavioral statements regarding their most clear and unclear teachers. These responses were then submitted to a discriminant analysis procedure to determine which items best differentiated between clear and unclear teachers. For the total sample, the best discriminant solution accounted for 61 percent of the variance. If you are bothered by the fact that these variables were based upon student perceptions, more recent research by Staybrook, Corno, and Winne (forthcoming) has found that accurate perceptions of effective teachers behaviors by students are necessary in order to establish causal links between effective teacher behaviors and student learning. Thus, on the basis of these studies, the following clarity PMs were generated.

PM3:   Effective teachers try to find out what students don't understand and then repeat the message until comprehension is achieved.

PM4:   Effective teachers repeat topics that are difficult to understand.

PM5:   Effective teachers answer questions.

PM6:   Effective teachers communicate at a rate appropriate to topics and students.

PM7:   Effective teachers give specific details about subject matter.

PM8:   Effective teachers allow adequate time for students to process information communicated.

PM9:   Effective teachers allow time to process information after explanations.

PM10: Effective teachers provide students with techniques for remembering information.

PM11: Effective teachers allow students time to practice using acquired information.

PM12: Effective teachers work examples (where appropriate) and explain them.

PM13: Effective teachers explain concepts in a clear, step-by-step fashion.

These PMs help to better define those communication behaviors that relate to the control of classroom learning structures. And it should be pointed out that these behaviors were not confused by students as only describing those teachers who award high grades (Kennedy et al., 1978).

Consideration of students is a construct that more clearly relates to interpersonal communication skills than does control of the classroom structure. Boser and Poppen (1978), defined verbal responses that teachers make when improving interpersonal relationships with students. In their study, 101 ninth-grade students were asked to rate the frequencies of interpersonal behaviors used by teachers with whom they had had good and poor relationships. These categories of interpersonal relationships were defined in previous research by Poppen (1975). Although the following PMs are based upon research using ninth-grade students, the interpersonal skills do not differ from those generally described for all age groups in the broader area of interpersonal communication (cf. Scott et al., 1978).

PM14: Effective teachers reflect their perceptions of students' feelings without evaluation.

PM15: Effective teachers do not express personal judgments or feelings about students' ideas.

PM16: Effective teachers make guesses about students' motives for past or present behavior without personal evaluation.

PM17: Effective teachers focus attention when interacting on students' behaviors and students' responsibilities for such behaviors.

PM18: Effective teachers express liking for students, unrelated to students' behaviors or success or failure in regard to academic tasks.

PM19: Effective teachers share personal ideas, opinions, or feelings with students without trying to impose them on students.

Thus far, I have focused specific teacher communication skills directed at specific classroom circumstances (e.g., clarity and interpersonal relationships). I am going to conclude by examining some general communicator style variables of effective teachers investigated by Norton (1978).

Norton was concerned with identifying those communication skills of effective teachers that tended to describe their generic communication behaviors across a variety of classroom situations. Norton studied the responses of 596 students takings courses from 65 University of Michigan professors. The students rated their professors on items relating to the command aspect of teachers communicator effectiveness. Norton's research is important because he treats communication style in a manner consistent with the descriptive criteria of instructional communication, as defined above. Specifically, he recognized that instructional communication effectiveness was a process that was ongoing, complex, and composed of interrelated sets of behaviors (Norton, 1977). So we can be assured that Norton's analyses of his style data took into account the systemic nature of the classroom communication process.

Ultimately, Norton described the communicator style of effective teachers as (1) creating a positive communicator image, (2) being attentive, (3) creating a positive impression, (4) being relaxed, (5) not being dominant, (6) being friendly, and (7) being precise. Of these seven style variables, four variables (numbers 3, 4, 6, and 7) are redundant (and confirmatory) of previous skills competencies discussed above. However, three of the variables (numbers 1, 2 and 5) provide descriptors that are useful for generating further PMs. In addition, the remaining PMs reflect communication skills that are prerequisites for the more situationally specific ones discussed above and thus reflect the importance of general communication skills training:

PM20: Effective teachers have a good communicator image.

PM20a: Effective teachers find it very easy to communicate on a one-to-one basis with strangers.

PM20b: Effective teachers are very good communicators in a small group of strangers.

PM20c: Effective teachers find it very easy to maintain a conversation with members of the opposite sex who they have just met.

PM21: Effective teachers are extremely attentive communicators.

PM21a: Effective teachers can always repeat back to someone else exactly what was meant.

PM21b: Effective teachers deliberately react in such a way that people know they are listening.

PM21c: Effective teachers enjoy listening carefully to others.

PM22: Effective teachers are not interpersonally dominant.

PM22a: Effective teachers do not generally speak very frequently in social situations.

PM22b: Effective teachers do not try to take charge of things when they are with others.

PM22c: Effective teachers do not try to "come on strong" in social situations.

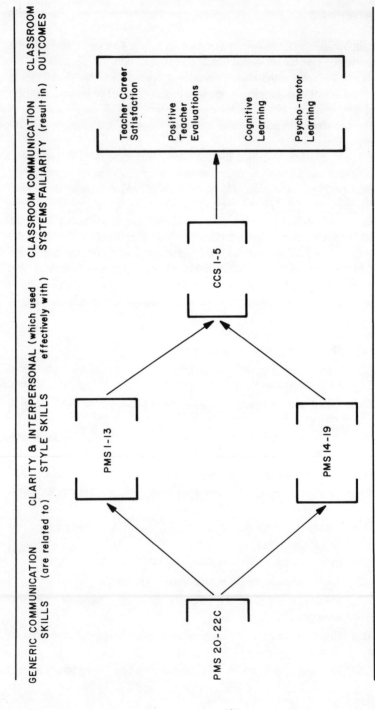

GENERIC COMMUNICATION SKILLS (are related to)   CLARITY & INTERPERSONAL STYLE SKILLS (which used effectively with)   CLASSROOM COMMUNICATION SYSTEMS FAILIARITY (result in)   CLASSROOM OUTCOMES

PMS 20-22c

PMS 1-13

PMS 14-19

CCS 1-5

Teacher Career Satisfaction

Positive Teacher Evaluations

Cognitive Learning

Psycho-motor Learning

Figure 7.7   A Hypothesized Causal Ordering of Communication Competencies for Teachers

With the inclusion of these PMs generated by Norton's research, I have gone full circle from cognitive competencies to specific communication skills that describe effective teachers. But lists of things do not always fit together clearly. So, I have summarized all of these for you in an hypothesized causal order in Figure 7.7.

What Figure 7.7 represents is the beginning of a set of criteria that will enable us to define the cognitive and skills competencies necessary to be achieved by perspective educators. More importantly, these competencies will enable professional educators to identify those troublesome communication behaviors of student teachers and in-service teachers in order to develop effective corrective training programs. And although I have argued against the concept of individual blame, teachers still remain responsible for communicating in such a way as to maximize students' learning potential. After all, effective communication is the difference between knowing and teaching, and aporia[5] has limited long-term utility in instructional environments.

NOTES

1. These works are otherwise well done and are cited only as examples of the psychological bias.

2. This is an outstanding and "cutting edge" review. I recommend it to the interested scholar.

3. Classrooms do have formal structures in which interpersonal relationships are based upon status norms, rather than solidarity (friendship) norms.

4. There are a variety of mathematical definitions that can be used to calculate social integration. See Knoke and Kulkinski (1982) for an excellent discussion of these.

5. Aporia is a philosophical term for the systematic generation of failure.

REFERENCES

Barton, A. Bringing society back in: Survey research and macro-methodology. *American Behavioral Scientist*, 68, *17*, 1-9.

Berlo, D.K. *The process of communication: An introduction to theory and practice.* New York: Holt, Rinehart & Winston, 1960.

Bernard, H. & Killwork, P. On the social structure of an ocean-going research vessel and other important things. *Social Science Research*, 1973, *2*, 145-184.

Boser, J. & Poppen, W. Identification of verbal response roles for improving student-teacher relationships. *Journal of Educational Research*, 1978, *72* (2), 90-93.

Bostrom, R. & Waldhart, E. Components in listening behavior: The role of short-term memory. *Human Communication Research*, 1980, *6* (3), 221-227.

Chapman, D.W. & Lowther, M.A. Teachers' satisfaction with teaching. *Journal of Educational Research*, 1982, *75* (4), 241-247.

Chermesh, R. & Tzelgov, J. The college instructor as a leader: Some theoretical derivations from a generalization of a causal model of students' evaluations of their instructors. *Journal of Educational Research*, 1979, *11* (2), 109-115.

Coleman, J. *The adolescent society: The social life of the teenager and its impact on education.* New York: The Free Press, 1961.

Cook, J.A. *The relationships among organizational communication structures and learning outcomes in college level basic communication courses.* Ph.D. thesis, North Texas State University, Denton.

Cook, J.A. & Hurt, H.T. *The relationships among organizational communication structures and learning outcomes.* Paper presented at the International Communication Association annual conference, Dallas, 1983.

Davis, J.A. Locals and cosmopolitans in American graduate schools. *International Journal of Comparative Society,* 1961, *2,* 212-223.

Hall, R. The concept of bureaucracy: An empirical assessment. *American Journal of Sociology,* 1963,*69,* 32-40.

Hurt, H.T. *Structure and instruction in organizational communication.* Paper presented at the Eastern Communication Association annual conference, Boston, 1978.

Hurt, H.T. & Preiss, R. Silence isn't necessarily golden: Communication apprehension, desired social choice and academic success among middle-school students. *Human Communication Research*, 1978, *4,* 315-328.

Hurt, H. T. & Sawyer, G. *Communication structures and learning outcomes.* Unpublished manuscript, Center for Communication Research, North Texas State University, Denton, 1983.

Hurt, H.T. & Teigren, C.W. The development of a measure of perceived organizational innovativeness. In B. Rubin (Ed.) *Communication yearbook 1.* New Brunswick, NJ: Transaction Books, 1977, 377-388.

Hurt, H.T., Scott, M.D., & McCroskey, J. *Communication in the classroom.* Reading, MA.: Addison-Wesley, 1978.

Inkson, J., Hickson, D., & Pugh, D. *Administrative reduction at variances in organizational and behavior.* London: British Psychological Association, 1968.

Kennedy, J., Cruickshank, D., Bush, A., & Myer, B. Additional investigations into the nature of teacher clarity. *Journal of Educational Research,* 1978, *72* (1), 3-10.

Kim, J.Y. Feedback in social sciences; Toward reconceptualization of morphogeneses. In B. Rubin and J. Kim (Eds.) *General System Theory and Human Communication.* Rochelle Park, NJ: Hayden, 1975.

Kincaid, L. The convergence model of communication. Honolulu, East-West Communication Institute, Paper 18, 1979.

Knocke, D. & Kulkinski, J.H., *Network analysis.* Beverly Hills: Sage, 1982.

Lashrook, V. & Wheeless, L.R. Instructional communication theory and research: An overview of the relationship between learning theory and instructional communication. In B. Rubin (Ed.) *Communication yearbook 2.* New Brunswick, NJ: Transaction Books, 1978.

McCroskey, J.C. Oral communication apprehension: A summary of recent theory and research. *Human Communication Research,* 1977, *4,* 78-96.

McCroskey, J.C. & Wheeless, L.R. An introduction to human communication. Boston: Allyn and Bacon, 1976.

National Commission on Excellence in Education. Open letter to the American people, a nation at risk: The imperative for educational reform. David P. Gardner (Chair), April, 1983.

Norton, R.W. Teacher effectiveness as a function of communicator style. In B. Rubin (Ed.) *Communication yearbook 1*. New Brunswick, NJ: Transaction Books, 1977.

Poppen, W.A. *Role-shifting: An eclectic model for improving relationships*. Paper presented at the Southern Association of Counselor Educators and Supervisors, October 1975.

Rogers, E. *The diffusion of innovations* (3rd ed.). New York: The Free Press, 1983.

Rogers, E. and L. Kincaid, *Communication networks: Toward a new paradigm for research*. New York: The Free Press, 1981.

Rogers, E. & Shoemaker, F. *Communication of innovations* (2nd ed.). New York: The Free Press, 1971.

Scott, M.D. & Elliott, S. *Innovation in the classroom: Toward a unified model for instructional communication research*. Paper presented at the International Communication Association annual convention, Dallas, 1983.

Scott, M.D., & Powers, W.G. *Interpersonal communication: A question of needs*. Boston: Houghton Mifflin, 1978.

Staybrook, N., Corno, L., & Winne P. Path analysis relating students' perceptions of teacher behavior to student achievements. *Journal of Teacher Education*, forthcoming.

Wheeless, L.R. & Hurt, H.T. Instructional communication theory and research: An overview of instructional strategies and instructional communication systems. In D. Nimmo (Ed.) *Communication yearbook 3*. New Brunswick, NJ: Transaction books, 1979.

Woolfolk, K.L. & Woolfolk, A.E. Effects of teachers verbal and nonverbal behaviors on student perceptions and attitudes. *American Educational Research Journal*, 1974, *11*, 297-303.

8

Judgments of Interpersonal Competence

How You Know, What You Know, and Who You Know

MICHAEL E. ROLOFF
KATHY KELLERMANN

To be described as competent should be a most valued compliment. But the warm inner feeling associated with receiving a positive evaluation may be replaced by an unsettling ambivalence when the term "competent" is preceded by the modifiers "merely" or "only." However, regardless of the emotional reaction, we argue that competence is inherently an evaluative judgment of a person's behavior rather than a skill or trait possessed by an individual. While a person may have certain characteristics that facilitate the production of behavior judged to be competent, that person is not a competent communicator unless he or she has been judged to be so by a perceiver. Therefore, competence is a judgment that a person's behavior corresponds to certain standards of performance. In the case of communication competence, the focus is upon the evaluative judgment of a person's verbal and nonverbal behavior. Consequently, the process of attributing competence to someone is influenced by two sets of variables: (1) those that influence how the judgment is made, and (2) those that influence the performance of the judged behaviors.

We approach interpersonal communication competency from the viewpoint of a cluster of theories associated with the study of social cognition (see Roloff & Berger, 1982a). Roloff and Berger (1982b, p. 21) defined social cognition as the "organized thoughts people have about human interaction." We will focus on how these thoughts are associated with both the behaviors of a communicator and the evaluative judgment of competence with respect to those behaviors. In other words, we advance the position that social cognition processes affect not only the communication behaviors being judged but also the judgment process itself.

This chapter will be divided into three sections. First, we will examine the nature of the judgment component of interpersonal communication competency by focusing on how people perceive and evaluate communication behaviors. Second, we will describe actor characteristics that may influence the behaviors being judged. Specifically, the influence of interpersonal awareness and social knowledge on judgments of competency will be explored. Finally, the results of an empirical investigation into interpersonal communication competency will be reported.

THE JUDGMENT OF INTERPERSONAL COMMUNICATION COMPETENCY

As noted earlier, to be judged as competent implies that one's behavior has been scrutinized and evaluated. To be described as a competent interpersonal communicator suggests that one's verbal and nonverbal behaviors observed within the context of an interpersonal relationship have been scrutinized and judged to be capable of achieving certain standards of performance. Thus, the evaluated communication behaviors have been sampled from those occurring within a broader relationship. We recognize that this definition is somewhat ambiguous and in order to more clearly explicate the construct, have developed six implications:

IMPLICATION 1: THE STIMULUS BEHAVIORS ARE OBSERVED WITHIN AN INTERPERSONAL RELATIONSHIP

As noted in other chapters, different types of communication competency may be studied (e.g., organizational or mass communication competency). The behaviors judged to be competent presumably occur in distinguishable contexts which in turn may require different behaviors. In the case of interpersonal communication competency, the critical context is that of an interpersonal relationship. Hinde (1979, p. 14) defined an interpersonal relationship as "some sort of intermittent interaction between two people, involving interchanges over an extended period of time. The interchanges have some degree of mutuality, in the sense that the behaviour of each takes some account of the behaviour of the other." Other than the obvious characteristic of being dyadic, interpersonal relationships are composed of interactions. They often have a history of interactions as well as the potential for future ones. As a result, several relational characteristics can be identified.

First, over the course of a relationship, partners come to form personal expectations about each other's behavior. By an expectation, we mean that individuals can make probability estimates about the likelihood each will perform certain behaviors. We recognize that people may not explicitly think about or describe these expectations; they may remain latent until the person is forced to justify or describe his or her judgment. During the initial stages of an interpersonal relationship, it is likely that the partner's probability estimates are based upon his or her experiences with people similar to his or her partner. These general expectations may result from observation of individuals belonging to the same groups or culture as the target person (Miller & Steinberg, 1975). As the relationship develops, personal expectations begin forming. While group or cultural membership still remains an important basis for inference, the relational partners begin to rely upon their observations and experiences with each other for formulating their probability estimates. In other words, we would expect that over the course of a relationship an individual's estimates about the likelihood that his or her partner would perform a given behavior either would begin to deviate from the probability estimates made for similar others or the probability estimates would become increasing conditional; that is, one's expectations that someone would engage in a given behavior become limited by specifiable boundary conditions. The personal expectations partly include allowances for idiosyncracies perceived in the partner through specification of conditional probabilities.

People are motivated to develop such personal expectations as a means of reducing their uncertainty about each other's behavior. If partners are incapable of accurately predicting their behaviors, interactions and exchanges could become uncoordinated and, hence, too risky. Consequently, we predict that partners will engage in information seeking until they reach some tolerable level of certainty in predicting their partners' behavior. Note that we have described a feeling of certainty, not accuracy in the activity of prediction. For some relationships, a less accurate picture of the partner does not impede the nature of the interactions. If partners choose to remain acquaintances, misperceptions may never produce difficulties because interactions remain somewhat superficial. However, should relational partners perceive that future interactions will likely occur or desire to escalate the relationship, the threshold of certainty may increase dramatically, that is, greater confidence is needed. The exact threshold for certainty in a given interpersonal relationship thus varies as a function of the type of relationship at present, the perceived development trajectory of the relationship, the purpose of the relationship, and a host of other variables. They key issue is that the certainty threshold does not necessarily correspond to accuracy in prediction. Indeed, some individuals perceive greater knowledge of their partner's preferences than is really the case. McCall and Simmons (1978) have noted that often relational partners engage in extensive impression management so that neither observes the other's transgressions. Consequently, we predict that as a relationship develops, the individual will engage in information seeking until expectations reach some level of confidence. After that time, information seeking becomes less active even if the expectations are fraught with error.

Second, the communication content observed in interpersonal relationships may be more varied than in other contexts. Interpersonal communicators are likely to share more information about their personal histories or predispositions. A number of theorists have predicted that as relationships develop, both the breadth and depth of self-disclosed information increases (e.g., Altman & Taylor, 1973; Miller & Steinberg, 1975). This tendency may reflect the desire to gain more information about each other and/or increased trust as the relationship escalates. In addition, the total number of topics discussed in an interpersonal relationship should be greater than in other contexts. Relational partners often need to coordinate daily activities in a number of different areas: eating, cleaning, shopping, working, and so on. It is likely that they will be required to interact about any number of phenomena associated with these tasks. The only common characteristic of this diverse content is that one or both partners believe the content is or should be available to both of them. In other words, the content of the communication is perceived to be relevant to their relationship.

Third, outside observers of an interpersonal interaction may not be able to fully comprehend its meaning to the relational partners by simply interpreting the verbal and nonverbal cues. This characteristic may seem counterintuitive. As long as an observer and relational partners are from the same subculture, one might expect the interpretation of the linguistic and nonverbal cues to be relatively error free. However, we argue that during the course of repeated interactions, relational partners have learned to interpret their cues in a somewhat unique manner. Their previous history of interactions have provided an information base for understanding, allowing the partners to communicate in a crisp and fluid manner with little amplification of intent. In other words, personal expectations have freed them from elaborate explanations about their goals and motives. For example, research conducted by Kent, Davis, and Shapiro (1978, 1981) discovered that friends could accurately and efficiently communicate when prohibited from asking questions of one another during an interaction while such a prohibition significantly disrupted the communication between strangers. Unless an observer has access to the interaction history of a relationship, he or she lacks the personal expectations about the partners to "fill in the gaps" in the conversation. Gottman, Markman, and Notarius (1976) discovered that having marital partners code their own interactions produced results different from previous research utilizing outside observers as coders. We note, however, that in some interactions the interpretations of the partners and observers may match; if the interaction history is limited, then both partners and observers may be equivalent in knowledge.

Finally, interpersonal relationships develop over time. As the number of interactions increase, we expect at least some of the changes described in this section (e.g., development of personal expectations, information base, etc.) to be observed. These changes may occur in a relatively slow manner and may even reach a plateau after which few if any changes in the relationship are found. Because interpersonal relationships develop, we recognize that one might study interpersonal communication competency at any number of places within their development. One might be interested in the dynamics of initial interactions as well as the interactions in more advanced relationships. While we argue that these two situations involve somewhat different processes, each is a valid area of inquiry. They are simply different stages of development in the history of an interpersonal relationship.

IMPLICATION 2: SALIENT VERBAL AND NONVERBAL BEHAVIORS OBSERVED WITHIN AN INTERACTION ARE THE TARGETS OF THE COMPETENCY JUDGMENT

At first glance, this implication may seem trivial; after all, it is obvious that competency judgments are inherently focused on behavior. However, this implication is more complex than initially surmised. An almost bewildering number of different verbal and nonverbal cues are emitted in interaction. Verbal cues such as words, phrases, and appeals can be observed. Nonverbal behaviors in the vocalization of the verbal cues as well as the movement of the face, body, and limbs are occurring simultaneously with the verbal cues. It seems unlikely, if not impossible, for a person to make a competency judgment about each individual cue in an interaction; there are simply too many. Consequently, the important question becomes, Out of myriad verbal and nonverbal behaviors contained in an interaction, which ones are the focus of the competency judgment? Our proposed answer to that question stems from a perspective advanced by Taylor and Fiske (1978) wherein most human decision making is characterized as a function of "top of the head" judgments. Taylor and Fiske write that "individuals frequently respond with little thought to the most salient stimuli in their environment. We believe that the causal attributions people make, the opinions people express, and the impressions they form of others in work or social situations is often shaped by seemingly trivial but highly salient information and that, accordingly, such attitudes and impressions show little cross-situational consistency" (p. 252). In other words, the attention of a judge is drawn to those characteristics of a situation that seem to stand out from other competing characteristics. These salient cues may or may not lead the scrutinizer to make veridical judgments.

Taylor and Fiske have argued that a number of different environmental stimuli may make a given cue salient (e.g., brightness, movement, etc.). Among those stimuli is the notion that novel cues are likely to become salient. This implies that novelty is a violation of what one expected to occur. We extend upon their analysis by arguing that a behavior is novel and, hence, salient when its observed frequency significantly violates the expectations for that particular communicator or class of communicators. In other words, a novel behavior is one which *violates expectations for a given communicator or group of communicators*, not necessarily behavior that is statistically rare in general. Our conception of expectation violation requires several amplifications.

First, not every deviation from an expectation will make that behavior salient. We noted that a violation must go beyond some threshold in order to attract attention. In other words, deviations of low magnitude may not be scrutinized at all. Unfortunately, we have no data upon which to exactly set the threshold. Indeed, the threshold may vary dependent upon the observer's state, the situation, and the purpose of the interaction. At this point, we simply note that if a given behavior is perceived to be too frequent or infrequent, it becomes salient and will be the focus of the competency judgment.

Second, environmental cues may increase the likelihood that a violation will be perceived as salient. In some cases, a judge may not have access to all of the cues emitted by a communicator. If one is watching a person communicating with another it is likely the vantage pont may be from the side. This particular view reduces the likelihood that the frequency of some facial cues could be accurately observed while certain other behaviors can be better observed than if facing the communicator directly. Consequently, different cues may be seen as violating expectations simply because of the vantage point of the perceiver.

Third, these violations are likely to be observed in the justifications or explanations of the judge. In other words, if we ask the person how he or she made the competency judgment, these salient behaviors should be reported as critical influences on the judgment. Langer (1978) has argued that in most cases, people mindlessly engage in tasks with little recognition of any stimuli in the situation. However, she notes that when deviations from expectations occur, the person becomes more mindful of what has occurred and awareness increases. It should be noted that our assertion is inconsistent with Taylor and Fiske's analysis. They argue that people may not be fully aware that they are responding to salient cues. Consequently, we only predict a probability of awareness, not a certainty.

Fourth, the salience of a given behavior may change during the course of relational development. Earlier, we argued that the expectations for initial interaction are of a general nature, acquired from experience with communicators similar to the target person. As the relationship progresses, personal expectations geared to experiences with that particular communicator form. In the initial stages of a relationship, any behavior that significantly violates expectations for the general class of communicators is likely to be salient. However, as the relationship develops and interaction experience accumulates, those behaviors that violate the personal expectations for that particular communicator will become salient. Interestingly, this suggests that if a communicator initially and consistently violated expectations for the class to which he or she belongs, a judge would come to expect that behavior as part of the personal expectation. If the communicator should suddenly start behaving according to expectations of the general class of communicators (or in violation of the personal expectation for him or her), the behavior that is consistent with the expectation for his or her group will be perceived as deviant and will become salient.

Fifth, judges having different experiences with the same class of communicators or a single communicator may perceive different behaviors as salient. We argue that these different experiences will create unique general or personal expectations. We do not wish, however, to give the impression that no overlap will exist among expectations of different judges. Given similar socialization experiences, significant areas of overlap may be found. However, because two individuals are inherently observing an interaction from different vantage points, we expect some level of difference to be found. As a result, individual judges may find different behaviors as significantly violating the expectation for the communicator and reach different conclusions about competency. In fact, we would argue that the less overlap in socialization experiences or in direct experiences with a given communicator or class of communicators, the greater the chance that judges will perceive different behaviors as being salient.

Sixth, a significant single violation of an expectation may prompt the individual to look for more. If Langer (1978) is correct, then a single significant violation should prompt mindfulness that could stimulate closer scrutiny. The judge may lower thresholds for what constitutes a violation or look for violations of related behaviors. For example, if one perceives a communicator as speaking much faster than expected, the judge may begin scrutinizing related behaviors he or she expects to be simultaneously occurring. Indeed, the judge may even be more willing to view moderate deviations from expectations as constituting salient behaviors.

Finally, if no significant violations are observed, the judgments may reflect the *expectations* for a given communicator or class of communicators rather than the target's *actual* behavior. In other words, if no salient cues are present, the judge may assume that the person behaved according to the expectation for the communicator or class of communicators even if slight violations actually could be observed. In essence, the judge engages in very little active scrutinization of the communicator's behaviors. For example, Langer, Blank, and Chanowitz (1978) observed that communications lacking adequate justifications but structured in a manner similar to those normally experienced by recipients were mindlessly accepted. In other words, when nothing salient was observed in the structure of a communication, people tended to obey its command even when the command was irrational. They responded to the command based upon the expectation they had formed for that type of communication rather than on the content of the actual communication.

IMPLICATION 3: SALIENT BEHAVIORS ARE EVALUATED IN TERMS OF STANDARDS OF PERFORMANCE

Thus far we have described the context in which behaviors are observed and what behaviors are sampled from those performed in the interaction. We have not yet addressed the issue of how they are evaluated. In other words, simply because a behavior is salient (i.e., significantly violated an expectation) does not indicate the direction of its evaluation (i.e., positive or negative) or the criteria along which it was evaluated (i.e., the precise standard of performance). Just as we argued that people have expectations about the frequency with which certain types of people perform behaviors, we also argue that judges have expectations about the probability that certain behaviors lead to outcomes and reflect desired processes. These expectations are termed standards of performance. For example, judges may believe that a relationship exists between the frequency with which one smiles during a conversation and how persuasive one will be (i.e., what impact one is having) or how attentive one is (i.e., what other processes are going on). When a given frequency of smiles is observed, the judge will be able to assess a predicted level of persuasiveness or attentiveness. Again, we feel compelled to amplify upon this definition.

First, a standard of performance reflects a perceived relationship between behavior and a criterion (e.g., persuasiveness). A number of types of relationships might be observed. One might expect that a positive linear relationship exists between a behavior and a standard. As the frequency of a behavior increases so does the perception of how successfully the behavior meets the standard. For example, a person may believe that the louder one talks, the greater is one's persuasiveness. Conversely, a negative relationship might exist between two variables; as the frequency of a behavior increases, then that behavior becomes less successful in meeting the criterion. For example, an individual might believe that the greater the frequency of nonfluencies in speech, the less persuasive is the individual exhibiting the nonfluencies. Finally, any number of nonlinear relationships might be expected. An inverted-U relationship might be expected by an individual between the amount of direct eye contact and friendliness such that at high and low levels of direct eye contact, a communicator is viewed as not being friendly.

While we have chosen to describe these relationships in social scientific jargon, we recognize that most people may be unable to do this. Yet, people do justify their competency judgments in ways that allow us to infer such relationships. For example, we have observed individuals watching the television program "Firing Line" when William F. Buckley faces his nemesis John Kenneth Galbraith. Not only do the two men possess different political views but they also engage in different debating styles. Buckley speaks rapidly while Galbraith is much slower and more deliberate. We have heard viewers of this debate respond that Buckley speaks too rapidly while Galbraith speaks too slowly; the point being that viewers seem to see an inverted-U quadratic relationship between speech rate and persuasiveness. Galbraith is less effective because he is at the low end while Buckley is also less effective because he is at the high end. This anecdotal evidence raises an interesting question for empirical research. Recently, Street, Brady, and Putnam (1983) noted that competency judgments were greater for individuals speaking at 376 and 253 words per minute than for communicators speaking at 140 words per minute. It would be of interest to see if the addition of speech rates between 140 and 253 words per minute and rates greater than 376 words per minute would cause the inverted-U nonlinear relationship to be evidenced and if naive judges could predict the exact form of the relationship. In other words, people might be able to describe in ordinary language the statistical relationships we observe.

While we have noted that a standard of performance is defined by the relationship between a behavior and some criterion, we have not noted what competency criteria might be employed. Initially, we anticipated that five sets of criteria could be employed in making competency judgments. A judge might evaluate the degree to which a communicator adapted his or her verbal and nonverbal communication to the relational partner, a criterion similar to the processes described in Accommodation Theory (Street & Giles, 1982). A judge might evaluate the degree to which a communicator has made him- or herself understood, a criterion reflecting not only clarity concerns but also issues of openness and disclosure. Another criterion that we anticipated might be employed in competency judgments relates to the persuasive impact a communicator might have, the idea being that a persuasive communicator is a competent communicator. The degree to which a communicator appears apprehensive or relaxed/comfortable might also be an important criterion on which judgments of competency are based (e.g., McCroskey, 1977). Competency judgments might also be a function of a communicator's style which could be differentiated according to Norton's (1978) dimensions of style—relaxed, friendly, animated, dynamic, dramatic, open, dominant—as well as being a function of attentiveness (Norton & Pettegrew, 1979) and fluency.

In order to determine whether these particular criteria are employed, Kellermann and Roloff (1983a) had persons evaluate both their own and their partners' competency on a 33-item questionnaire immediately after having interacted. Two sets of factor analyses were done on these ratings. First, items pertaining to the degree to which persons both *thought* they had been competent and believed they would be *perceived* by their partners to have been competent were factor analyzed. Five factors explaining 71 percent of the variance emerged: comfortableness, friendliness, activity in the conversation, ability to be understood, and persuasiveness. Second, items pertaining to perceptions of competency of the *relational partner* were factor analyzed, yielding three factors—other-directedness, comfortableness, and activity in the conversation—explaining 63.4 percent of the variance. Interestingly, persons used fewer criteria when judging the competency of others than when judging the competency of self. It can therefore be concluded that there are distinguishable standards on which judgments of competency are based.

Second, these standards reflect subjective observations about the relationship between behaviors and outcomes or processes; consequently, no statement can be made about their accuracy. Hewes and Planalp (1982) have noted that a number of "forgivable" biases influence human decision making. Research also indicates that these biased judgments tend to persist even after they have been discredited (e.g., Jennings et al., 1981; John-Smith, 1982). Thus, the relationships are only as accurate as the observations upon which they are based and the methods by which the data from the observations are processed.

Third, a given standard of performance may be related to a number of different communication behaviors. For example, one may perceive several behaviors as related to persuasiveness. A person who talks loudly, rapidly, and with few disfluencies may be expected to be persuasive. These behaviors in conjunction or in isolation may be related to a given standard. We believe that this cluster of behaviors related to a given standard constitutes what Hewes and Planalp (1982) have referred to as an implicit theory. In other words, they are propositions relating variables to one another in a manner similar to scientific theories. For example, one could discover an implicit theory of persuasion that would reflect all of the behaviors and their perceived relationship to that criterion.

Fourth, a given behavior may be perceived as related to a number of different standards. In other words, a given behavior may be part of several different implicit theories. For example, one may perceive a relationship exists between amount of eye contact and persuasiveness, attentiveness, and friendliness. Consequently, a given salient behavior can be evaluated along more than one standard of performance. It is conceivable that a given frequency of behavior may be related in different fashions to more than one standard. For example, if one perceives a positive linear relationship between the frequency of eye contact and attentiveness but an inverted-U relationship between frequency of eye contact and friendliness, then a given level of eye contact can be evaluated differently along the two standards; a high frequency may be judged attentive but not friendly.

Fifth, not all standards are operative in a given situation. Just as we noted not all behaviors performed in an interaction are judged, we now note that a judge will not employ all of the potential standards of performance. Indeed, we view the selection of salient behaviors and appropriate criteria as being in a mutually causal relationship. In some cases, a judge enters a situation with certain criteria in mind that will make given behaviors salient. Dependent upon the goal a communicator may have for entering into a social interaction (Cronkite & Liska, 1980), a person will be cognitively tuned so that he or she is more likely to see violations of expectations for certain types of behaviors and not others. For example, a person may enter into a situation to gather information about another's sincerity. Consequently, he or she may be cognitively tuned to scrutinize certain behaviors assumed to be indicators of sincerity. This cognitive tuning may increase the probability that a person will see deviations from expectations as being significant since he or she is *looking* for them. Upon reaching the situation, however, a given behavior may be so different from latent ("untuned") expectations that not only will it be judged according to entry standards but may prompt new standards to become relevant. However, if the behaviors are consistent with expectations for that person, only a few standards will be employed. In other words, the manner in which the behavior is sampled and processed varies not only according to the type of standard applied, but the quantity of standards applied. The more behaviors are salient, the more likely it will be that persons more carefully scrutinize the situation and apply multiple standards; the more behaviors there are that fulfill expectations, the less fine-grained will be the observation and the fewer standards applied.

Sixth, behavior that violates an expectation may or may not be negatively evaluated. We often think of violations of expectations as implying a negative judgment. Such a statement suggests that the usual behavior of a given communicator or class of communicators is also perceived to be maximally related to a given standard. We do not believe this assumption to be universally true. Imagine that a person has an expectation that an inverted-U relationship exists between how fast a person speaks and his or her persuasiveness. In other words, the greater the number of words spoken per given time unit, the greater the persuasiveness up to some rate, after which persuasiveness begins to decline. Let us further assume that maximal persuasiveness is perceived to be around 200 words per minute. If one's expectation for a given class of communicators is that most speak at or around 200 words per minute, then significant deviations from that amount should indeed be salient and negatively evaluated. However, if a person has come to expect that a given class of communicators are "slow talkers" (i.e., speak at about 100 words per minute), then an individual who is part of that class but speaks at 200 words per minute may have his or her speech rate viewed as both salient and positive (i.e., persuasive). In other words, behavior that is salient (i.e., significantly violates general or personal expectations) may be positively evaluated if it conforms to the standards of performance. Behaviors consistent with personal or general expectations may be negatively evaluated if they do not correspond to standards and no competing salient cues are present.

IMPLICATION 4: RELATIONAL PARTNERS OBSERVING THE SAME INTERACTION MAY REACH DIFFERENT CONCLUSIONS ABOUT EACH OTHER'S COMPETENCE

Communicators often have the frustrating yet interesting experience of leaving an interaction confident of what had transpired only to find that the other person had an equally confident but radically different impression of the same events. We argue that the same phenomenon can be observed with competency judgments. One person may leave the interaction feeling that he or she had been very persuasive as a result of any number of behaviors enacted. That person may even perceive that the interaction partner felt the same way. However, upon later discussion, the person finds that the partner found him or her to be extremely unpersuasive. Varying perceptions about a situation such as this may exist for a number of reasons.

First, a communicator may have inadequate information about how he or she behaved in an interaction. When we say inadequate, we mean that a communicator may be unaware of the behaviors he or she enacted. This last statement may sound peculiar. How can a person do something without being aware of it? Actually, this is quite easy in an interaction. As we noted earlier, myriad behaviors are enacted in even a short interaction. It is no more reasonable to assume that a source is aware of all he or she has done any more than it is reasonable to assume that an observer judges each behavior for there are simply too many behaviors. In addition, Argyle (1975) has argued that some communication behaviors, especially nonverbal cues, occur at low levels of awareness. Just as an observer might not be able to discern a micromomentary facial cue, there is little reason to believe that a source is aware he or she engaged in one. Furthermore, to the extent behaviors of the communicator do not violate personal expectations for self, it is unlikely that the communicator's *exact* behavior would be given extensive attention. In a sense, the communicator's behavior is likely to be scripted (Abelson, 1976, 1981) to the extent that the communicator does not engage in significant violations of expectations. Enactment of scripted behaviors has been said to be not only mindless but the action sequences themselves have been said to be difficult to tap and recall specifically (Langer, 1978). As a result, a communicator may have inadequate information about how he or she *actually* behaved in a specific interaction.

Second, the relational partners may become focused on different things during the interaction. Duval and Wicklund (1972) have argued that individuals focus their attention on either self or the environment but are unable to focus on both simultaneously. Consequently, the relational partners must shift their attention between self and other during the conversation, which may result in missed or misperceived behaviors. In addition, self-focus is viewed to be a negative state for the individual, implying that attention is generally focused outward. In other words, partners are focusing on each other more than on themselves, thereby allowing for differences in judgments due to differences in attentional focus.

Third, relational partners may enter the interaction with general or personal expectations for each other that diverge from the ones they hold for themselves. In other words, one partner might expect the other smiles frequently during interactions while the other perceives him- or herself to be a serious individual who rarely smiles. Consequently, one person might view his or her smiling to be nonsalient while the partner views it as a violation of expectation. This would seem to be quite likely in initial interactions where parties have little knowledge of one another but greater knowledge of themselves.

Fourth, the two partners view each other from different vantage points. It is extremely difficult to view oneself during an interaction. One may rarely have insight into what exactly one is doing because the opportunity for self-observation is so rare. It is interesting to watch students viewing videotapes of themselves in an interaction. They are frequently embarrassed by what they see. Small verbal and nonverbal slips cause loud and pained groans from the viewers! It becomes obvious that they are observing behaviors they had no idea they had enacted. Further, research by Storms (1973) seems to confirm this anecdotal evidence. He discovered that actors and observers reach different conclusions about the causes of the actors' behavior. However, these differences are attenuated when the actor is allowed to view his or her own behavior on videotape. In other words, the actor is given the opportunity to view self as an observer and differences in judgments tend to dissipate.

Finally, the relational partners may enter the interaction with different standards of performance. If one expects that a positive linear relationship exists between the amount of eye contact and perceived friendliness while the other thinks an inverted-U relationships exists, then the two may evaluate their behaviors differently even if they accurately perceive the frequency of the behaviors.

IMPLICATION 5: ONE'S POSITION AS A PARTICIPANT OR OBSERVER OF AN INTERACTION WILL INFLUENCE THE COMPETENCY JUDGMENT

While we recognize that an interpersonal relationship is dyadic, it is sometimes the case that an outside observer will make a judgment about the relational partners. For example, a counselor may look for communication problems between two dissatisfied spouses. In addition, a researcher may ask outside observers to code a dyadic interaction. Or perhaps most common is the informal observation individuals undertake prior to meeting others for the first time. We view the roles of participant and observer as distinct and expect that the judgments of people occupying the two roles may differ. We see several arguments supporting this position.

First, we noted earlier that individuals may have different expectations about a communicator's behavior. Two relational partners may have formed personal expectations about each other that an observer has had no opportunity to form. Particularly in developing or developed relationships, the role of participant or observer is likely to produce different expectations about a communicator's behavior as the observer is generally limited to cultural level information for the class of communicators to which a participant belongs whereas a participant has access to information on which personal expectations can be based.

Second, participants and observers view the interaction from different vantages. By the nature of being a participant in an interaction, the relational partners usually cast most of their gaze upon each other and focus their listening on their talk. Consequently, they are spending some time thinking about what each of them has said and reacting to it. Even if the conversation is highly scripted (Abelson, 1976) the relational partners must pay enough attention in order to enact the scripted behaviors. Observers are only required to listen and make judgments. They do not have to enact communication behaviors. This may mean that some judges may be better able to perceive violations of expectations than the interactants. However, this "alleged" advantage may turn into a disadvantage if the observer scrutinizes the conversation so closely that he or she reacts to violations of expectations not perceived by the interactants to be salient. In other words, the observer may perceive things unrelated to the experience of the interactants.

Finally, an observer may evaluate the interaction with standards of performance different from those used by the interactants. Therapists or researchers may differ from the partner as to what constitutes an appropriate behavioral enactment. In a developed relationship, the standards of performance of the participants may have been modified during the development period in a mutually influenced manner that no longer coincides with potential observers' standards of performance.

IMPLICATION 6: COMPETENCY JUDGMENTS MAY MEDIATE OTHER COGNITIVE AND BEHAVIORAL REACTIONS

While competency judgments may in and of themselves be interesting, it would seem that their relationship to other variables would be of great interest. Although a number of variables might be explored, we shall focus on two. First, to the extent that one attributes competency to self, the greater will be one's willingness to communicate with others. In other words, self-perceived competency judgments should be predictive of other cognitive variables such as communication apprehension (McCroskey, 1977), shyness (Zimbardo, 1977), or self-esteem. People who see themselves as competent may have a self-related "halo effect" whereby they are more confident of their communicative abilities and are consequently more likely to communicate. Second, to the extent that one attributes competency to another, the more likely one might attribute other related characteristics to the communicator. This also implies a "halo effect." In other words, we argue that people see certain communication behaviors as related to other traits. For example, a judge may well see extreme fluency related to traits such as intelligence or even Machiavellianism. Consequently, the standards of performance may be related to other traits and constitute implicit theories of personality (e.g., see Wegner & Vallacher, 1977).

Thus, we view the competency judgments as a matching process. We are somewhat reluctant to use the term "matching" as it might imply that this process is a deliberate and self-conscious one. We recognize that competency judgments may often occur so rapidly that a deliberative process is not possible. Consequently, the "matching" may be something of which we are not highly aware. However, we propose that an individual has expectations about the probability a given communicator will enact certain behaviors. When the behavior of the communicator significantly violates these expectations, that behavior becomes salient and becomes the target of a competency judgment. In addition, behaviors are perceived to be related to certain processes and outcomes. The salient behaviors are compared to these standards of performance and an evaluation is made. The evaluations may be related to other cognitive and behavior variables, creating implicit theories. Hence, the judgment of competency is a complex cognitive process dependent upon information evaluated, personal expectations, standards of performance, and implicit theories. Actor characteristics can also influence the judgment of competence by altering the behaviors enacted and available for processing.

ACTOR CHARACTERISTICS AND INTERPERSONAL COMMUNICATION COMPETENCY

From the outset, we noted that two sets of variables influence judgments of interpersonal communication competency. We examined those affecting the judgment process in the previous section. Now we turn to those variables influencing the performance of the judged behaviors. We have chosen not to provide a "laundry list" of prescriptive behaviors likely to be judged as competent. Without extensive empirical research examining the standards of performance, such a list would be premature. Indeed, given differing personal expectations and differing standards of performance, such a list would be difficult if not impossible to construct. Instead, we have chosen to focus on social cognition processes which may facilitate the production of behaviors judged to be competent. We will examine three different and competing perspectives concerned with the production of competent behavior.

PERSPECTIVE 1: INTERPERSONAL AWARENESS

We define interpersonal awareness as the degree to which an actor focuses his or her attention on and consequently adapts his or her communication to stimuli in the interaction. In simplified terms, interpersonal awareness is concerned with how much a person pays attention in the interaction and behaviorally reacts to what is observed. We see several implications arising from this definition.

First, an interpersonally aware communicator focuses on a variety of different stimuli in the interaction. In other words, such a person does not focus exclusively on one particular aspect of the interaction. A person who is exclusively self-focused is not interpersonally aware. A person may be daydreaming or so wrapped up in the performance of his or her behavior that he or she has little idea of what is transpiring in the interaction in which he or she is allegedly part. Nor is an interpersonally aware communicator focused exclusively on the environment. Such a communicator may have a great deal of knowledge about what the partner is doing but have little self-awareness or control over his or her own behavior. Such a person may spend an extraordinary amount of interaction time listening or watching with little time spent talking. If, as Duval and Wicklund (1972) have noted, attention cannot be simultaneously focused on self and environment, then the interpersonally aware communicator engages in rapid and frequent attentional shifts from self to partner. Thus, the interpersonally aware communicator can scrutinize the behavior of the partner for what is appropriate and then control his or her own behavior so that it adapts to some degree to the partner's.

Second, an interpersonally aware communicator is more cognitively active than is a less aware communicator. Because of the rapid shifts in attention and subsequent alterations in behavior, it would seem that such a communicator would not be allowed the luxury of mindlessness (Langer,

1978). Lapses in cognitive activity would cause a mismatching of interaction behavior. On the other hand, the interpersonally aware communicator cannot be totally mindful either, without script or plan for conducting the interaction. No knowledge of how to conduct the interaction requires such constant attention to self and other, that the rapid shifts would prohibit the smooth operation or understanding of the interaction (e.g., Chiesi et al., 1979; Spilich et al., 1979).

Third, not only is an interpersonally aware communicator actively scanning the interaction, but he or she is using the results of these observations in the production of his or her communication behaviors. This implies that his or her behavior is a function of self and other perceptions. We recognize that from time to time both own and other demands will coincide so that they equally influence the person's behavior. However, it other situations the two sets of demands diverge and the person must reach some accommodation between them. In such cases, the interpersonally aware communicator may decide to adopt one or the other rather than compromise; importantly, he or she is aware of both sets of demands and considered them before adopting his or her behavior.

Fourth, the interpersonally aware communicator will alter his or her behavior across different contexts. The communicator is able to recognize that interactions involving different stimuli require alterations in behavior. Consequently, the interpersonally aware communicator adapts his or her behavior and, if observed across many interactions, appears inconsistent. A noted absence of cross-situational consistency in the performance of a given behavior may be a hallmark of interpersonal awareness.

Fifth, the interpersonally aware communicator is likely to be perceived as a competent communicator. Because the interpersonally aware communicator is reactive to situational cues, he or she is capable of adapting his or her communication behavior to the particular partner. This tendency toward audience analysis should increase the probability that the communicator engages in behaviors consistent with standards of performance. He or she may be better able to understand and enact behaviors consistent with the standards held by a particular judge.

Sixth, not only is the interpersonally aware communicator likely to be judged competent, but he or she may actually be more skillful in accurately perceiving the situation and creating desired impressions. In other words, a person might accidentally be judged competent for a number of reasons (e.g., the judge misreads communication cues or one's mindlessly enacted behavior accidentally corresponds to standards of performance). In the case of the interpersonally aware communicator, he or she actually possess the competency attributed to him or her.

Finally, the interpersonally aware communicator is assumed to be aware of his or her competency. In other words, the communicator is aware of the degree to which he or she scrutinizes the interaction and performs appropriate behaviors. Consequently, the interpersonally aware communicator should be able to accurately describe what impressions he or she attempted to create and the likelihood that they were understood by the partner. This assumed ability to understand the basis of own competency is reflected in the tendency of theorists to measure interpersonal awareness through self-report questionnaires.

We will focus on three measures of interpersonal awareness: interaction involvement, attentiveness, and self-monitoring. We recognize that none of the three were explicitly constructed to measure interpersonal awareness. However, all three incorporate to some degree the implications we just made about the construct of interpersonal awareness.

Cegala (1981, p. 112) defined interaction involvement as the "extent to which an individual partakes in a social environment." The attentional focus of individuals varies as a function of their involvement:

> Highly involved people typically integrate feelings, thoughts, and experiences with the ongoing interaction of which they are assumed to be part. Their consciousness is directed toward the evolving reality of self, other and topic of conversation. As such, they are viewed by others as generally competent communicators. On the other hand, characteristically low involved people are removed psychologically from the ongoing interaction. When low in interaction involvement, individuals may appear preoccupied with other thoughts or goals, distracted, uncertain, and/or withdrawn from the immediate social context. Their speech may be marked by vagueness, ambivalence, inconsistency, or misunderstanding. Also, they may typically demonstrate poor recollection of details, pertaining to past conversations. In general, they appear less competent in their interactions with others [Cegala et al., 1982, p. 229].

In essence, a highly involved person's attentional focus is aimed at all aspects of the interaction. While interaction involvement is most frequently measured as a trait, in some cases, a situation may arise that will increase further a person's chronic level of interaction involvement. Furthermore, some components of interaction involvement have been identified as being situationally induced (Cegala et al., 1976).

Interaction involvement is operationalized through a self-report questionnaire. A person is asked to indicate on a seven-point scale the extent to which a number of statements are like him- or herself. A number of attempts have been made to factor analyze the questionnaire responses. Most have discovered three factors (Cegala, 1978, 1981; Cegala et al., 1982). Although names of the factors have shifted across studies, the most current labels are perceptiveness, attentiveness, and responsiveness. However, a recent factor analysis indicated that the scale should be characterized as unidimensional (Kellermann & Roloff, 1983b).

Other than attempts at scale refinements, only a few studies have been done with interaction involvement. Cegala et al. (1976) discovered significant relationships between interaction involvement measured as a trait and the degree of involvement in a specific situation. Cegala (1981) reported that individuals high in interaction involvement were more effective in gaining information through indirect means, thereby avoiding loss of face. Finally, Cegala et al. (1982) found that individuals high and low in interaction involvement differ in their nonverbal communication.

While interaction involvement could be related to both actual and apparent awareness, Norton and Pettegrew's (1979) attentiveness construct is only concerned with the degree to which one tries to appear to be attentive. They define attentiveness as "a constellation of verbal and paraverbal signals which indicate that a person's message is being noticed in an alert and or understanding manner" (p. 16). This definition implies that a person who self-reports that he or she creates the impression of being attentive may or may not actually be paying attention. Similarly, a person who reports not acting like he or she is paying attention may or may not actually be.

Attentiveness has been measured on a 30-item self-report questionnaire. A person is asked to indicate on a six-point scale how much a number of statements are like him- or herself. Norton and Pettegrew discovered that the scale is multidimensional, reporting four interpretable factors: attentiveness signals, evaluation, sensitivity, and inactivity. A recent factor analysis conducted by Kellermann and Roloff (1983b) discovered five interpretable factors: listening, talk encouragement, inactivity, activity for understanding, and cognitive certainty. Norton and Pettegrew not only developed the scale but included data that suggested that attentiveness was created through posture, verbal behaviors, and eye contact. In addition, they discovered that attentiveness varied with hypothetical role relationships.

While most of the research associated with self-monitoring has been conducted by social psychologists, communication scholars have noted its potential for studying interaction (e.g., Berger & Roloff, 1980). Snyder (1974, 1979) has argued that people vary in the degree to which they can and do monitor their self-presentations and communication. Individuals who are high in self-monitoring are highly sensitive to what constitutes an appropriate self-presentation from the viewpoint of others. In addition, they are motivated and able to enact such presentations. The low self-monitor is sensitive to situational cues but from a different perspective. Instead of seeking the appropriate self-presentation from the viewpoint of others, the low self-monitor determines the presentation most consistent with his or her own disposition or attitudes. While the high self-monitor does what others expect him or her to do, the low self-monitor does what he or she sees as being consistent with his or her own standards. Snyder (1979) noted that when a high self-monitor confronts a situation he or she asks the question: "Who does this situation want me to be and how can I be that person?" The low self-monitor asks: "Who am I and how can I be me in this situation?"

Self-monitoring is operationalized through 25 true-false, self-descriptive statements. Three studies have found the scale to be multidimensional. Briggs et al. (1980) discovered three factors: extraversion, acting ability, and other-directedness. Gabrenya and Arkin (1980) report four factors: sociability/social anxiety, acting ability, other-directedness, and speaking ability. Kellermann and Roloff (1983b) found three interpretable factors: acting ability, extraversion/sociability, and stability of self-presentation.

While the self-monitoring construct has been investigated in a number of different research areas (see, Snyder, 1979), it has three important implications for communication. First, high self-monitors are more active participants in interactions than low self-monitors (Ickes & Barnes, 1977; Dabbs et al., 1980). Highs appear to regulate the interaction more so than lows though the speech of high self-monitors tends to be more glib and facile. In addition, Lippa (1976) and Elliot (1979) both discovered that high self-monitors were more effective at portraying accurate and inaccurate self-presentations. Second, research suggests that high self-monitors are sometimes more sensitive to their partners than are lows. High self-monitors are more likely than lows to notice and accurately recall traits of a prospective date (Berscheid et al., 1976) and to seek highly personalized information about another (Elliot, 1979). However, this sensitivity has not been universally found. Zuckerman et al. (1981) discovered in a thorough review of research related to the ability to detect deception that as many studies have found that low self-monitors are better able to detect deception as have found that highs are superior. Recently, Comadena (1982) discovered that self-monitoring was unrelated to the ability to detect deception in one's spouse and Dabbs et al. (1980) reported that *low* self-monitors appeared more sensitive to their interaction partners than did highs. Third, high self-monitors are often more adaptive to their relational partners than are lows. High self-monitors are more likely than lows to mold their communications to be consistent with their relational partner's attitudes (McCann & Hancock, 1983) and to match the intimacy, emotionality, and descriptive content of the partner's self-disclosures (Shaffer et al., 1982). However, Dabbs et al. (1980) found that *low* self-monitors seemed to adapt their communication to their partners more so than highs.

While we have treated interaction involvement, attentiveness, and self-monitoring as similar conceptualizations of interpersonal awareness, our research indicates that statistically they are somewhat distinct. Kellermann and Roloff (1983b) had interaction partners complete the three interpersonal awareness scales where attentiveness and interaction involvement were based on the interaction the persons had just experienced. Correlations among the three scales indicated that attentiveness and interaction involvement were significantly and positively correlated ($r = .60$, $p < .001$). Interestingly, self-monitoring was not significantly correlated with attentiveness ($r = -.03$) and negatively and significantly correlated with interaction involvement ($r = -.20$, $p < .048$). While the latter correlation explains little variance, its direction is counterintuitive. Further, we discovered that several of the self-monitoring subscales were also significantly and negatively correlated with interaction involvement and its subscales but at higher magnitudes ($-.24$ to $-.41$). We believe that these negative correlations may be explained in two ways. The first explanation arises from what a person might focus on in an interaction. When subjects responded to the attentiveness and interaction involvement scales, they indicated the degree to which they perceived they were oriented toward the relational partner. The self-monitoring scale accessed the degree to which the person attempts to manage impressions and adapts his or her behavior to the general situation. It is plausible that the high self-monitor may not have been totally oriented toward the interaction partner but also looked to the experimenter for signs of appropriate behavior. In other words, the self-monitoring scale may access more than orientation toward the partner, thereby creating significant and negative correlations of low magnitude. Second, it is also possible that the attentiveness and interaction involvement scales better tap one's *self*-perception of interpersonal awareness whereas self-monitoring better taps the perception of *how one will be perceived*. Given that perceptions may vary as a function of the role of the observer, the potential for negative correlations exists. In this case, the high self-monitor may *appear* to be involved to the partner but may *not* truly be involved whereas the low self-monitor may *appear* to be involved to the partner and *is* involved.

Thus, the interpersonal awareness perspective argues that the interpersonally aware communicator is actively involved in an interaction. Because of this increased activity, he or she is more likely to be seen as engaging in behaviors that conform to standards of performance. The judgment of competence is thus a function, in this perspective, of behaviors enacted indicating interpersonal awareness.

PERSPECTIVE 2: SOCIAL KNOWLEDGE

Our first perspective assumed that the key to interpersonal communication competency was to be highly aware of and reactive to cues in the interaction. Prior knowledge had little if any effect in that process. Our second perspective focuses primarily upon the information that a communicator brings to the interaction. In other words, our second perspective assumes that sensitivity to cues in an interaction is less important than the knowledge with which one enters the situation. We define social knowledge as the information one has prior the communication situation about one's relational partner and topic of interaction. There are several implications of this definition.

First, social knowledge is a product of a number of types of experiences. One acquires information through direct experience with the partner or topic. In other words, one has previously communicated with the person or about the issue. Information may also be acquired through observation. Instead of directly communicating one might observe others communication with the relational partner or about a topic. In addition, social knowledge might be acquired through mental rehearsal. This inference process involves a communicator in advance of the interaction practicing what he or she would say. This practice may be purely cognitive with no communication with another.

Second, two types of information constitute social knowledge: information about the relational partner and information about topics. Berger and Calabrese (1975) argued that people are motivated to acquire information about their relational partners. As we noted earlier, this information reduces uncertainty about the interaction and subsequent risk. As the relationship escalates, personal expectations tend to develop which further reduce uncertainty (Miller & Steinberg, 1975). However, we also note that people acquire information about topics of interaction. For example, a given person may have certain topics about which he or she has a vast store of information and, consequently, feels comfortable talking about. One may have encountered people who have "pet" topics of conversation; regardless of the situation, these people tend to steer the conversation to those "pet" topics. A "workaholic" whose whole life revolves around career may only discuss job-related topics just as new parents may focus their interactions on their infants. Because these issues are confronted on a day-to-day basis, persons may have acquired more information about them and will tend to discuss them more frequently than rarely encountered topics.

Third, the accumulation of social knowledge reduces the necessity of interpersonal awareness. When knowledgeable, one does not need to be as sensitive to the cues in the interaction because they can be anticipated. We have noted that after repeating a lecture a number of times, it is no longer necessary to pay strict attention to the communication situation. One can reach the point where even questions can be anticipated. All aspects of the interaction become highly predictable. A person can effectively carry out the lecture without an extreme degree of awareness. This low awareness does not mean that a person is *entirely* mindless. Abelson (1976) noted that when a person engages in such scripted behavior, he or she must at least recognize cues in the situation that point to the appropriate script and then move from an observer of the situation to the role of an actor. However, once the script has been engaged, the mindless behavior described by Langer (1978) may be observed.

Fourth, a person with high social knowledge may be unable to describe how or why he or she communicates in the manner in which he or she does. We noted earlier that high social knowledge may involve little interpersonal awareness. We also argue that it may involve little self-awareness. A person may have interacted with a communicator so many times or communicated about a given topic so often that he or she has forgotten how he or she is communicating. One may have had the frustrating experience of asking an expert to describe how his or her job is done only to find the explanation to be incomplete or incomprehensible. The problem is not with the expert, but with the tendency of increased experience to make behavior automatic and mindless.

Fifth, there is a nonlinear relationship between the amount of social knowledge and communication competency. At first glance, this implication may seem counterintuitive. We usually assume that with increasing experience comes both increased knowledge and competency. Most would accept the argument that low knowledge communicators might be perceived as incompetent but would balk at the notion that knowledgeable communicators might also be perceived as less competent. We argue that as a communicator acquires social knowledge he or she becomes increasingly perceived to be competent up to some point of knowledge after which there are no increases in attributed competence (i.e., a plateau is reached) or the communicator's perceived competence actually begins to decrease. In situations involving low social knowledge, the communicator is faced with some uncertainty. As he or she knows little about the interaction partner or topic, some awkward sequences are expected as the communicators attempt to mesh ideas. As they become increasingly knowledgeable, the intermeshing becomes much easier. However, at high levels of knowledge problems may occur. Specifically, we see three problems emerging form for the communicator having high social knowledge. One problem concerns the fact that he or she may become increasingly bored with the enactment of the script. We noted earlier that after having performed a lecture several times, it can be done on "automatic pilot." However, we also note that too many lectures can make the material and presentation style quite stale and the communicator's lack of enthusiasm may begin to appear. Even the receiver of such messages can become quite bored. A second problem occurs wherein as social knowledge increases, the communicator becomes less aware of cues in the interaction. This low awareness implies that he or she may miss important cues that had not been incorporated into his or her script. The person may move toward the completion of his or her presentation with little or no acknowledgment of feedback. Last, because the information upon which social knowledge is based is not static, a high social knowledge communicator who does not update his or her knowledge store may find it "out of date." We noted that the high social knowledge communicator may not process cues in the situation but instead rely upon expectations. This implies that the person is not updating his or her expectations with new experiences. Consequently, he or she may encounter script violations which prompt sudden mindfulness (Langer, 1978) and attributions of incompetency. For example, Langer and Weinman (1981) discovered that individuals who had overlearned a task and were encouraged to think about how they performed the task before describing their behavior were less fluent than those not encouraged to become mindful or those describing their performance on a novel task.

Thus, a communicator possessing moderate social knowledge may perform most competently in the eyes of a judge. Such a person has enough knowledge so that he or she can enact certain behaviors confidently and has had sufficient experience so that the behavioral enactment is fluid. On the other hand, such a communicator still reacts to interaction cues and may be able to continue to "update" his or her knowledge store. Unfortunately, without extensive research, we cannot precisely specify the degree of social knowledge most conducive to attributions of competence.

PERSPECTIVE 3: THE INTERPERSONAL AWARENESS BY SOCIAL KNOWLEDGE INTERACTION

Thus far we have treated interpersonal awareness and social knowledge as though they were main effects in an analysis of variance. In other words, they are variables operating independently of one another and to some degree negate the other's existence. If one is interpersonally aware, social knowledge does not matter and vice versa. However, a third perspective that assumes that the two interact to influence attributions of competency is plausible. The form of this interaction is such that interpersonal awareness is of critical importance in situations about which the actors have low social knowledge. As noted earlier, when communicating with a person about whom one has little information or communicating about a novel topic, one may find him or herself groping for something to say; uncertainty is high. The communicator may retreat to superficial, "safe" topics or when venturing into other topics, accidentally create conflicts. In such situations, an interpersonally aware communicator may be at an advantage. He or she is reacting to the situation in such a way so as to discern appropriate topics and styles of communication. Indeed, high self-monitors are more likely than low self-monitors to seek individuated information about an unfamiliar target of persuasion (Elliot, 1979) and to remember more experimenter supplied information about a future dating partner (Berscheid et al., 1976). In other words, the information processing skills of the interpersonally aware communicator are a distinct advantage in situations about which the communicator has low social knowledge. However, in situations in which the communicators have increased amounts of information, the advantages of being interpersonally aware become less. In fact, given the Langer and Weinman (1981) study, the cognitive activity of the interpersonally aware communicator may become a distinct disadvantage in situations in which he or she has high social knowledge. In other words, the interpersonally aware communicator may think too much about what is transpiring in the interaction, leading to hesitations and editing of behavior.

AN EMPIRICAL ADVENTURE INTO INTERPERSONAL COMMUNICATION COMPETENCY

As each of the three perspectives seems plausible, we conducted an empirical study to gather evidence on their validity. Because we could not integrate all of the ideas presented in the previous two sections into one study, we chose only to investigate the viability of the three perspectives on actor characteristics. We leave the other implications for future research and note that their exclusion does not lessen their importance. In addition, we chose to hold social knowledge as to partner constant to examine the independent effect of the impact of social knowledge as to topic. This section will be divided into four parts: hypotheses, methods, results, and conclusions.

HYPOTHESES

As we noted in the previous section, three perspectives on actor characteristics could be identified. Our perspective on interpersonal awareness suggested two hypotheses. First, regardless of social knowledge, the more interpersonally aware (high scores on self-monitoring, interaction involvement, and attentiveness) the communicator, the more likely he or she will be perceived to be competent by a judge. Second, regardless of social knowledge, the more interpersonally aware the communicator, the greater the convergence of competency perceptions by several judges (including self, partner, and outside observer). While the first hypothesis is straightforward, the second requires some explanation. We are predicting that the perceptual skills of the interpersonally aware communicator make it more likely that he or she can actually predict and describe how he or she is being perceived by others. In other words, the perceptions of the interpersonally aware communicator correspond to reality to a greater extent than a communicator not interpersonally aware. It should also be noted that neither interpersonal awareness nor competence should vary as a function of social knowledge in this perspective.

Our perspective on social knowledge suggests the following hypotheses. First, as one's social knowledge about a topic increases, one's perceived competency increases up to some point of knowledge after which attributions of competency level off or decline. Second, in an initial interaction situation, convergence of competency judgments across judge roles is expected for observers and partners but not for social actors. If social knowledge is key to judgments of competence, and personal expectations have not had a chance to form, then observers and partners will tend to be viewing the interaction from a similar vantage pont. In developing relationships, no clear position emerges as to the convergence of different judgment perspectives. It should also be noted that the social knowledge perspective implies that interpersonal awareness either does not vary as a function of social knowledge or it decreases as social knowledge increases.

Our perspective on the interaction between interpersonal awareness and social knowledge suggests one hypothesis. When communicating about topics for which a person has low information, the more interpersonally aware the communicator, the more competent he or she will appear to be. This hypothesized difference should be attenuated or reversed when communicating about topics for which one has high social knowledge.

METHODS

In order to create a test of these competing perspectives, we chose to investigate the communication competency among acquaintance dyads. We note that these dyads were at an initial stage of relational development and might behave differently than dyads at later stages. However, this allowed us to focus on interaction about *topics* of differing levels of social knowledge. In other words, we chose to focus on that part of social knowledge arising from the topic of interaction and have reserved that portion arising from knowledge about the relational partner for future research.

In order to examine the impact of social knowledge as it pertains to the topic of an interaction, it was necessary a priori to locate topics *varying* in familiarity. Seventeen topics, all related to university life, were developed and pretested on three dimensions: (1) degree of interest, (2) extent of knowledge, and (3) extent of past discussion. Given that we did not want interest in a topic to confound our analysis of the impact of social knowledge, four topics were chosen that were found to be relatively similar in interest (M = 2.82; 1 = low, 5 = high) but varied widely in social knowledge and past discussion. The four topics meeting these criteria were, in ascending order of extent of social knowledge: (1) university required community volunteer service (M = 1.06), (2) drug abuse at the university (M = 2.25), (3) food service at the university (M = 3.75), and (4) social life at the university (M = 3.94).

There were 68 college students, 42 females and 26 males, who volunteered to participate in the study. The participants were asked to sign up in pairs with persons who were strangers to them. All participants were told when they volunteered that the study concerned the effects of differing communication environments, requiring the videotaping of conversations on various assigned topics with persons who were strangers to them. Upon arriving for the experiment, the participants were provided written instructions indicating the topic they were to discuss with their conversational partners. One of the four topics was randomly assigned to each dyad. Prior to reading the instructions, each participant completed three scales designed to measure the person's interest, knowledge, and extent of past discussion of the assigned topic. Upon completing the scales and reading the instructions, the participants were brought to an experimental room for the videotaping of their conversations. Each dyad was taped for six minutes and each conversation commenced with the reading of identification numbers. At the end of the six minute taping session, each participant was taken to another room where he or she completed a questionnaire consisting of the interaction involvement (Cegala, 1981), attentiveness (Norton & Pettegrew, 1979), self-monitoring (Snyder, 1974), and competency (Kellermann & Roloff, 1983a) scales. All scales but self-monitoring were modified or designed to apply to the situation the participants had just experienced rather than attempting to elicit their general feelings about their behavior across multiple situations in the past. We chose not to transform the self-monitoring scale into a situated form because the integrity of the items of the scale could not be maintained. In addition, the self-monitoring scale was measured on a five-point Likert scale instead of the usual true-false format. In coding the questionnaires, we made higher values represent a higher perception of the characteristic. After completing the questionnaire, each participant was debriefed and thanked for his or her help in the study.

Three observers each made ten full rating passes of the videotapes. A full rating pass is defined as viewing each conversation and making a judgment about *one* of the two persons in the dyad for *all* conversations, then repeating the entire process for the other member of each dyad. The ratings the observers completed were designed to correspond to the items on the competency scale (fluency, understanding, persuasiveness, comfortability, openness, dominance, dramaticism, adaptation, animation, friendliness, degree of relaxation) as well as to the construct underlying each of the four scales the participants had completed (involvement, attentiveness, sensitivity, competency).

RESULTS

Procedural Checks. The four topics employed in this research varied significantly (measured on five-point scales; $1 = \text{low}$, $5 = \text{high}$) in terms of the participants' social knowledge ($F = 39.48$, $df = 3/64$, $p < .0001$) and the degree to which the topics had been discussed in the past ($F = 9.02$, $df = 3/64$, $p < .0001$). Newman-Keuls tests indicated that social knowledge of each of the four topics was uniquely different than all the other topics. Social knowledge was greatest for the social life topic ($M = 3.50$), next highest for the food service topic ($M = 2.81$), lower for the drug abuse topic ($M = 2.22$), and lowest for the volunteer work topic ($M = 1.06$). Social knowledge as to topic was therefore successfully varied in this study through the assignment of the four topics. While participants' interest in their assigned topic was not identical for all topics ($F = 9.02$, $df = 3/64$, $p < .0001$), the food service, volunteer work, and drug abuse topics were equivalent in interest ($M = 2.50$) whereas the interest in the social life topic was significantly higher ($M = 3.7$). As a result, persons' interest level in their assigned topics became a covariate in all analyses to prohibit confounding the analysis of social knowledge. It should be noted, however, that the statistical results did not differ when analyses ignoring interest as a covariate were conducted.

The interpersonal awareness measures completed by the participants ranged in internal consistency from alpha coefficients of .59 for self-monitoring to .77 for attentiveness to .83 for interaction involvement. The scale for self-perceived competency had an alpha coefficient of .90 and the partner-perceived competency scale's internal consistency was .85. Observer reliabilities were generally strong with only four of 15 having Pearson correlation coefficients less than .70.

Tests of Perspective 1: Interpersonal Awareness. The interpersonal awareness perspective on communication competence suggests that *regardless* of social knowledge as to topic, the interpersonally aware communicator is a competent communicator. This perspective on communication competence would require a pattern of results such that

(1) interpersonal awareness and competence are positively and significantly correlated, with these correlations remaining stable across differing levels of social knowledge;
(2) the competency perceptions of actors, partners, and observers should converge for highly aware interpersonal communicators whereas no convergence in these perceptions is anticipated for individuals not interpersonally aware;
(3) no main effects for interpersonal awareness across topics should occur;
(4) no main effects for competence across topics should occur.

Interpersonal awareness was measured by the three self-report scales and three corresponding observer ratings. Competency was measured in terms of self, partner, and observer perception. In the interest of parsimony, results will be presented only for the overall measures of competency (self-perceived, partner-perceived, and observer-perceived) as the subscales of these measures followed the pattern of results of the overall measures and the overall measures are viewed to be more stable indices of competency judgments.

The correlations of the interpersonal awareness and competency measures are presented in Table 8.1 for the group as a whole. In general, interpersonal awareness is significantly and positively correlated to communication competency. Twelve of eighteen correlations for the group as a whole are significant at $p < .05$. While not contained in Table 8.1, cor-

TABLE 8.1
Interpersonal Awareness and Overall Competency Correlations

| | Perceiver of Competency | | |
Interpersonal Awareness	Self	Partner	Observer
Self-Perceived			
Self-Monitoring	.05	.27*	-.04
Interaction Involvement	.68**	.34*	.47*
Attentiveness	.33*	.26*	.35*
Observer-Perceived			
Sensitivity	.16	.28*	.52**
Involvement	.31*	.43*	.72**
Attentiveness	.16	.22	.58**

*p < .05
**p < .01

relations were computed for each topic for each type of interpersonal awareness and competency judgment. Only two of the eighteen *sets* of correlations (correlations of a given awareness and competency judgment for each of the four topics) varied significantly across topics using a chi-square test of significance (Cohen & Cohen, 1975). Hence, the results indicate that as interpersonal awareness increases, judgments of competency increase *regardless* of social knowledge of the topic. This same pattern of results was obtained for the various subscales of self-perceived and partner-perceived competence as well.

It is interesting to note, however, the type of competence associated with the various measures of interpersonal awareness. For example, interaction involvement is related far more to self-perceived competency than it is to partner-perceived competency ($z = 2.71$, $p < .003$) or observer-perceived competency ($z = 1.82$, $p < .036$). In contrast, self-monitoring correlates somewhat better with partner-perceived competency ($z = 1.30$, $p < .097$) than with self- or observer-perceived competency. Attentiveness, on the other hand, correlates equally well with all three types of competency. These relationships also vary as a function of the role of the person making evaluations of interpersonal awareness. In the case of observers' judgments of awareness, observer ratings of competency consistently correlate more strongly than either self- or partner-perceived judgments. Indeed, it appears that interpersonal awareness is a strong standard of performance for observers in making competency judgments. For actors, interpersonal awareness may not be a standard of performance for making competency judgments. However, given the *varying* correlations of self-perceived awareness and self-perceived competency, it is difficult to reach a strong conclusion in this matter. For partners, it is unknown whether interpersonal awareness is a standard of performance in judgments of competency as partners' perceptions of actors' awareness was not measured. However, given our theoretical outlook, we would expect partners to hold such a standard. Even though interpersonal awareness is a standard of performance in making competency judgments, there is no guarantee that the *same* standard is applied by actors, partners, and observers; the relationship embodied in the standard may vary greatly as a function of the role of the perceiver. It can therefore be concluded that one's role vis-à-vis the interaction alters the judgments that will be made about the relationship of interpersonal awareness and competency.

The issue of convergence or divergence of perceptions, however, requires the examination of competency ratings separated for persons high and low in interpersonal awareness. It was predicted that for persons high in interpersonal awareness, the role of the judge would not alter perceptions of competency whereas for persons low in awareness, divergence of judgments would occur. Almost precisely the inverse of this prediction occurred as can be seen in the correlations presented in Table 8.2. In general, for individuals low in interpersonal awareness, greater convergence of perceptions of competency occurred than for individuals high in interpersonal awareness. It is noteworthy that the coorientation of social actors and their partners accounts for the greatest change in the convergence between persons low and high in interpersonal awareness. While this result seems counterintuitive and certainly opposite of what the perspective would suggest, perhaps persons low in interpersonal awareness have better knowledge of how they will be perceived by conversational partners due to the cross-situational consistency of their behavior. During the course of many interactions, it is possible that the consistency of enactment creates a generalized perception of competence that is in part based upon feedback from conversational partners. In contrast, the highly aware individual enacting cross-situationally inconsistent behavior does not have the same advantage of past feedback to guide his or her perceptions of a given enactment. While such an explanation clearly requires investigation, the reversal of predicted convergence results is not only fascinating but brings the interpersonal awareness perspective into serious question. It is simply not the case that the interpersonally aware communicator is necessarily more accurate in predictions of competence.

As to the main effect of interpersonal awareness across topics of varying social knowledge, it can be stated that awareness does not appear to be a function of social knowledge. Self-perceived attentiveness and self-monitoring, and observer rated attentiveness and sensitivity exhibited no

TABLE 8.2

Correlations of Competency Between Perceivers for
High and Low Levels of Interpersonal Awareness as Perceived by Self

Level of Interpersonal Awareness	Type of Interpersonal Awareness	Perceivers of Competency		
		Actor/Partner	Actor/Observer	Partner/Observer
Low	Self-Monitoring	.40*	.35*	.42*
	Attentiveness	.30*	.27*	.49
	Involvement	.23*	.42*	.44*
High	Self-Monitoring	.18	.34*	.42*
	Attentiveness	.01	.16	.18
	Involvement	.09	.20	.35*

*p < .05

significant differences across the topics. However, interaction involvement perceived both by the actor (F = 2.37, df = 3/64, p < .08, eta squared = .10) and by the observer (F = 5.48, df = 3/64, p < .002, eta squared = .20) varied as a function of social knowledge as to topic. Basically, when social actors have greater knowledge of a topic, they become more involved in the conversation. In plain English, it's hard to be involved when you don't have a lot to say. It is particularly interesting that *only* involvement exhibited differences across topics for the awareness measures. In another investigation (Kellermann & Roloff, 1983b), involvement was found to be an indicator of certainty/uncertainty as it pertains to the interaction. Uncertainty about the topic is therefore likely to be high when you *must* discuss it (as participants here had to do) and persons lack the needed information to continue the conversation. Therefore, as social knowledge as to topic increases, uncertainty *should* decrease. Furthermore, follow-up analyses revealed that only the responsiveness dimension of interaction involvement varied significantly across the topics. This is precisely the dimension Kellermann and Roloff found to be highly associated with uncertainty. Hence, an individual's certainty may vary as a function of social knowledge as to topic but his or her *awareness* does not appear to do so.

The issue of whether communication competency varies in relation to social knowledge not only speaks to the interpersonal awareness perspective (e.g., there should be no relationship between competency and social knowledge) but also speaks to the second perspective of social knowledge. In the second perspective, differences in knowledge were expected to create differences in perceived competency. As these predictions are in direct opposition to each other and as the results are necessary for the first perspective although less central to its test, they will be presented with the tests on the second perspective.

Tests of Perspective 2: Social Knowledge. The social knowledge perspective argued that communication competency was a function of the information individuals have about the topic of a conversation and about the relational partner. By investigating initial interactions, relational knowledge was held constant. For social knowledge as it pertains to the topic to be the primary determinant of competency requires a pattern of results wherein

(1) a nonlinear relationship between competence and social knowledge should occur;
(2) interpersonal awareness either does not vary as a function of social knowledge or decreases as social knowledge increases;
(3) convergence of competency judgments across judge roles is expected for observers and partners but not for social actors.

The discussion of tests of the interpersonal awareness perspective indicated that the second criterion for the results required by the social knowledge perspective was for the most part supported. Criteria (1) and (3) will be discussed together.

Overall perceptions of competency vary significantly as a function of social knowledge for observers' ($F = 4.80$, df $= 3/64$, p $< .004$, eta squared $= .18$) and for partners' judgments ($F = 2.23$, df $= 3/64$, p $< .09$, eta squared $= .10$). In both cases, Newman-Keuls tests indicated that for the lower social knowledge topics of volunteer work ($M_O = 4.5$, $M_p = 54.6$) and drug abuse ($M_O = 4.8$, $M_p = 56.0$), competency was significantly less than for the topics of higher social knowledge, those being the topics of food service ($M_O = 5.4$, $M_p = 63.13$) and social life ($M_O = 5.7$, $M_p = 60.11$). In essence, this nonlinear "stretched-S" relationship evidences plateaus on each end of the continuum of social knowledge. Although not meeting conventional levels of significance, it is interesting to note that the data support a weak trend for the highest level of social knowledge (e.g., social life topic) to be related to lower judgments of competency than the second highest social knowledge topic.

Also telling is the failure of self-perceptions of competency to vary as a function of social knowledge. It may very well be that when faced with topics of low social knowledge, individuals who "make the best of it" view themselves as having "made the best of it" *competently.* Conversely, given topics of high social knowledge persons expect to be competent because they are practiced in the interaction script that topic mandates. In other words, the *more* the social knowledge, the *less* persons might base their competency judgments on situational cues and the *more* they might base their competency judgments upon whether the enacted sequence of behavior flowed in an uninterrupted manner. The *less* the social knowledge, the *more* persons might base their competency judgments on situational cues, however, these judgments are affected by whether the behavior sequences enacted "made the best of a difficult situation," rather than whether the behavior sequences were actually competent. Outside observers and conversational partners, on the other hand, view competency to be a function of the social knowledge of the actor. It might very well be that partners and observers expect *actual* competent performances rather than allowing for competency judgments to reflect the difficulty of the situation. Supportive of this reasoning are the relatively small standard deviations in self-perceived competency ratings across the four topics.

In addition to examining the issue of convergence of perceptions of competency according to the average competency perceived for individuals speaking on topics of varying social knowledge, correlations of an actors, his or her partner's, and an observer's judgments of competency were computed for the group as a whole and by topic. These correlations are presented in Table 8.3. As is quite noticeable, actors and their partners tend to agree on the actors' competency only when social knowledge is very low. In general, observers' competency judgments agree with both actors' perceptions of their own competency and their partners' perceptions of their competency though observers and partners converge somewhat more than observers and actors. The one exception to this general statement concerns judgments of competency for individuals discussing the drug abuse topic. For some inexplicable reason, observers of actors discussing drug abuse perceived the actors' competency to be high when both self-perceived and partner-perceived judgments of competency were low, and vice versa. While the reason for this divergence in competency judgments in the drug abuse topic is unknown, we tend to believe it is due to some peculiarity of the topic rather than social knowledge. On the basis of the analysis of means and the correlations, it can be said that social knowledge is a key determinant in the perception of overall competence and that convergence of perceptions between partners and observers, though not actors, generally occurs.

Not only were overall ratings of competence analyzed across the four topics but the subscales of the self- and partner-perceived competency measures were also examined for differences due to the varying levels of social knowledge. Self-perception subscales of comfortableness, friendliness, and ability to be

TABLE 8.3

Correlations of Perceivers' Judgments of Competency

Perceivers	Overall	Social Knowledge Topic			
		Volunteer Work	Drug Abuse	Food Service	Social Life
Observer/Actor	.34*	.49*	−.32*	.35*	.50*
Observer/Partner	.42*	.53*	−.29*	.55*	.37*
Actor/Partner	.27*	.41*	.01	.04	.22

*p < .05

understood exhibited no significant differences across the four topics. However, self-perceived conversational activity (F = 2.95, df = 3/64, p < .04, eta squared = .12) and persuasiveness (F = 2.75, df = 3/64, p < .049, eta squared = .11) were found to differ significantly across the varying levels of social knowledge topics. For conversational activity, the same spread-S nonlinear relationship was manifested (M_{vw} = 14.4, M_{da} = 14.3, M_{fs} = 19.0, M_{sl} = 17.9). Again, the potential for high social knowledge to be debilitating is indicated in the mean conversational activity rating for the social life topic being less than that for the food service topic, although in this case the difference did not reach conventional levels of significance. A somewhat different pattern is uncovered for the persuasiveness subscale: Persons discussing the highest social knowledge topic of social life (M = 20.2) viewed themselves to be significantly more persuasive than persons discussing any of the other topics (M_{fs} = 17.8, M_{da} = 16.9, M_{vw} = 16.8). Self-perceptions of competency thus manifest no overall differences as a function of social knowledge but two dimensions of self-perceived competency (conversational activity and persuasiveness) suggest nonlinear relationships with social knowledge.

From the perspective of partner-perceived competency, conversational activity also was viewed to differ across topics of varying social knowledge (F = 4.50, df = 3/64, p < .006, eta squared = .17). Newman-Keuls tests revealed the same nonlinear "spread-S" relationship as reported for self-perceptions (M_{vw} = 6.5, M_{da} = 7.1, M_{fs} = 8.9, M_{sl} = 9.0). The partner-perceived other-directedness and comfortableness dimensions failed to differ as a result of increasing levels of social knowledge. It can therefore be concluded that regardless of role, participant or actor, conversational activity is an important determinant in perceptions of communication competence.

Observers not only made a general rating of competence for each participant but they also made eleven other judgments corresponding to items on the self- and partner-perceived competency scales. While observer judgments of competency failed to differ significantly across levels of social knowledge for adaptiveness, understanding, persuasiveness, animation, degree of relaxation, dominance, and dramaticism, judgments of *fluency* ($F = 12.19$, df = 3/64, p < .001, eta squared = .36), *comfortableness* ($F = 2.40$, df = 3/64, p < .07, eta squared = .10), *friendliness* ($F = 8.79$, df = 3/64, p < .0001, eta squared = .29), and *openness* ($F = 4.89$, df = 3/64, p < .004, eta squared = .19) exhibited significant differences. Friendliness follows the spread-S nonlinear relationship with social knowledge, whereas openness, fluency, and comfortableness follow a somewhat different nonlinear path wherein persons discussing the highest social knowledge topic (social life) were perceived by observers to be more fluent, open, and comfortable than persons discussing the other three topics.

In general, perceptions of competency are related in nonlinear fashions to social knowledge. However, the role of the judge alters which components of competency are weighted in the judgment. On overall judgments of competency and on persuasiveness, observers and partners, converge fairly well in their judgments. On activity dimensions of competency, however, observers fail to converge with partners or actors while actors and their partners converge in the perception that activity is a result of the extent of social knowledge. Other-directedness judgments (friendly, open, etc.) are important to observers, though not to actors or partners for judgments of competency. For the most part, the social knowledge perspective receives support due to competency varying across topics of differing social knowledge. However, inconsistencies remain in the relationships between the role of the judge and the importance of the components of the competency judgment. It should be noted, however, that the single *best* observer rating of competence is the *direct* one which converges with partners' perceptions exactly. The inconsistencies arise in the item by item observer rating analyses which may not be as *stable* indices of competence as is the overall judgment.

Tests of Perspective 3: Interpersonal Awareness by Social Knowledge Interaction. This interaction perspective argued that competence was a result of both interpersonal awareness and social knowledge. When social knowledge is low, interpersonal awareness is viewed in this perspective to be the key to communication competence; when social knowledge is high, awareness and competence are unrelated. As was discussed in the tests for the interpersonal awareness perspective, correlations for awareness and competence did not generally vary across the topics. Even in the two instances in which correlations of awareness and competence differed as a function of the topic, the pattern of the correlations does not match the pattern predicted by this interaction perspective. Instead, the *lowest* social knowledge topic exhibited a *negative* correlation between self-perceived attentiveness and self-perceived competency while the correlations for the remaining topics were positive and essentially similar. A somewhat similar pattern is found in the case of self-perceived involvement and observer-perceived competence: The second lowest social knowledge topic yielded a negative correlation whereas the other topics exhibited similar positive correlations. Hence, the interaction model fails to explain even those instances where topic differences were located in correlations between awareness and competence. Moreover, the prediction of differences in the relationship of awareness and competence as a function of social knowledge is not supported.

CONCLUSIONS

These data shed light upon the validity of the three perspectives described in the second section of this chapter. We found mixed results for the first perspective which posited a direct effect of interpersonal awareness on judgments of communication competency. Significant positive correlations were observed between the measures of interpersonal awareness and overall competency judgments. However, these results must be weighed against several problems. First, the three measures of interpersonal awareness did not have a uniform effect on self-perceived, partner-perceived, and observer-perceived judgments of competency. Self-monitoring had a somewhat larger association with partner-perceived judgments of competency than with either self-perceived or observer-perceived judgments of competency. Interaction involvement had a significantly stronger relationship with self-perceived competency than with either partner-perceived or observer-perceived judgments (although the latter two correlations were significant). Finally, attentiveness evidenced similar correlations with competency regardless of the role of the perceiver, although the correlations were smaller in magnitude than those observed for interaction involvement. Thus, the three measures seemed to tap into competency judgments differently dependent upon the role of the perceiver. One exception should be noted, however, in that observers' perceptions of interpersonal awareness were strongly correlated with their perceptions of competency. Such a result speaks to the application of different standards of performance and different personal expectations being applied by perceivers in different roles.

Second, these data do not entirely support the notion that people who are interpersonally aware (at least as measured by self-reports) are really more accurate perceivers of the interaction. When we compared the correlations between self-perceived, partner-perceived, and observer-perceived competency, we discovered larger correlations for people low in interpersonal awareness than for those high in interpersonal awareness. It would seem that individuals high in interpersonal awareness have self-perceived judgments that are less related to those judgments made by others than is the case for those less interpersonally aware. This raises an interesting question: Why would people scoring high on measures of interpersonal awareness be perceived to be competent communicators (by self, partner, and observer) but also have levels of self-perceived competency that differ from judgments made by others? A partial answer to this question may arise from the type of questionnaire items used. The three self-perceived measures of interpersonal awareness are only indicators of attempts to be sensitive to cues in the situation rather than assessments of a person's actual ability to be sensitive to such cues. Each of the measures asks the person to indicate the degree to which he or she thinks that certain behaviors have been performed. As the scales do not test *actual* sensitivity, a person who is unaware of his or her behavior should contribute to significant error. The person may think he or she has been sensitive or wish that he or she had been sensitive when in reality the person had not been particularly sensitive.

While the preceding analysis explains why the interpersonally aware person's self-perceived competency does not correlate with the judgments of others, it does not explain why that person might also be perceived as competent. This aspect seems most important because it calls into question whether the correlations between the measures of interpersonal awareness and communication competency are really a function of actual interpersonal awareness. In other words, it may be the case that these measures are actually tapping into other constructs which are related to the performance of behavior judged to be competent but those constructs do not include interpersonal awareness.

Another potential explanation for the correlations of awareness and competency and the convergence for low aware communicators in perceptions of competency concerns the extent to which people are *aware* of their success or failure in their behavioral enactments. It may be the case that when persons *think* they have not been competent communicators, they *actually* have not been whereas when persons *think* they have been competent communicators, they may or may not actually have been. In other words, the communicator low in interpersonal awareness may *not* be as competent and *know* it, whereas the communicator high in interpersonal awareness may think of him- or herself as competent and may or may not be. Basically, we would argue that accurate perceptions of competence are more likely to occur when the person indicates he or she has been incompetent. This is not to say that all perceptions of competence are inaccurate, only that many may reflect an *illusion* rather than a reality. Other research has indicated that those individuals who are most depressed have the most verdical perceptions of how they are perceived by others whereas individuals who have an "illusion of control" often have a view of themselves that is distorted in a positive direction (Alloy et al., 1981). Thus, the interpersonally aware communicator *may* be more competent but may also have perceptions that do not agree with other perceivers.

A third problem with the interpersonal awareness perspective concerns the fact that the competency judgments were not solely a function of awareness. Competency was found to alter in relation to actors' social knowledge of the topic. In this perspective, competency was assumed to be produced by interpersonal awareness *regardless* of social knowledge.

Thus, interpersonal awareness plays a significant role in influencing judgments of competency but does not necessarily reflect accuracy in perceptions. It may be the case that this finding will not be replicated with other measures of interpersonal awareness. We urge future researchers to explore measures such as rhetorical sensitivity (Hart & Burks, 1982; Hart et al., 1980) and interpersonal orientation (Swap & Rubin, 1983) for similar findings. We would note, however, that both of these scales utilize items similar to those of the scales employed here (i.e., self-reports) and we would expect similar results.

Our second perspective of social knowledge received the most empirical support from the data. We discovered the predicted nonlinear relationships between level of social knowledge and competency judgments. However, the form of the nonlinear relationship was not as dramatic as we expected. Instead of an inverted-U relationship, we discovered that competency judgments tended to plateau at our highest level of social knowledge. This plateau may have been a function of the highest level of social knowledge that our topics measured. While a pretest and manipulation check indicated that the topics did differ in social knowledge, the highest social knowledge topic was not at the upper bound of our scale and, in fact, evidenced a significant decrease in knowledge between the pretest and the manipulation check. In a number of instances, nonsignificant trends in the direction of an inverted-U relationship were detected that lead us to believe that had we been able to employ a topic of higher social knowledge, competency judgments may have decreased to create the inverted-U relationship.

The third perspective positing an interaction between interpersonal awareness and social knowledge received no support. Most of the correlations between interpersonal awareness and judged competency did not vary significantly across levels of social knowledge and in the two cases in which they did vary, the pattern of correlations were not consistent with our hypothesis. Thus, our data suggest that interpersonal awareness and social knowledge operate independently of one another. While both influence competency judgments, they are not without some difficulties.

While our study was primarily focused on the influence of actor characteristics on competency judgments, the data also shed some light into the judgment process itself. The predicted actor-observer differences were present. The relational partners and observers did not consistently perceive competency in a similar fashion. We strongly urge researchers to avoid making conclusions about competency based solely on actor, partner, or observer judgments. They represent different perspectives and could lead to different conclusions. In addition, and perhaps most importantly, these data suggest that actor characteristics do not account for a large proportion of variance in the competency judgment. When looking at overall judgments of competency, self-perceived interpersonal awareness only explains from 0-46 percent of the variance for actors perceiving their own behavior, 7-12 percent of the variance for partners' perceptions of the actors' competence, and 0-22 percent of the variance for observers' judgments of competence. However, for observer judgments of interpersonal awareness, 27-52 percent of the variance in observer-perceived competency is explained 5-18 percent of partner-perceived competency, and 2-9 percent of self-perceived competency. Regardless of the perceiver of awareness and competence, it is clear that interpersonal awareness explains at best only half of the variance in competency judgments and generally explains only 10-20 percent of the variance. Social knowledge as to topic does not explain a great deal of variance in judgments of competency either, ranging from 0 percent for actors to 18 percent for observers. This leads us to believe that researchers should focus more attention on the *dynamics* of the decision-making process rather than solely studying actor characteristics. Both would seem to be important, but we predict that those factors that influence the judgment process may be more important than actor characteristics that produce the behavior. We anxiously anticipate research shedding light upon our conjecture.

REFERENCES

Abelson, R.P. Script processing in attitude formation and decision-making. In J.S. Carroll & J.W. Payne (Eds.) *Cognition and social behavior.* Hillsdale: Lawrence Erlbaum Associates, 1976.

Abelson, R.P. Psychological status of the script concept. *American Psychologist,* 1981, *36,* 715-729.

Altman, I., & Taylor, D.A. *Social penetration: The development of interpersonal relationships.* New York: Holt, Rinehart & Winston, 1973.

Alloy, L.B., Abramson, L.Y., & Viscusi, D. Induced mood and the illusion of control. *Journal of Personality and Social Psychology,* 1981, *41,* 1129-1140.

Argyle, M. *Bodily communication.* London: Metheun, 1975.

Berger, C.R., & Calabrese, R.J. Some explorations in initial interaction and beyond: Toward a developmental theory of interpersonal communication. *Human Communication Research,* 1975, *1,* 99-112.

Berger, C.R., & Roloff, M.E. Social cognition, self-awareness and interpersonal communication. In B. Dervin & M. Voight (Eds.) *Progress in communication sciences* (vol. 2). Norwood: ABLEX, 1980.

Berscheid, E., Graziano, W., & Monson, T. Outcome dependency: Attention, attribution, and attraction. *Journal of Personality and Social Psychology,* 1976, *34,* 978-989.

Briggs, S., Cheek, J., & Buss A. An analysis of the self-monitoring scale. *Journal of Personality and Social Psychology,* 1980, *38,* 679-686.

Cegala, D.J. *Interaction involvement: A necessary dimension of communicative competence.* Presented at the annual meeting of the Speech Communication Association, Minneapolis, November, 1978.

Cegala, D.J. Interaction involvement: A cognitive dimension of communicative competence. *Communication Education,* 1981, *30,* 109-121.

Cegala, D., Fischbach, R., Sokuvitz, S., Maase, S., & Smilter, R. *A report on the development and validity of the social orientation scale.* Presented at the Speech Communication Association Convention, San Francisco, November, 1976.

Cegala, D.J. Savage, G.T., Brunner, C.C., & Conrad, A.B. An elaboration of the meaning of interaction involvement: Toward the development of a theoretical concept. *Communication Monographs,* 1982, *49,* 229-248.

Chiesi, H.L., Spilich, G.J., & Voss, J.F. Acquisition of domain related information in relation to high and low domain knowledge. *Journal of Verbal Learning and Verbal Behavior,* 1979, *18,* 257-273.

Cohen, J., & Cohen, P. *Applied multiple regression/correlation analysis for the behavioral sciences.* Hillsdale, NJ: Lawrence Erlbaum, 1975.

Comadena, M. Accuracy in detecting deception: Intimate and friendship relationships. In M. Burgoon (Ed.) *Communication yearbook 6.* Beverly Hills: Sage, 1982.

Cronkhite, G., & Liska, J. The judgment of communication acceptability. In M. Roloff & G. Miller (Eds.) *Persuasion: New directions in theory and research.* Beverly Hills: Sage, 1980.

Dabbs, J.M., Evans, M.S., Hopper, C.H., & Purvis, J. Self-monitors in conversation: What do they monitor? *Journal of Personality and Social Psychology,* 1980, *39,* 278-285.

Duval, S., & Wicklund, R. *A theory of objective self-awareness.* New York: Academic Press, 1972.

Elliot, G. Some effects of deception and level of self-monitoring on planning and self-presentation. *Journal of Social Psychology,* 1979, *37,* 1282-1292.

Gabrenya, W., & Arkin, R. Self-monitoring scale: Factor structure and correlates. *Personality and Social Psychology Bulletin,* 1980, *6,* 13-22.

Gottman, J., Markman, H., & Notarius, C. The topography of marital conflict: a sequential analysis of verbal and nonverbal behavior. *Journal of Marriage and the Family*, 1977, *39*, 461-478.

Hart, R.P., & Burks, D.M. Rhetorical sensitivity and social interaction. *Speech Monographs*, 1972, *39*, 75-91.

Hart, R.P., Carlson, R.E., & Eadie, W.F. Attitudes toward communication and the assessment of rhetorical sensitivity. *Communication Monographs*, 1980, *47*, 1-22.

Hewes, D.E., & Planalp, S. There is nothing as useful as a good theory . . .: The influence of social knowledge on interpersonal communication. In M. Roloff & C. Berger (Eds.) *Social cognition and communication*. Beverly Hills: Sage, 1982.

Hinde, R.A. *Towards understanding relationships*. New York: Academic Press, 1979.

Ickes, W., & Barnes, R. The role of sex and self-monitoring in unstructured dyadic interactions. *Journal of Personality and Social Psychology*, 1977, *35*,315-330.

Jennings, D., Lepper, M., & Ross, L. Persistence of impressions of personal persuasiveness: Perseverance of erroneous self-assessments outside the debriefing paradigm. *Personality and Social Psychology Bulletin*, 1981, *7*, 257-263.

John-Smith, M. Cognitive schema theory and the perseverance and attenuation of unwarranted empirical beliefs. *Communication Monographs*, 1982, *49*, 118-126.

Kellermann, K., & Roloff, M. *Communication competency? It depends*. Unpublished manuscript, Northwestern University, 1983.(a)

Kellermann, K., & Roloff, M. *Measures of communication sensitivity: I wonder what condition my dimensions are in?* Presented at Speech Communication Association Convention, Washington, D.C., November, 1983. (b)

Kent, G.G., Davis, J.D., & Shapiro, D.A. Effect of mutual acquaintance on the construction of conversation. *Journal of Experimental Social Psychology*, 1981, *17*, 197-209.

Kent, G.G., Davis, J.D., & Shapiro, D.A. Resources required in the construction and reconstruction of conversation. *Journal of Personality and Social Psychology*, 1978, *36*, 13-22.

Langer, E.J. Rethinking the role of thought in social interaction. In J.H. Harvey, W. Ickes, & R.F. Kidd (Eds.) *New directions in attribution research*, Vol. 2. Hillsdale: Lawrence Erlbaum, 1978.

Langer, E.J., Blank, A., & Chanowitz, B. The mindlessness of ostensibly thoughtful action: The role of "placebic" information in interpersonal attraction. *Journal of Personality and Social Psychology*, 1978, *36*, 635-642.

Langer, E., & Weinman, C. When thinking disrupts intellectual performance: Mindfulness on an overlearned task. *Personality and Social Psychology Bulletin*, 1981, *7*, 240-243.

Lippa, R. Expressive control and the leakage of dispositional introversion-extroversion during role-played teaching. *Journal of Personality*, 1976, *44*, 541-559.

McCall, G., & Simmons, J. *Identities and interactions: An examination of human associations in everyday life* (rev. ed.). New York: MacMillan, 1978.

McCann, C., & Hancock, R. Self-monitoring in communicative interactions: Social cognitive consequences of goal-directed message modification. *Journal of Experimental Social Psychology*, 1983, *19*, 109-121.

McCroskey, J.C. Oral communication apprehension: A summary of recent theory and research. *Human Communication Research*, 1977, *4*, 78-96.

Miller, G.R., & Steinberg, M. *Between people: A new analysis of interpersonal communication*. Palo Alto, CA: Science Research Association, 1975.

Norton, R.W. Foundations of a communication style construct. *Human Communication Research*, 1978, *4*, 99-112.

Norton, R.W., & Pettegrew, L.S. Attentiveness as a style of communication: A structural analysis. *Communication Monographs*, 1979, *46*, 13-26.

Roloff, M., & Berger, C. *Social cognition and communication*. Beverly Hills: Sage,1982.

Roloff, M., & Berger, C. Social cognition and communication: An introduction. In M. Roloff
    & C. Berger (Eds.) *Social cognition and communication*. Beverly Hills: Sage, 1982.

Shaffer, D., Smith, J., & Tomarelli, M. Self-monitoring as a determinant of self-disclosure
    reciprocity during the acquaintance process. *Journal of Personality and Social Psychology*,
    1982, *43*, 163-175.

Snyder, M. Self-monitoring processes. In L. Berkowitz (Ed.) *Advances in experimental social
    psychology* (vol. 12). New York: Academic Press, 1979.

Snyder, M. Self-monitoring processes. *Advances in Experimental Social Psychology*, 1979, *12*,
    85-128.

Spilich, G.J., Vesonder, G.T., Chiesi, H.L., & Voss, J.F. Text processing of domain-related
    information for individuals with high and low domain knowledge. *Journal of Verbal
    Learning and Verbal Behavior*, 1979, *18*, 275-290.

Storms, M.D. Videotape and the attribution process: Reversing actors' and observers' points of
    view. *Journal of Personality and Social Psychology*, 1973, *27*, 165-175.

Street, R.L., Brady, R.M., & Putnam, W.B. *The influence of speech rate stereotypes and rate
    similarity on listeners' evaluations of speakers*. Presented at the International Communica-
    tion Association Convention, Dallas, May, 1983.

Street, R.L., & Giles, H. Speech accommodation theory: A social cognitive approach to
    language and speech behavior. In M. Roloff & C. Berger (Eds.) *Social cognition and
    communication*. Beverly Hills: Sage, 1982.

Swap, W., & Rubin, J. Measurement of interpersonal orientation. *Journal of Personality and
    Social Psychology*, 1983, *44*, 208-219.

Taylor, S.E., & Fiske, S.T. Salience, attention, and attribution: Top of the head phenomena. In
    L. Berkowitz (Ed.) *Advances in experimental social psychology*, vol. 11. New York:
    Academic Press, 1978.

Wegner, D., & Vallacher, R. *Implicit psychology: An introduction to social cognition*. New
    York: Oxford University Press, 1977.

Zimbardo, P. *Shyness*. Reading, MA: Addison-Wesley, 1977.

Zuckerman, M., DePaulo, B., & Rosenthal, R. Verbal and nonverbal communication of
    deception. In L. Berkowitz (Ed.) *Advances in experimental social psychology* (vol. 14).
    New York: Academic Press, 1981.

9

Skills for Successful Bargainers

A Valence Theory of Competent Mediation

WILLIAM A. DONOHUE
MARY E. DIEZ
DEBORAH WEIDER-HATFIELD

In their recent review of the negotiation literature Putnam and Jones (1982) lament the scholarly dependence on researching distributive (win-lose) models of negotiation. They argue for the need to explore more integrative (win-win) models of bargaining that have demonstrated greater long-term viability as problem-solving mechanisms. The movement toward integrative approaches to negotiation has gained a great deal of momentum as illustrated in Derek Bok's (President of Harvard University) annual report to the Harvard Board of Overseers. He urged that law-school curricula place more emphasis on "the gentler arts of reconciliation and accommodation, work at "tapping human inclinations toward collaboration and compromise rather than stirring our proclivities for competition and rivalry," and institute courses "devoted to methods of mediation and negotiation" designed to explore voluntary, non-court-based approaches to dispute resolution ("Excerpts from the Report," 1983). A prime example of the shift in popularity from win-lose to win-win approaches to dispute resolution in the American legal system is in the field of divorce and family mediation which is designed to provide "a means for resolving disputes, restructuring family relationships, and prompting the best interest of children once divorce has become inevitable" (Brown, 1982, p. 9).

One of the most popular means of achieving integrative solutions to disputes is to employ some form of third-party intervention (Brown, 1983; Frost & Wilmot, 1978; Pruitt, 1981; Rubin & Brown, 1975). Of these forms of intervention, mediation is helpful in achieving the most integrative solutions because the intervenor works with the disputants to help them reach their own agreements instead of imposing agreements. Thus, it would seem useful for communication scholars to identify how mediators use communication to accomplish integrative agreements.

The process of mediation and the role of the mediator in that process has long been described as understudied, inaccessible to investigation, and devoid of sound theory. For example, Podell and Knapp (1969) argued that the lack of empirical verification of mediation processes rendered theory in the area rather speculative. Kochan and Jick (1978) noted that mediation is probably the most widely practiced and least researched conflict resolution procedure in collective bargaining due to a lack of theory, and to the widely held view that mediation is an art unsuited to systematic analyses. Gulliver (1979, p. 210), in building his case for mediation as an integrated part of negotiation, noted that "the process of mediation and the roles and strategies of mediation have been rather neglected in studies of negotiation; consequently, there is a good deal of confusion and misapprehension conceptually and analytically." In addition, Wall (1981) concluded that despite the ubiquity of the process of mediation, it remains understudied and unrefined.

The purpose of this chapter is to address some of these concerns and provide a theory of mediator communicative competence that will enable researchers to understand better how mediators are able to use communication to create collaborative, integrative decision-making environments and resolve parties' disagreements. The theory will be a variation of the valence models presented in previous work in the area (Hoffman, 1979; Poole, McPhee, & Siebold, 1982) and will rely heavily on research in linguistics that focuses on how communicators use language to mark contexts as collaborative and create the appropriate decision-making environment. To begin laying the foundation for this valence theory, the discussion will focus on mediator competence by reviewing and critiquing the research in the area. The chapter will conclude by outlining the basic principles of a valence theory of mediator communicative competence.

MEDIATOR COMMUNICATIVE COMPETENCE

As indicated previously, mediation is often viewed in relation to other third-party interventions. Rubin (1981) indicates that third-party intervention in a bargaining event signals that competitive inclinations dominate the interaction to the extent that parties are unable to settle their dispute themselves. However, the disputants are sufficiently cooperative that they are willing to accept the intervention of a third party. However, as Rubin points out, the third party is spawned by the relationship between the original two parties. As a result, the role and involvement of the third party is typically peripheral to the primary relationship. Often, however, the third party can become very involved in the process, transforming the dyad into a triad in which case bargaining is likely to dissolve unless the third party continues to be involved in the negotiation process. Regardless of the level of involvement, the third party must maintain a relationship with the other two parties that requires fundamentally different communication choices than the two parties maintain between themselves. It is within this cooperative-competitive negotiation framework that the third party must be able to draw upon a level of communicative competence that allows the mediator to maintain the appropriate sort of relational distance from the other two parties while continuing to work toward dispute resolution.

THE PRIMARY ROLE OF THE MEDIATOR

Perhaps the least involved, and the least interesting third-party role from a communication standpoint is the arbitrator who simply listens to the opposing views and makes a binding settlement. At the other end of the continuum is the mediator who is very involved in assisting the parties in making a decision, suggesting that of the third-party intervention roles, the mediation role is most interesting from a communication standpoint. However, it is clear from reviewing the literature that working with parties to reach their own agreements has different meanings. For example, Gulliver (1979) proposes a useful continuum illustrating the range of mediator roles. The continuum is not intended to be typological, but simply indicative of common mediator performances. At one end of the continuum is the passive mediator who uses mere presence to simply prevent the parties from insulting one another. Next is the chairman who keeps order and directs procedures. The enunciator increases involvement by clarifying and emphasizing general rules and norms to facilitate interaction. The prompter keeps suggestions tentative and limited, yet interprets comments for parties to encourage coordination. Finally, at the opposite end of the continuum is the leader who more or less directly injects opinion and evaluates the demands made by either party.

Clearly, within Gulliver's (1979) continuum of mediator roles is the implication that the mediator does whatever necessary to assist in agreement making. For example, Maggiolo (1971) argues that mediation goes beyond the simple catalytic agent stage into an active role of making affirmative suggestions and recommendations for developing agreements. In adapting Pruitt's (1971) view of the mediator as persuader, Rubin and Brown (1975) view third parties as influence agents who see themselves as functioning in a bargaining role. As a result, the mediator is conceptualized as simply another party to the bargaining relationship whose main interest is to promote agreement.

PHASES IN THE MEDIATION PROCESS

As noted by Kochan and Jick (1978) many writers have acknowledged that conflict resolution processes, no matter in what context they occur or for what purpose they are undertaken, can usually be divided into several stages or phases. Gulliver (1979) for example, proposes a seven phase developmental model of negotiation involving "a series of overlapping sequences or phases, each with its particular emphasis and kind of interaction and each opening the way for the succeeding one in a complex progression" (p. 82). The phases include (1) the search for an arena for the negotiations; (2) formation of an agenda and working definitions of the issues; (3) preliminary demands and offers and limits of the issues with particular emphasis on the differences between the parties; (4) the narrowing of differences, agreements on some issues, and the identification of the more unyielding ones; (5) preliminaries to final bargaining; (6) final bargaining; (7) ritual confirmation of the final outcome; and, in many cases, (8) the implementation or arrangements for the outcome.

According to Margerison and Leary (1975) the role of the mediator in the process is to move the interaction into phases that promote more of a problem-solving interaction with less of a competitive orientation. Gulliver (1979) found that the mediator is probably most useful during the transition from one phase of negotiation to the next or back to prior phases. While all transitions are likely to be difficult, Gulliver expects the transition from phase 3 (preliminary demands and offers with an emphasis on differences) to phase 4 (narrowing of differences with an emphasis on agreement) to be most problematic because it involves a shift from opposition and hostility to coordination with some trust and even cooperation.

Haynes (1981) explains the divorce mediation process in terms of issues covered at each session with a session lasting anywhere from one to five hours depending on the phases of the negotiations and the characteristics of the parties.

While the phases identified by Gulliver (1979) and Haynes (1981) are similar, one important difference between labor and divorce mediation situations is the point at which the mediator's is likely to enter the process. Kressel (1972) found that labor mediators preferred later entry into the negotiation process presumably because the parties' motivation to use the mediator's services at that time was highest. Pruitt (1981), however, explains that a mediator's assistance is more likely to be sought early in efforts to reach a divorce settlement possibly because past experiences make it clear to the couple that they have been unable to resolve their problems on their own. In addition, the size or degree of conflict, along with the parties' concerns about losing face, will influence the point at which a mediator is engaged (Rubin, 1980).

This discussion suggests that any conceptualization of mediator communicative competence include: (1) an identification of the unique phases through which a particular type of mediation is likely to progress, and (2) an identification of the types of communicative behaviors occurring throughout those phases.

COMMUNICATIVE FUNCTIONS: PRIOR RESEARCH

Generally, the communicative behaviors employed by mediators to control an interaction have been classified as either content or process oriented. Bartenuek, Benton, and Keys (1975) indicate that process mediation seeks to develop conditions and skills that facilitate concession making and problem solving, while content mediation addresses specific issues. Margerison and Leary (1975) and Kochan (1980) indicate that process actions are frequently emphasized in the earlier stages of mediation perhaps in order to restructure the emotional conflict that often arises at the beginning of mediation (Walton, 1969).

Much of the research that discusses process and content interventions is in the form of anecdotes and suggestions that mediators might use to be more effective. For example, the following list contains common process suggestions:

(1) *Refereeing the interaction* by terminating repetitive discussions and providing equal air time for participants (Walton, 1969); being nonevaluative when parties speak (Fisher, 1972); or clarifying parties' views by restating positions (Walton, 1969).

(2) *Encouraging interpersonal feedback* by asking parties to exchange perceptions of each other (Walton, 1969); or instructing parties in the use of role reversal (Johnson, 1971).

(3) *Inducing a problem-solving orientation* through humor (Kressel, 1972) and by encouraging parties to see common goals (Sherif, Harvey, White, Hood,

& Sherif, 1961); or creating deadlines to increase time pressures (Pruitt, 1981).

(4) *Planning and preparing for the future* by teaching parties how to use the mediation techniques so they can continue to use them to solve their own problems and decrease the need for third-party interventions (Walton, 1969; Pruitt, 1981).

In addition, a list of content-oriented communication suggestions has been proposed:

(1) *Initiating agenda* by placing less controversial issues first so that concessions and agreements come easily at the outset (Pruitt, 1981; Rubin, 1981); identifying issues under dispute (Erickson, Holmes, Frey, Walter, & Thibaut, 1974); or introducing superordinate goals to modify parties perceptions of the conflict (Rubin, 1981).

(2) *Diagnosing conflict* by identifying the pitfalls of the aggressor-defender mode of conflict and educating the parties in the logic of flexible rigidity, i.e., maintaining aspirations while taking a problem-solving approach (Pruitt, 1981).

(3) *Presenting options* in order to encourage concessions, especially formulating these options, so that neither party loses face (Pruitt, 1981; Rubin, 1981).

From this discussion of prior research, it should be readily apparent that scholars interested in examining mediation processes have had little interest in developing theoretical perspectives on communication processes in mediation, and less interest in generating any data that even describe how communication functions in mediation contexts. Several conditions are probably responsible for the lack of interest in learning more about communication processes in mediation. First, most of the writing focusing on communicative functions has been done by scholars who are generally not interested in focusing on microscopic communication processes that contribute to effective mediation (Coogler, 1978; Haynes, 1981; Pruitt, 1981; Rubin, 1981). Second, most of the interest in the topic of mediation has been generated recently as evidenced by the tremendous upsurge in legislation passed by many states requiring mediation for disputing parties before court appearance are possible (Comeaux, 1982). Third, most of the research in the area of conflict management in communication has focused on the two-party negotiation process (see Putnam and Jones, 1982). As the typical negotiation context is quite different from the mediation context, it is difficult to simply transfer theories and research results.

As a result of these impediments, three primary weaknesses of the research cited above can be identified. First, and most importantly, it is not useful to list suggestions that may or may not facilitate communication without some attempt to theoretically specify how and why these suggestions work. For example, the suggestions cited above uniformly point to the need to create a cooperative decision-making environment within which to resolve the dispute. As Scherer and Giles (1979) indicate in their book on social markers in speech, there are a great many communicative acts that can create cooperative or competitive contexts, and a large number of ways in which language choices can be sequenced to structure context. Yet, there has been no attempt to specify theoretically how communication processes function collectively to create the context needed for decision making. We need a theoretical mechanism to guide an empirical sorting out of the mediation process and to assist professional mediators in dispute resolution.

A second problem with the approaches to mediation cited above is the lack of any systematic consideration of the role of context in the mediation process. Several contextual variables have been mentioned such as conflict intensity (Rubin, 1980), logistical considerations (Walton, 1969), rules specification (Wall, 1981) or resource control (Frost & Wilmot, 1978). How do all of these and possibly other contextual features influence the kind of communication patterns that are likely to emerge in mediation? The answer to this question will be central to the development of any theory concerning how communication processes influence mediation.

A third weakness of the research relates specifically to the confusion over phases in mediation. The review of mediation phases presented previously indicates that some of the approaches are prescriptive while others are descriptive. There is little empirical support for the consequences of not adhering to various phase restrictions. There is also very little conceptual effort devoted to what kinds of communicative acts prevail during specific phases, or what kinds of messages or procedures mark the transition from one phase to another. Providing some theoretical specification of how communication creates cooperative contexts may permit a more careful assessment of how phases emerge in mediation.

Given these problems this chapter will present a theory of mediator competence that works toward specifying how communication functions in the mediation context, and what kinds of communicative choices are likely to lead toward more successful mediation efforts. To accomplish this goal, we will begin by identifying contextual parameters that might influence the ways in which the participants communicate. After these contextual parameters have been identified, the specific code choices that facilitate mediator objectives given the various contextual patterns will be specified. Finally, the manner in which these language choices can be placed into a valence model of communicator competence will be displayed. A brief example will conclude this chapter.

CONTEXTUAL PARAMETERS IN MEDIATION

Defining what is meant by context or situation often stirs controversy among scholars, probably because there are a number of perspectives from which a definition can be formulated. Fortunately, there is some consensus among social psychologists and sociolinguistics that certain features of situations or context can be readily identified. By drawing upon the works of Argyle (1981), Avedon (1981), Brown and Fraser (1979), Hymes (1964), and Levinson (1978), context can be defined as "The set of elements that, by convention, operate to make a given interaction-type recognizable—both to interactants and to observers—as one type of interaction rather than another" (Diez, 1983). Participants do not necessarily share the same awareness of the elements; rather, participants develop what Goffman (1959) calls a "working consensus" (see also Raush, 1972). The contextual parameters that will be discussed in this paper include: conflict intensity, participant role relationships, procedural enforcements, and mediation subject matter. Each of these will be discussed in turn.

Conflict Intensity. Rubin's (1980) review of the experimental research in third-party intervention indicated that the intensity of the conflict had a very large impact on which intervention strategies were likely to be selected. Conflict intensity can be defined as the degree of goal discrepancy in the interaction with respect to both substantive or issue-centered conflict, and relational, or person-centered conflict (Raven & Kruglanski, 1970). If participants have extremely discrepant goals or interactional purposes both in regard to the topic of mediation, and in regard to attacking the other participant personally, then the conflict will be viewed as intense. Thus, consistent with the works of Gregory and Carroll (1978), Brown and Fraser (1979), and Graham, Argyle, and Furnham (1981), it is conceivable that participants in mediation can have a number of purposes operating simultaneously. The purposes that seem to be most relevant to the mediation situation include coming to agreement on the issues in the interaction, and managing the relational goals of participants for one another.

Participant Role Relationships. According to Rubin (1981), role relationships are problematic in mediation because only the role of the mediator *seems* relatively formal and clearly defined, often by some legal authority, or by some prearranged consensus about the role of the mediator by the disputants. The other roles may be more fluid. For example, in a divorce mediation, participants may start out as husband and wife, but the goal of the interaction is to change that relational role structure into some other form that is manageable for the disputing couple. Thus, as Brown and Fraser (1979) and Ervin-Tripp (1980) point out, role relationships with respect to power valance, interaction history and the like can have a significant impact on code choice. In the mediation context, the mediator must constantly monitor the role relationships to determine if they are changing in a way that is productive for the mediation to accomplish its goals.

Procedural Enforcements. As Levinson (1978) indicates, there are constraints imposed on situations such that a particular *form* for the interaction will be expected, and in many cases, even enforced. In many cases, after a mediator has been introduced into the conflict, a set of procedural choices may include the neutrality of the place selected for meetings and the time limits for the mediation (Walton, 1969). Or, rules might be established with regard to how the interaction will proceed logistically, such as whether parties ought to meet together or separately with the mediator. Massengill (1982) argues that the mediator should not hold any single-party sessions. Haynes (1981) maintains, however, that private interviews to discuss a variety of issues are necessary. At the same time, Haynes encourages involvement of the children in the decision-making process once a basic agreement on the custody, visitation, and support issues have been reached in a divorce mediation context. In addition, Brown (1982) and Haynes make specific suggestions about the seating arrangements and the use of outside experts in mediation situations.

Mediation Subject Matter. Hymes (1964) indicates that topic has a substantial impact on code choice in conversation. Brown and Fraser (1979) include topic as one of the elements of the situation that helps participants define the purpose of the interaction. It is quite conceivable that the subject matter of the mediation efforts will greatly affect code choices by the mediator and the participants. For example, discussions about child custody problems in divorce mediations may be quite different from discussions about working conditions in a labor-management mediation situation. Some topics simply require more or less formality, self-disclosure, use of directives, and so on, than other topics.

To review, this chapter contends that contextual parameters influence the extent to which the mediator can competently perform the job of dispute resolution. The goal of the mediator is to create a sufficiently cooperative communication context by manipulating these parameters. That is, the competent mediator will attempt to adjust the level of conflict intensity so the issues can be discussed and handled. When person-centered conflict abounds, the mediator must shift the resulting energy to focus on specific issues. Or, the mediator may have to increase conflict intensity if the participants are unwilling to communicate their desired outcomes. In addition, the mediator must enforce a set of procedures that will lead to a mutually satisfying decision. Imposing discussion rules or establishing meeting schedules might be included in such procedural adjustments. Topic and topic order should also be considered when managing mediation effort. Some topics are more readily discussable at some stages of mediation and not at others.

Finally, managing role relationships is critical for the mediator. This task is made problematic for the mediator because the mediator is stepping into a situation in which the other parties have already admitted that their current set of role relationships will not permit them to solve the dispute. The mediator must not only redefine the role relationships between the disputing parties, but also establish such role relationships between the disputing parties and him/herself. To accomplish this, the mediator can remain neutral or use him- or herself. Influence strategies to encourage agreement. Nevertheless, one of the major tasks is relational redefinition for the mediator. We now turn to a discussion of this problem.

NEGOTIATING RELATIONAL PARAMETERS

This chapter will argue that relational redefinition in a mediation task is conducted as a negotiation at the metamessage level. That is, participants do not generally discuss in specific detail the ongoing changes in role relationships that emerge from the discussion. Rather, these changes are a function of a subtle negotiation process in which a participant proposes a certain relational definition by marking some action in a way that communicates that relational definition. The other person responds to that proposal by either accepting or rejecting it through a similar marking process. For example, as Scherer and Giles (1979) note, communicators always mark or label their actions so that others will know how to judge the intention of the action, and subsequently respond to it. Politeness markers (Brown & Levinson, 1978) make the relational proposal of equality or deference because when a communicator uses a polite form of address or request, the communicator is giving the metamessage "I do not have the relational right to threaten your face with my form of address or request." The other can accept that relational definition by matching the marking strategy or by not specifically pursuing that marking device as a topic of conversation. Thus, relational redefinition is a subtle negotiation process in which participants propose and counterpropose particular relational states by marking their linguistic (and extralinguistic) forms. Two questions remain: What specific relational dimensions are being negotiated? How does the mediator manage these dimensions?

The problem of managing the relational redefinition is complex for the mediator. Not only is the mediator forced to manage the relationship between the two conflicting parties, but the mediator must develop a functional relationship with each of the two parties individually. In addition to handling these three relational problems, the mediator must be concerned with how each of the participants is viewing the mediator's relationship with the other disputing party. As a result, the mediator has five distinct relational problems to handle. For example, as a tactic to influence the mediator one of the disputants may attempt to comply with a mediator's request even if the request is undesirable to that person. In so doing, the person may wish to create the impression of cooperation with the mediator, thereby forming the appearance of a coalition. The mediator often wishes to avoid the appearance of taking sides to maintain cooperation. The problem is that the appearance of taking sides may occur through the subtle negotiation of the meta-messages participants are sending to one another. Thus, the competent mediator must learn to control the relational negotiation process by monitoring the ways in which he or she is making and responding to relational proposals by various marking strategies.

The relational parameters that are being negotiated in a mediation situation appear to include control, trust, and intimacy (Morton, Alexander, & Altman, 1976). Each of these parameters will be considered individually, after which their interrelationships will be discussed.

Control. Relational control, or the right to direct, delimit, and define the actions of the relationship has been discussed frequently in communication research (see O'Donnell-Trujillo, 1981). Controlling metamessages are detected by examining how individuals attempt to structure the other's prior utterance. Accepting the control of the other produces complementary relational forms while rejecting control or competing for control produces symmetrical relational forms. In mediation, control of the interaction is a key objective for the mediator to increase his or her flexibility in pursuing some particular pattern of questioning or topic development. The opposing parties may also be trying to compete with the mediator for control depending upon their objectives. Nevertheless, negotiating control is one of the relational parameters that the mediator must be able to manage.

Trust. Morton, Alexander, and Altman (1976) discuss trust in terms of the development of relational constraints. They argue that relationships create constraints and that we develop some sense of probability about the likelihood that the other person will adhere to those constraints. Trust is the attributed sense of consistency in the other person's communicative performance within specific contexts. That is, we develop expectations that in specific contexts people will mark their behavior in particular ways. For example, certain levels of politeness, or certain forms of directives will be expected to be selected over others. Or, specific code choices and address forms will be used given the ways in which the contextual parameters outlined previously develop over time.

Trust is negotiated frequently in mediation from at least two perspectives. First, before the mediator enters the interaction the disputants attribute some level of trust to the other. The level may be low, with the disputants looking to the mediator to increase that level of trust. Clearly, the mediator must negotiate an increase in the level of trust so that the parties will cooperate sufficiently to form an agreement. Second, the mediator must encourage each of the disputants to attribute trust to him or her so that both parties will comply with the mediator's requests. In addition, as suggested previously, the mediator's behavior toward each disputant will be scrutinized carefully by the other disputant to determine the mediator's communicative choices, particularly at the initial stages of interaction.

Intimacy. Intimacy is generally treated as the extent to which participants in a relationship engage in a mutual sharing of personal products (Morton, Alexander, & Altman, 1976). By focusing on the process of sharing, it becomes possible to conceptualize relational intimacy as the number of illocutionary acts and sensory modes people use to exchange information. An illocutionary act is the act performed in making an utterance (as distinct from simply uttering the words). Stiles (1981), following Searle's (1976) lead, identified eight illocutionary acts: disclosures (reports of the speaker's subjective experiences); advisements (advice, orders, commands); edifications (statements of fact, assertions or descriptions); confirmations (expressions of shared attitudes); questions; interpretations (judgments, labeling); acknowledgments (greetings, back-channel responses); and reflections (repetitions, rephrasings, summaries, clarifications). The use of several of these acts in interaction marks relational intimacy. For example, making a disclosure or giving advice may indicate that the person is making a proposal to increase interpersonal intimacy. Certainly, being able to use most or all of these acts indicates that the couple is quite flexible in its ability to exchange information.

This definition is particularly useful for the mediation context because one of the objectives of the mediator may be to renegotiate intimacy and change the way disputants exchange information. For example, if the couple uses advice to exchange information and produces dysfunctional conflict, the mediator may try to move the interactants to use disclosure or simple edification or some other less intimate mode of exchange.

It should be obvious that control, trust, and intimacy do not operate independently. Rather, all three relational parameters operate simultaneously in the mediation context. For example, in negotiating control the mediator may also be negotiating intimacy because the control mechanism the mediator uses might also mark a change in the level of intimacy in the interaction. In addition, the form of control selected may be inconsistent with prior forms which may have trust implications. Thus, these relational parameters are being continuously negotiated by the mediator in attempting to build a context that will facilitate decision making and commitment to the decision by the disputants once the decision has been reached.

At this point it is appropriate to identify the specific language choices that mediators have to negotiate these relational parameters and create a felicitous interactive condition. This chapter now turns to that task.

THE LANGUAGE OF MEDIATOR COMPETENCE

While the idea of speech markers previously has not been applied directly to a theory of mediator competence, work based on Hymes's (1974) definition of communicative competence provides the basis for such a link. Following Hymes, Diez (1983) discussed the ability of the adult speaker in negotiation settings to call upon his or her developed understanding of communicative code choices (1) to interpret the linguistic and other communicative code choices of others, making inferences and judgments about that other's definition of the situation and expectations of what rights and obligations are in force for the interaction, as well as (2) to use their own linguistic and other communicative code choices to influence the ongoing definition of the situation and the set of rights and obligations mutually negotiated.

Extending the definition to a more specific type of negotiation—mediation—the competent mediator must first have a developed awareness of the gestalt created by the communicative behavior of others, a clear yet flexible ability to read cues. Equally important is the development of a sophisticated control over his or her own communicative behavior, such that he or she can make choices that will adjust the situation appropriately and move the parties toward the goal of the mediation, deciding on a mutually agreeable outcome.

Mediation competence implies the development of complex communicative skills, given both the contextual parameters described earlier and the critical relational parameters discussed in the previous section. Basic to this ability of the mediator is the nature of communicative competence as interpretation and production. The mediator cannot pull out a "recipe" that may be applied in every case. Rather, he or she must be able to constantly adjust, by assessing the interaction of the others, the communicative means by which he or she will guide the decision-making process.

While the skill is complex, that is not to imply that it is either "magic" or otherwise unavailable for examination. Considerable work in exploring the multiple functions of language (Halliday, 1973; Giles, Scherer & Taylor, 1979) and in describing the situated nature of language (Brown & Fraser, 1979; Diez, 1983), for example, have broken important ground in allowing communication researchers to examine behavioral evidence of communicative competence. In this section, we will use one such framework to illustrate how interpretation skills and communicative code choices are likely to be employed by competent mediators.

One way to view the multiple functions of language is to probe the kinds of "work" performed by communicative code choices. While the emphasis here will be on linguistic choices, we hasten to note that additional cues about the meaning of interactional choices are always present in the paraverbal and nonverbal cues as well. Ordinarily, what the mediator takes into account is not the individual cues but the overall "display package" that creates a sense of the definition of the situation for that interactant.

Diez (1983) outlined three kinds of interaction work evident in two-party negotiation interaction, contrasting competitive and cooperative group settings. We will extend her definitions of distance, coherence, and structuring work here as a way to illustrate the range of linguistic choices under the control of the competent mediator.

Distance work, as defined by Diez, is a primary means by which speakers establish rights and obligations between and among each other. It involves communicative code choices that signal psychological distance (immediacy/nonimmediacy), social distance (relative formality/informality), and role distance (power/solidarity). Psychological distance is signalled by what Weiner and Mehrabian (1968) call "immediacy," the degree of directness and intensity of the interaction between communicators and referents. Varying relationships, then, are caught in encoding differences. The notion of "directness" can be expanded to illustrate the work of the mediator. First, in assessing the directness of the orientation of the two parties, the mediator gains a sense of the conflict intensity. Hostility may manifest itself in overly direct, confrontational communication or in overly indirect allusions (constituting a sort of denial or repression). Alternatively, in low conflict situations, the mediator may observe an open, direct relationship, manifested in their code choices, between the parties and the issues involved in their settlement process.

Depending upon the assessment of the nature of the communication patterns, the mediator makes choices about his or her own directness of orientation to each party, to the relationship between the parties, and to the issues involved in the dispute. It may be appropriate for the mediator to encourage immediacy in relationship to specific issues, for example, asking each person to speak only for him- or herself and to address what he or she feels in regard to the issue, while encouraging the parties to distance themselves from the emotional feelings they have formerly directed at the other person. The mediator's own relationship to each party may be aided by his or her directness of reference to each party's statements and proposals; this same action establishes nonimmediacy or lack of involvement/agreement with the party's emotional bias—that is, the mediator may acknowledge the feeling level of each person, while controlling where that feeling level fits in the overall decision-making process.

Social distance is marked by overall "register" or the sense of relative formality/informality conveyed. Again, the mediator assesses the contextual elements initially through cues related to social distance. The higher the conflict intensity, the more likely the parties are to choose "stiff" and "righteous" (i.e., formal) communicative code elements. The mediator's choices must match the seriousness of the participants, while moving the tone of the interaction to a more neutral state. Moreover, he or she must establish a social distance from each that will not jeopardize his or her relationship with the other. Reference to each is a significant marker of relationship—use of name, choice of first name or title and last name, nonverbal reference through eye contact—all may be subtle cues of social distance. Goffman's (1959) discussion of front and back region behavior is apropos here; the mediator must maintain the front region "role" of mediator. To lapse into humor or relaxation with one party (i.e., back region behavior) would be to destroy the trust of the other and the seriousness of the decision-making setting.

In contrast, in relatively low conflict situations, the tenor of the whole interaction may be more informal. However, the mediator needs to assess the ongoing definition of rights and obligations even though the situation appears to be more informal.

Role distance is defined in terms of the dimensions of power and solidarity involved in the relationships between the parties. The mediator must be careful to maintain the balance of power, not appearing to "side" with either party. Subtle linguistic choices are called upon to create and maintain impartiality and balance, including again references to each with equal frequency, references to the contributions of each to the discussion, and so on. The mediator must also be very careful in his or her assessment of the parties' responses to his or her own communicative behavior. For example, if one of the parties is more effective at "matching" the linguistic choices and tone of the mediator, the other may begin to perceive that the mediator and that party are united against him/her. The mediator's task in making communicative choices, then, is to constantly create the necessary balance for the two parties to trust him or her and to focus on the issues to be resolved.

There are, then, a range of distance cues which a mediator must balance according to the contextual parameters, the stage of the interaction, and the goal of the parties. Three important continua capture the broad scope of the types of communicative code choices related to distance work and linked with the establishment and adjustment of relational parameters.

First, the range of formal/informal relates clearly to the relational parameter of intimacy. At the formal extreme, appropriate to high conflict situations, the mediator may make formal register choices in order to create distance between the parties, thereby defusing their emotional conflict. Carefully structured sentences, neutral or technical vocabulary, and a serious tone are examples of formal register markers (Gregory & Carroll, 1978). Such code choices also move the focus from the conflict between the parties to the goal of their reaching a mutually acceptable settlement.

At the other extreme of low conflict orientation, the mediator may adopt a more informal register, still indicating the seriousness of the task of agreeing to a settlement, but encouraging the sense of amicability and solidarity cued by the interaction of the participants. Generally, of course, the mediator will find him- or herself somewhere in between, or will need to assist the parties to move from relatively formal to a more mid-position in the register and tone of the interaction. To do so, the mediator draws upon a range of communicative options—again, not as from a recipe book, but out of his or her awareness of the present definition of the situation and of the subtle cues that may signal a change or new understanding.

A second range is indirect/direct, relating primarily to control as a relational parameter. The more intense the involvement in the conflict appears to be, the more the mediator may at the beginning take charge in sorting out the orientation of the parties, indicated in their immediacy cues. The mediator will generally use nonimmediacy, cued by tentativeness of expression, in considering possible solutions. The mediator will be direct, however, in indicating to each that he or she is aware of their contributions.

Finally, the range of supportive/impartial code choices provides the means by which distance work assists the mediator in establishing trust.

Backchannels, restatements, and the like, are supportive moves, indicating to the parties that the mediator is operating in the interest of their settlement. However, these same cues must be carefully monitored so that impartiality is also created. A mediator perceived as not neutral (i.e., favoring one party over the other) will have difficulty establishing a relationship of trust with the other party. One means of establishing the supportive/impartial balance is to adopt neutral language, stating observations clearly, without judgment. Even with feelings the mediator can objectively accept each party's right to the feelings while not endorsing the feelings in relationship to the potential settlement.

Through distance work, the mediator assesses the communicative code choices of the parties and makes his or her own choices in such a way that initial relationships are established in trust and that the ongoing movement of the parties toward their mutual settlement can be facilitated. By striving for a neutral tone and an objective sifting of the issues, the mediator provides a linguistic model for the participants. He or she not only indicates relationally the impartiality with which he or she will deal with the two persons, but also sets linguistic expectations for their talk as the interaction progresses.

Coherence work is the disambiguating or sense-making function of language in interaction. Diez (1983) describes it as the need to make connections, both with the flow of discourse and between the discourse and elements outside of it. The former concerns the clarity of any part of the discourse; the latter is the means of specifying what is given and what is new.

Again, the mediator's first task (although it quickly becomes simultaneously operative with the second) is to assess the communicative cues of the participants' own coherence work. In the initial stages, coherence cues may indicate the degree of conflict intensity. Given a highly charged, emotionally laden dispute, there is greater danger that the parties will take short cuts to conclusions, based on their emotional set. Because any equivocality on the part of the other will be interpreted out of the bias of past experience, they will tend to miss possible connections leading to a settlement. The mediator, then, uses his or her skills to listen for potential links, to sort and analyze elements of the discourse, synthesizing or structuring the information to delete the "hidden" principles clouding the assessment of potential solutions. This is a critical interpretation skill, requiring the ability to analyze and synthesize on the spot.

In terms of linguistic choices, the mediator faced with such a situation needs to build carefully whatever elements he or she will set forth, tieing them to specific referents in the parties' talk. Coherence work in this sense draws upon skill in subordination of sentence structure, as well as the use of links between ideas and their antecedents and subsequent references.

Clearly, some distance work is also involved in coherence work, as the mediator defuses the information by sorting out the factual from the emotional

With less intense conflict, the parties may be less prone to exploit ambiguity, but the work of the mediator still involves the clarifying and examining of the relationships between elements of the solution and the careful referencing of those elements to data and sources. In both instances, the mediator works with a continuum of explicit/implicit information. He or she often draws out the implicit elements in the contributions of the parties, and carefully constructs explicit relationships and potential relationships among the varied aspects of the situation. By its very nature, the settlement in both conflict extremes needs to be spelled out clearly as a legal document in the end. The mediator's skill at building coherent relationships assists parties to reach their goal, regardless of the contextual parameters at the beginning.

Coherence work, thus, impacts on the relational parameters in a way less direct than that of distance work. It contributes to the sense of trust, in that the parties must recognize their contributions in the elements drawn out by the mediator. Moreover, it depends on distance work in the equal treatment of the parties to get out the data important to each side in the dispute.

Coherence work is less related to intimacy, except insofar as the mediator works to promote issue- or position-centered discussion. Fisher and Ury (1982) note that a focus on positions prevents parties from becoming "locked in" to one solution. And the fact that the mediator can provide the means to adjust positions by linking elements within them is face-saving to the parties.

Coherence work is crucial to control in that the mediator's careful building of the elements and relationships allows the parties to be in control of their own decision. It is a primary means by which the mediator serves as facilitator to the agreement. The mediator's use of linguistic choices that indicate tentativeness (e.g., I think; What do you think about . . .; Let's assume that . . .; If this were the case, what would that mean?) reinforces the idea that the relationships between ideas being proposed is open to adjustment and reframing—is in fact to be determined by the action of the parties rather than by the mediator. Again, this aspect of coherence work models for the participants that their own language should be tentative until they have arrived at a mutually acceptable solution.

In coherence work, the mediator helps get clear what the issues are, sorting out where agreement is possible or already present. He or she uses clear statements to provide perspective, thus allowing the participants to focus on the problems rather than on the emotional backlog surrounding the issues that have divided them. This use of connecting and linking both clarifies the work of the parties in negotiating their agreement and allows them to begin to change their positions, because these have been separated—by the mediator—from the emotional baggage.

Regarding structuring work, Diez (1983) discusses the larger interactional tasks of management of floor time and of processing techniques used in decision making. As described earlier in relationship to mediator roles, there is a continuum from highly involved to monitoring that the mediator may assume in the macroorganization of the interaction. Early in the establishment of the ground rules, the mediator again needs to assess from the interaction of the participants what the best procedure for this particular mediation situation would be, and he or she uses language to set forth a proposal for that structure.

The overall process of the mediator is guided by his or her ability to do the structuring work required to build a cooperative front allowing the parties to negotiate their dispute. Bearing in mind that the two parties retain control of the outcomes in mediation, the mediator makes structuring choices that direct the flow of the interaction, help the parties to negotiate, and assist the parties to cooperate to solve their conflict.

Initially, structuring work must set the tone (along with the language choices involved in distance work) and establish a working pattern of interaction. It is important that mediators explain their role and talk explicitly about what they will and will not do in assisting the parties in coming to an agreement. This may be done in establishing ground rules, for example, about what is "fair" for discussion.

Given the establishment of a good working relationship and a set of ground rules, the mediator's structuring work guides the movement of the interaction across the meeting or set of meetings. Mediators need a repertoire of many types of moves that they can use to direct the parties to elicit the elements needed for an agreement to be reached. For example, they may ask questions that direct the parties to explain their proposals for a certain aspect of the settlement. Combining structuring work with distance work and coherence work, the mediator will attempt to keep the discussion objective, clear, and directed toward the settlement. For example, if the parties have been asked to share their proposals, but digress into more feeling statements, the mediator may redirect the interaction. Specifically in relationship to structuring work, the mediator must be sensitive to the question of "equal time." Again, distance work cannot be clearly separated here, for the message of giving more time to one side may imply a lack of impartiality toward the other side.

In the patterns of the larger structure, directed by structuring work, the mediator might ask for clear proposals for agreement, identify what still needs to be done, act as an agent of reality in establishing consequences or confronting inconsistencies, draw conclusions, ask the parties to imagine how their solutions would work, or use any other means of framing and shaping the interaction toward the parties' ability to reach an agreement.

Because structuring work relates to the larger language patterns, at and beyond the speech act level, it is primarily focused on the relational parameter of control. Through structuring, the competent mediator directs, delimits and defines actions; and initially the mediator may use structuring to manage many aspects of the interaction. Gradually, however, in successful mediation, the structuring work is aimed at allowing the parties to take charge of their own direction toward the decision, and the mediator moves toward the monitoring role.

While structuring is clearly related to control, it cannot be completely divorced from the relational patterns of intimacy and trust. In directing the exchange of information, for example, the mediator is also directing the degree to which interpersonal intimacy is negotiated by structuring the kinds of illocutionary acts that are most appropriate for exchanging information. The perception of structuring moves as "fair" to both parties increases the developing sense of trust each places on the mediator. To the extent that the mediator uses inconsistent structuring mechanisms trust may be compromised.

On this more macroscopic level of influence through language choices, the mediator uses his/her skill to keep the potential agreement clear and objectively before the parties, directing their contributions and promoting their cooperation. Structuring work choices are not separate, discrete choices from those involved in distance and coherence work—often, as Halliday (1973) has pointed out, several functions of language are embedded within the same surface structure of the spoken words. Analytically, however, it is clear that the mediator needs to attend to three separate aspects of interaction work, impacting on the relational parameters of intimacy, trust, and control, in building the cooperative front between the parties involved in negotiating the agreement.

To review, this chapter argues that competent mediators must rely on an ability to interpret the linguistic and other communicative code choices of others while using their own code choices to influence the ongoing definition of the situation. The mediator's goal is to resolve the dispute by creating an agreement that the opposing parties will adopt and adhere to in the long run. To form this agreement, the mediator must be able to reduce conflict intensity by creating a more functional set of role relationships among all parties, establishing appropriate negotiation procedural rules, and managing the order of issue discussion. Of the mediator's resources to reduce conflict intensity, creating functional role relationships is perhaps the greatest communicative challenge since the disputing parties have already admitted that their role relationships are dysfunctional by asking the third party to mediate the negotiations. The mediator's task in creating functional role relationships is to select and implement appropriate levels of control, trust, and intimacy among all parties. These relational parameters are created by selecting various distancing, coherence, and structuring code choices throughout the course of the mediation process. What is needed at this point is some theoretical perspective that would explain how the distance, coherence, and structuring code choices can affect the mediator's ability to construct an integrative decision-making context over the course of the mediation. We now turn to a review of valence theory of group decision making since that theory will be used to explain the link between code choice and cooperative context construction.

MEDIATOR EFFECTIVENESS AS VALENCE ACCUMULATION

As indicated previously, one of the greatest communicative challenges for the mediator is to create a functional set of role relationships among all three parties involved in the mediation. This chapter argues that the mediator creates these role relationships by manipulating distance, coherence, and structuring code choices. This argument suggests that the more general objective of the mediator is to encourage the disputing parties to align themselves with his/her code choices so that the interaction will be pursued with language that will create a more cooperative communicative context. This suggests that the mediator attempts to influence the conflicting parties to yield control of the interaction, develop a sense of trust for the mediator and the other party, and make use of a level of intimacy that facilitates the exchange of information. This influence process can be termed *linguistic alignment* and can be defined as the coselection of language codes. (This is not to be confused with Stokes and Hewitt's (1976) term of "conversational alignment" which deals more with repairing conversational miscues.)

Influencing the conflicting parties to align their code choices with the mediator's can take three directions. First, the mediator can increase the level of cooperativeness by encouraging the conflicting parties to match his or her level of distance. In most cases the mediator will be trying to create distance between the individuals emotional involvement and the issues surrounding the mediation. However, the mediator must be careful to monitor the extent to which each party adopts the recommended level of distance because one party might attempt to comply with the mediator, sensing that the other is not complying, in an attempt to form a coalition against the other. Second, the mediator can increase the degree of compliance with requests to be tentative, yet clear in the course of the negotiation to create an appropriate level of coherence in the interaction. Often the mediator will create connections between issues/emotional expressions and hope to receive confirmation concerning the validity of the connections. Thus, the mediator generally seeks to encourage the conflicting parties to align themselves with his or her coherence objectives. Third, seeking compliance with the mediator's structuring attempts is important for the mediation task since the mediator must begin control of how floor time is allocated, for example, and how certain procedural issues are resolved. To the extent that the mediator accomplishes these objectives, the conflicting parties can be viewed as aligning themselves linguistically with the mediator.

What is needed at this point is an explanation concerning how this linguistic alignment builds toward creating a cooperative context. Valence theory in group interaction (Hoffman, 1979) will be used as that theoretical foundation. However, before valence theory can be detailed, it will be useful to review some of the perspectives explaining interpersonal influence processes in groups.

Several researchers have attempted to sort out competing claims for how group decision shifts occur (Davis et al., 1974; Burnstein & Vinokur, 1977; Sanders & Baron, 1977; McPhee et al., 1982; Poole et al., 1982). Three competing perspectives that appear to explain decision shifts include: attitude change resulting from the exchange of persuasive arguments, normative pressures resulting from social comparison processes, and social decision schemes based on initial preferences and the use of various decision rules. While Sanders and Baron found that social influence occurs as a result of both attitude change and normative pressures to conformity, Poole and his associates found that the distribution of positive valence toward various proposals was the best predictor of decision outcomes. Based on Hoffman's (1979) work they concluded that positive valence, or the force (Lewin, 1935) generated by comments accumulating in support of various propositions, provides the most parsimonious explanation of group decision-making behavior. Given the valence theory's dependence upon interaction structure, it is a useful starting place to answer the question posed previously of how linguistic alignment builds toward creating a cooperative context for mediation.

In his book, Hoffman (1979) uses the concept of valence to account for the manner in which groups reach decisions. According to Hoffman (1979, p.6),

> Valence is used here, analogously to Lewin's usage with respect to attraction of goals (1935), to represent the degree of acceptability a cognition may have for a problem-solving unit; that is, the likelihood that it will be accepted by the unit, be it individual or group. Positive valence would indicate an acceptable cognition, and negative valence an unacceptable cognition. A cognition may acquire positive valence from a variety of sources, and the effects of

these sources may be presumed to accumulate to increase the valence of the cognition.

Further, according to Stein, Hoffman, Cooley, and Pearse (1979, p. 131),

The generation of valence for both the definition of the problem and for the adopted solution, as measured from members' statements in the discussion, have been shown to be implicit processes. By implicit, we mean the group may never explicitly state the definition of the problem or how much it favors a particular solution. Yet an implicit problem definition is used as a criterion for adopting a solution.

The research strategy as reported by Hoffman is to code statements made in creative group decision-making situations that respond either positively or negatively to a decision proposal. These statements are assigned either positive or negative points, and the accumulation of the points predicts which proposals will be adopted. In Hoffman's research a decision threshold was discovered in that over 80% of the adopted proposals required an accumulated valence of at least 15 to gain adoption.

In their research Poole et al. (1982) found that not only is valence accumulation necessary for decision acceptance, but the distribution of valence accumulation among group members is critical. The more evenly distributed the valence, the more likely the acceptance according to the authors. In another study, McPhee et al. (1982) supported the finding in the prior study that valence distribution, as opposed to simply total accumulated valence, was a better predictor of decision outcome. In addition, McPhee et al. supported Hoffman's (1979) finding that an acceptance threshold does exist for the adoption of a decision alternative, adding support to the primary assumptions of the valence model. However, no theoretical explanation was offered (and Hoffman does not provide any) for why such a threshold should exist at a particular level.

One of the central implications of this research is that decision shift in a group interaction, like a typical mediation interaction, can be conceptualized as a product of the amount of accumulated valence. The objective of the mediator is to create valence for some alternative(s) that will successfully resolve the dispute. However, the extent to which the mediator can accomplish this objective is dependent upon the mediator's ability to emerge as the leader of the group. Stein et al.'s (1979) research applied the valence concept to the problem of leader emergence by assigning points to individuals (instead of to proposals) for initiating certain leader behaviors, and for receiving support for those behaviors from other group members. Stein et al.

hypothesized certain leadership emergency thresholds such that a certain amount of valence had to be accumulated for a person to be a leader candidate and for the person to finally emerge as the group leader. Their valence theory of leader emergence was built on Hollander's (1958, 1961, 1964) idiosyncrasy credit theory. Stein et al. (1979, p. 128) summarize Hollander's position as follows:

> Hollander considers status to be the consequence of the positive regard, idiosyncrasy credit, in which a member is held by his peers. Initially, credits are based on the personal characteristics (e.g., social status) which shape first impressions. As time passes, credits are gained or lost depending upon conformity to group expectations and contributing to the task. Deviance and poor performance reduce the credit balance. As long as positive balance is maintained, group membership is assured.

If these perspectives are applied to the mediation context, a theory begins to emerge explaining why some mediators are more successful than others at resolving disputes in ways that increase the chances of compliance with the agreements. The basic assumption of the theory is that a mediator cannot achieve effectiveness without accumulating a sufficient quantity of valence to emerge as the leader of the group. Valence for the leader candidacy of the mediator accumulates as the mediator draws upon developed skill to achieve linguistic alignment of the disputing parties. The greater the alignment by both parties, the greater the force endorsing the role relationships the mediator is trying to affect, (i.e., the mediator as leader and the disputing parties as individual decision makers formulating a specific contract).

Given that the ultimate goal of the mediator is to accumulate valence for some particular decision option so that option can be selected and ultimately resolve the dispute, a question of order arises. That is, must the mediator accumulate some amount of valence to merge as leader *before* valence can accumulate for the acceptance of some specific decision proposal? In Hoffman's research, the process of leader emergence and decision emergence is simultaneous. For example, the person who makes a proposal receives positive valence and then continues to receive positive valence if that proposal receives support. In that way the leader and the proposal emerge at once. There are no data available that describe the way in which the dual emergence occurs, but conceptually, the leader uses the proposal as the vehicle for emergence.

For the mediation context, the process may not work that way for a number of reasons. First, the mediator ought to achieve linguistic alignment before the proposals are discussed so that a context for creating proposals can be developed. Without the proper context established, the chances of proposal acceptance are probably quite weak. Second, the mediator may not have the primary responsibility for making proposals. Either of the conflicting parties may make a proposal that ultimately gains support and acceptance. According to the Hoffman model, either of the three parties could emerge as leader because leader emergence is tied directly to proposal acceptance. This model breaks down in the mediation context because the role relationships necessary to make a decision between the disputing parties have been destroyed before the mediator enters the group. Otherwise, the mediator would not be needed. If the mediator does not manage control, trust and intimacy so that functional role relationships can be created, then it is unlikely that either party would accept a proposal created by the other party. Thus, this chapter argues that the mediator must accumulate valence and emerge as leader *before* proposals for agreement can be forwarded and accumulate valence. Once this has occurred, either disputing party can emerge as a sort of leader (in the sense that the leader is the person whose proposals gain valence). However, this emergence can occur only under the sanction of the mediator. In fact, it is probably desirable that the mediator not be responsible ultimately for proposal making since it is the disputing parties who must live with the agreement.

Accumulating Valence. One of the critical questions posed by a valence theory approach to mediator competence is how to operationalize both the mediator's valence accumulation as the emergent leader and the decision valence accumulation that leads toward an agreement. While it is beyond the scope of this chapter to present an extensive discussion of the methodological issues surrounding the testing of this valence theory, it would be useful to highlight some of the more critical issues surrounding the operationalizing of the valence accumulation.

There are probably several ways in which it would be possible to assign points to a mediator's performance. It would seem most useful to begin this task by assigning points based on the mediator's distancing, coherence, and structuring code choices. However, it does not seem reasonable to have valence accumulate based only upon the mediator's code choices. The accumulation ought to be more interactive as it is in Stein et al.'s. (1979) leader emergence research. In this approach the mediator gets a certain quantity of points for certain behaviors, then adds or subtracts points based on the individual's responses to those behaviors.

To adapt that system to the present chapter it would be necessary to identify certain distancing choices, such as the use of certain levels of immediacy, or the use of certain illocutionary acts, or the use of certain levels of politeness, and then assign points to the mediator based on the frequency with which these choices are made. The mediator would then accumulate or lose valence based upon the extent to which the other parties would match these levels of immediacy, types of illocutionary acts, or levels of politeness. With coherence and structuring dimensions of mediator competence a similar system could be developed. With coherence the mediator could accumulate points based upon the number of times the mediator attempted to summarize the interaction, for example. These points would increase or decrease based upon the extent to which the other parties supported or rejected these summary attempts. With structuring the mediator could accumulate points by managing the topic through certain turn allocation procedures, for example. If the others complied with the structuring attempts the mediator's valence would accumulate further. The goal of this chapter is to suggest the kinds of behaviors that might be seen as instrumental in the accumulation of valence related to mediator competence. The procedures articulated by Poole et al. (1982) specify procedures for determining decision valence accumulation.

At this point it might be helpful to illustrate the manner in which valence accumulation is likely to occur with respect to leader emergence and decision emergence. Figure 1 illustrates valence accumulation that leads toward agreement. As Figure 1 indicates, the mediator and the disputing parties begin the interaction with no accumulated valence. As the interaction progresses, the mediator is likely to initiate some distance, coherence, and structuring moves in an attempt to gain control of the interaction, the trust of the participants, and a functional level of intimacy. These initiations will result in the modest accumulation of valence for the mediator, but it will not result in the dramatic increase in valence because the disputing parties have not yet begun to align their code choices with that of the mediator. In fact, in the initial periods of interaction it is likely that the disputing parties will continue to make code choices that are counter to the objectives of the mediator which may result in the negative accumulation of valence. For example, the disputing parties may not comply with the mediator's structuring or coherence attempts. Or, the parties may use distancing markers that are dysfunctional, (e.g., informal accusatory remarks or directives that are not marked with politeness). This creates a divergence of valence accumulation for the mediator and the disputing parties and indicates the initial conflict stage of the interaction.

At some point, however, the mediator becomes successful in achieving linguistic alignment, and instead of valence accumulation diverging, it begins to converge with the mediator's, and the lines become more parallel. The point at which the alignment occurs might be termed the "alignment marker." At this point, the mediator's valence will begin to increase a great deal because the disputing parties are complying with the mediator's distance, coherence, and structuring attempts. The alignment marker is very

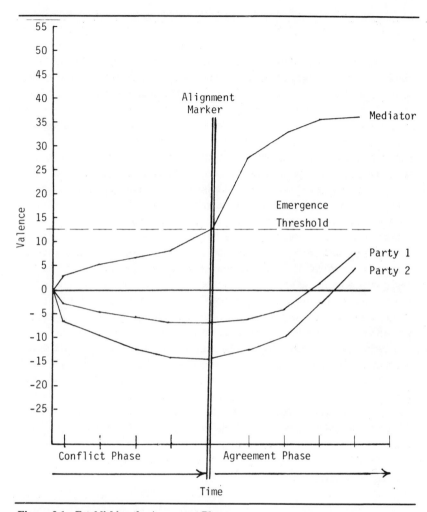

Figure 9.1 Establishing the Agreement Phase

important to identify because it helps define a number of other points. First, the marker identifies some amount of accumulated valence for the mediator. That amount can be viewed as the threshold that the mediator must cross to emerge as the group leader. Empirically, it will be of significant interest to determine if that threshold is consistent across interactions, or varies with the nature of the contextual parameters. This chapter has already suggested that this threshold will vary with the contextual parameters, which will in turn affect the location of the alignment marker. In addition, it will be inter- esting to explore which kinds of code choice enable the mediator to reach the threshold more quickly. In some circumstances, distance markers may facilitate compliance whereas in other situations, structuring code choices may result in greater compliance.

The second point that the alignment marker identifies is the transition in the interaction from a conflict phase to an agreement phase. The conflict phase is characterized by diverging valence accumulation whereas the agreement phase is characterized by greater alignment, thereby creating the context for an agreement.

The third point identified by the alignment marker is the hypothesized point at which positive decision valence will begin to accumulate. At or near the intersection of zero valence and the alignment marker it is proposed that the context will become more amenable for the parties to discuss the main issues in the mediation since the role relationships have begun to get sorted out. In the optimal decision-making context the decision valence will proceed in a line somewhat parallel with the mediator's increased valence.

This discussion suggests that the establishment of an alignment marker is a necessary condition for decision emergence. Figure 9.2 illustrates the circumstance in which an alignment marker never emerges in the interaction. The group stays in the conflict stage, and the opportunity for positive decision valence to accumulate is attenuated. In addition, neither of the disputing parties emerges into the positive valence position since neither complies with any of the mediator's attempts to create functional role relationships.

Finally, one of the objectives of the mediator relative to the valence accumulation of the disputing parties is to equalize the amount of valence each party acquires. If one of the parties acquires too much valence, or their valence begins to diverge as in Figure 9.2, then the mediator runs the risk of violating trust between the disputing parties and the mediator. In addition, the discussion could possibly return to the conflict stage until the role relationships are sorted out once again.

RESEARCH EXAMPLE

To illustrate the way in which this valence theory of mediator competence functions, it is useful to present two portions of a mediation transcript and indicate how an analysis of the transcript would begin to test the theory. The two bits of transcript will be taken from a divorce mediation tape created by Haynes (1981). The transcript is not an actual mediation interaction, but represents actors playing the parts of the disputing parties with Haynes (who is an actual mediator) serving as the mediator. The two segments are from the beginning of the tape and from a spot about one-third of the way through the interaction.

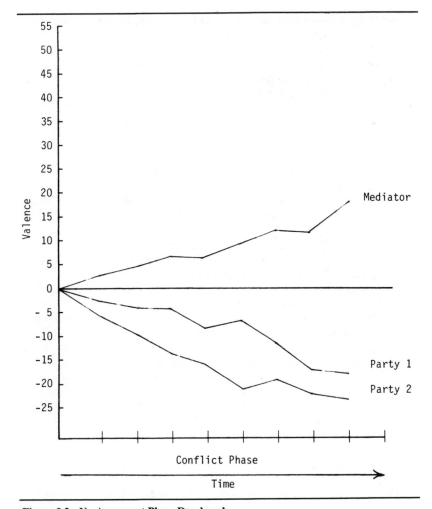

Figure 9.2 No Agreement Phase Developed

Segment 1:
(1) Wife: I just want you to tell him to be honest. He is not honest and he hasn't been honest and I have been honest.
(2) Mediator: O.K., if I understand what the difference is, it's that a third party has emerged in the situation.
(3) Wife: Wheww!
(4) Husband: Let me make it clear, only since Gwen has said she wanted out of the relationship.

(5) Wife: We don't have any formal agreement. Mark had been to visit John and someone else was there that I do not know and I don't like it.

(6) Husband: I didn't leave.

(7) Wife: You left the relationship emotionally years ago.

(8) Husband: Suffer. I'm not asking you to like it.

(9) Mediator: O.K. so there's a third party. So there's a third party.

(10) Wife: Right.

(11) Husband: How does this impact the things we had talked about?

Segment 2:

(12) Husband: You're making it sound . . .

(13) Wife: You are playing dirty with me and I'm not playing dirty with you. I'm being honest. I'm laying it on the line.

(14) Husband: That's a lot of crap, Joan. You're not playing dirty . . . Where were you when I asked for us to really work on the relationship? Out with . . .

(15) Wife: John, it's water, that is water under the bridge.

(16) Mediator: Now you're both hurting very much from this, I see.

(17) Husband: She has no idea, no idea whatsoever.

(18) Mediator: I suspect that Gwen does and Gwen also hurts and perhaps neither of you quite understand how much the other one hurts in this process. And that's a new key in one sense because that really is part of the process, the, and that each of us will, will have some of those feelings as we go along. I'm trying to understand how this all fits in what you want to do which is to negotiate your separation agreement. And it seems to me that we had agreed that we would focus this week on the issue of Mark and, uh, the parenting questions. If I understand it, not, you both have very strong feelings about Mark, and, uh, about the parenting. Uhm, why don't you share some of those with me at this point.

(19) Husband: When you said strong feelings, that's an understatement, John. This is the one issue, that, uh, I feel extremely, uh, strong about and I'm really going to struggle to get custody of Mark.

(20) Mediator: Um hm.

(21) Husband: I think one thing needs to be remembered here. It is Gwen who made the decision to leave the relationship. It's Gwen that's looking for out of the relationship. It's Gwen that's looking for out of the relationship, and that really needs to be considered when we talk about custody.

(22) Mediator: O.K., we're not, however, going to look at the past in terms of fault or responsibility. We're only going to look at the future in terms of what's best for Mark, right?

(23) Wife: It's true, I know I I I have initiated. I really uh I don't think you can ignore however, that the two of us have been thinking along these lines for a long time. I was the one who had the the ability to make a first move . . .

(24) Husband: First of all, I hardly feel that you leaving the relationship, uh, needs to be classified as an ability. I'm not looking for leaving the relationship . . .

(25) Mediator: Let me cut you off right here because it doesn't seem to me to be very productive to talk about who left the relationship so much as what's going to happen to Mark. How are you going to parent Mark?

(26) Right. That's exactly how I feel. I don't think it really is important who made the decision to make the first move. My concern is that that Mark remain where he's been comfortable all along. And he's used to having me be there and . . .

(27) Mediator: John, exactly what is your proposal in terms of Mark?

(28) Husband: Well, Gwen is looking to go back to school . . .

Contextual Parameters. A cursory analysis of these segments indicates that conflict intensity appears to be relatively high, particularly in the first segment. Both parties have expressed a desire to have child custody and are very explicit about their intention to fight to get custody. This conflict intensity is illustrated clearly in utterances four through eight in which the couples are engaging in active, escalating disagreement, and again in utterances 13 and 14 when the couple is engaging in a great deal of evaluative, accusatory talk.

To manage the intense conflict, the mediator has imposed a number of rules on the interaction to facilitate agreement making. One of the rules, illustrated in utterance 22 is that it is inappropriate to attribute fault to the other about some event in the past. Only the present and future is discussable. The mediator makes ample use of these rules in other parts of the complete transcript.

It is also quite apparent that the role relationships exhibited in these two segments of interaction remain quite problematic. The mediator has trouble establishing his role as illustrated in the first segment when the couple pays little attention to the mediator and continues to argue. In fact, after utterance 11 the mediator has difficulty encouraging the couple to talk specifically about the implications of a third party in the maintenance of prior agreements. In fact, the question is ignored. By the end of the second segment the mediator seems to be more successful at gaining control of the interaction. By gaining control the mediator can get the couple out of the husband/wife role relationship and into the contractual partner role relationship. Certainly, the level of conflict intensity, and the nature of the topic make it more difficult for the mediator to establish a working relationship between the couple. Nevertheless, these appear to be the primary contextual parameters that will tend to constrain the code choices for the mediator in reaching an agreement.

Code Choices. As indicated previously, one of the mediator's primary tasks is to manage distance in a way that facilitates the decision-making context. To deal with verbal immediacy the mediator, in utterance two, begins establishing his role by creating distance between himself and the conflict. For example, he modifies his utterance ("*if* I understand"), and uses a nonimmediate temporal code choice ("a third party *has emerged*"). To create formality in social distance the mediator uses rather formal language that clearly contrasts with the level of formality used by the disputing parties, particularly in the first segment. For example, in utterance 2 the more complex sentence structure ("a third party has emerged" vs. "John is seeing some other woman") encourages greater neutrality. In fact, throughout the mediator's interaction he uses nonimmediate and formal code choices to create more "business-like" role relationships. By the end of the second segment the woman seems ready to align herself with the mediator's distance code choices (utterance 26) as she is using more modifying immediacy cues ("I don't think" vs. "it isn't important") than in segment 1.

One of the more interesting distancing mechanisms being used in this transcript is the way in which the parties choose various illocutionary acts, particularly directives, to affect various power advantages. In the first segment the disputing couples are using illocutionary acts that signal an intimate role relationship such as a husband and wife. Both the husband and wife are using disclosures, advisements and interpretations, interpretations—acts that tend to make a relationship more intimate. The mediator, on the other hand, is careful to avoid using these kind of intimate acts. He relies more on edifications, confirmations, questions and reflections. The advisements (directives) that the mediator uses are marked with a great deal of politeness, particularly in the first segment, when the mediator states, "So there's a third party." In the second segment, to gain control, the mediator intensifies his advisement strategies and marks his directives with a bit less politeness, but still avoids the rather imperative tone of the couple in the first segment (e.g., utterance 8). For example, the mediator's advisements in utterance 18 ("why don't you share . . ."), and utterance 25 ("let me cut you off . . .) are still marked with some politeness, but are intended to establish the mediator in the power position to decrease the intimacy level and create functional role relationships. By utterance 25 the mediator appears to have accomplished this objective as the woman has restricted her acts to reflections and edifications. Similarly, the man is beginning to decrease intimacy by restricting his acts to similar forms. Thus, the mediator appears to have made some progress in his ability to create a level of distance that will facilitate the switch in role relationships and provide him with the resources to create a more favorable climate for agreement making.

The mediator's frequent use of reflections, particularly in the second segment, illustrate his reliance on the needs to create coherence in the discussion. Ambiguity generally does not facilitate decision making, so it is important to create the appropriate connections among ideas, and gain confirmation of positions that have been ostensibly established. In the first segment the mediator is quite redundant in his interaction to gain confirmation that a third party has emerged. In the second segment the mediator is trying to establish the level of commitment on the part of both parties to accept parenting responsibilities.

The use of coherence mechanisms is very useful for the mediator in creating the appropriate set of role relationships because the disputing parties will come to rely upon the mediator's ability to disambiguate the interaction. As the mediator gains confirmation about the perceptions he has established, the mediator begins to solidify his role which in turn helps to establish the roles of the disputing parties as agreement makers.

Similarly, the mediator's use of structuring mechanisms can serve to bolster his role as the mediator who is there to direct the interaction. In the first segment the mediator engages in little structuring. However, by the second segment the mediator is much more directive. For example, in utterances 22 and 25 the mediator specifically cuts off the discussion's direction and restructures it by reminding the parties that they are to adhere to a rule agreed upon previously that only the future is to be discussed. The two most common structuring mechanisms that the mediator relies upon are topic management and turn taking. The mediator appears to make very little use of disagreement, disconfirmation, or other structuring mechanisms that might tend to compromise trust. To the extent that the mediator succeeds in gaining compliance from the disputing parties about his topic choices and his turn allocation choices, his ability to establish his role increases. By the end of the second segment, the mediator gains compliance on his topic suggestions and turn allocations, and it is at about this point that a proposal is beginning to emerge that can begin to accumulate valence and be selected by the disputing parties.

Relational Parameter Outcomes. While the end of the transcript is not presented here, it appears from reading the transcript that the mediator terminates the discussion before a specific decision has been reached. This may be due to the fact that the transcript is not an actual display of mediation, but a simulation. However, it appears that at the end of the transcript not much positive decision valence has accumulated for any specific proposal. It may be possible to turn to an analysis of some of the relational parameters that the mediator has attempted to establish to determine some possible explanations for this lack of success.

As indicated previously, it is imperative that the mediator establish a sense of trust between himself and the disputing parties. To the extent that this happens early in the interaction with both parties, the mediator will be able to establish the kind of role relationships that will be functional for agreement. In a situation such as the one presented here there are some forces working against the accumulation of trust. As each side is interested in developing a personally favorable agreement, either party may look for a way to manipulate the mediator to side with him or her against the other person. As indicated previously, the mediator must avoid such coalition formation. However, in the transcript provided here, the woman may have attempted to manipulate the mediator. An analysis of both segments of interaction reveals that nearly all of the structuring attempts made by the mediator to focus on some topic, or reject the direction of another topic, are made immediately following a statement by the man. As an example, utterance pairs 17 and 18, 21 and 22, and 24 and 25 indicate that the mediator structures the interaction only in response to the man and not the woman. In utterance 26, the woman may have picked up on this structuring pattern and identified an opportunity to form a coalition with the mediator by appearing to cooperate with the mediator. This pattern continues throughout the interaction until, near the end, the man indicates that "It sounds like things are working to Gwen's favor. That's what it sounds like to me." The inconsistent ways in which the mediator handles his relationship with the husband and with the wife may have compromised the trust and attenuated the mediator's ability to begin building decision valence.

On the other hand, the mediator appears to have been a bit more successful at gaining control of the interaction through his various structuring and coherence-making attempts. At the beginning of the interaction the mediator struggled to gain control of the interaction. Segment one indicates that the disputing parties were dictating topics and allocating turns while excluding the mediator from the interaction. By the second segment the mediator is able to use coherence and distancing code choices to solidify his role as mediator so that he could introduce various structuring mechanisms into the interaction that might help gain control of the interaction.

As indicated previously, one of the outcomes the mediator wanted to affect was intimacy. Creating an intimacy level that is typical of professional agreement-making contexts was the mediator's goal. For example, in utterance 25 the mediator cuts off the man's use of evaluation in an attempt to reduce the level of intimacy. If relational redefinition is going to take effect for the couple in the long term it is important for the mediator to acquaint the couple with an intimacy level that will allow them to negotiate in the future.

SUMMARY

This chapter has argued that current attempts to understand the communicative competence of mediators are underdeveloped, and as a result, theoretically weak. We contend that the competent mediator must be able to read the other party's cues while remaining sensitive to the contextual parameters that will influence the ability of the mediator to affect an agreement. One of the first objectives of the mediator is to create a functional set of role relationships among the three communicating individuals. To accomplish this objective the mediator tries to control the interaction, create trust among all parties, and encourage parties to adopt a level of intimacy that will allow them to make an agreement. The communicative resources the mediator can use to affect these outcomes can be separated into three sets of code choices. First, the mediator must create an appropriate level of interpersonal distance. Second, the mediator must disambiguate the interaction through various coherence code choices. Third, the mediator must be successful at structuring pragmatic features of the interaction.

Valence theory accounts for how the use of distancing, coherence, and structuring code choices lead to the creation of more integrative decision-making contexts. It was argued that the mediator must manipulate code choices to accumulate a sufficient quantity of positive regard, or valence, to emerge as the leader/controller of the interaction. This leadership role is assumed when the disputing parties align their choices with that of the mediator. It is at this pont that the decision proposals can begin to accumulate support, or positive valence, so an agreement can be reached.

REFERENCES

Argyle, M. The experimental study of the basic features of situations. In D. Magnusson (Ed.) *Toward a Psychology of Situations: An Interactional Perspective.* Hillsdale, NJ: Erlbaum, 1981.

Avedon, E.M. The structural elements of games. In A. Furnham & M. Argyle (Eds.) *The Psychology of Social Situations.* New York: Pergamon Press, 1981.

Bartenuek, J.M., Benton, A.A., & Keys, C.B. Third party intervention and the bargaining of group representatives. *Journal of Conflict Resolution*, 1975, *19*, 532-557.

Brown, D.G. Divorce and family mediation: History, review, future directions. *Conciliation Courts Review*, 1982, *20*, 1-44.

Brown, L.D. *Managing conflict at organizational interfaces.* Reading, MA: Addison-Wesley, 1983.

Brown, P., & Fraser, C. Speech as a marker of situation. In K. Scherer & H. Giles (Eds.) *Social Markers in Speech.* Cambridge University Press, 1979.

Brown, P., & Levinson, S. Universals in language usage: Politeness phenomena. In E. Goody (Ed.) *Questions and politeness: Strategies in social interaction.* Cambridge Papers in Social Anthropology, 8. Cambridge, 1978.

Burnstein, E.B., & Vinokur, A. Persuasive argumentation and social comparison as determinants of attitude polarization. *Journal of Experimental Social Psychology*, 1977, *13*, 315-332.

Comeaux, E.A. Procedural controls in public section domestic relations mediation. In H. Davidson, L. Ray, & R. Horowitz (Eds.) *Alternative means of family dispute resolution.* Washington, DC: American Bar Association, 1982.

Coogler, O.J. *Structured mediation in divorce settlement: A handbook for marital mediators.* Lexington, MA: D.C. Heath, 1978.

Davis, J.H., Kerr, N., Sussman, M., & Rissman, A.K. Social decision schemes under risk. *Journal of Personality and Social Psychology*, 1974, *30*, 248-271.

Diez, M.E. Negotiation competence: A conceptualization of the constitutive rules of negotiation interaction. Paper presented at the Annual Meeting of the International Communication Association, Dallas, Texas, 1983.

Erickson, B., Holmes, J.G., Frey, R., Walker, L., & Thibaut, J. Functions of a third party in the resolution of conflict: The role of a judge in pretrial conferences. *Journal of Personality and Social Psychology*, 1974, *30*, 293-306.

Ervin-Tripp, S. Speech acts, social meaning and social learning. In H. Giles, W. Robinson, & P. Smith (Eds.) Language: *Social Psychological Perspectives*. New York: Pergamon Press, 1980.

Excerpts from the report. *The Chronicle of Higher Education*, May 4, 1983, pp. 8-9.

Fisher, R.J. Third party consultation: A method for the study and resolution of conflict. *Journal of Conflict Resolution*, 1972, *16*, 67-94.

Fisher, R., & Ury, W. *Getting to yes*. Boston: Houghton Mifflin, 1981.

Frost, J.H., & Wilmot, W.W. *Interpersonal conflict*. Dubuque, Iowa: Wm. C. Brown, 1978.

Giles, H., Scherer, K.R., & Taylor, D.M. speech markers in social interaction. In K. Scherer & H. Giles (Eds.) *Social Markers in Speech*. Cambridge: Cambridge University Press, 1979.

Goffman, E. *The presentation of self in everyday life*. Garden City, NY: Doubleday, 1959.

Graham, J., Argyle, M., & Furnham, A. The goal structure of situations. In A. Furnham & M. Argyle (Eds.) *The psychology of social situations*. New York: Pergamon Press, 1981.

Gregory, M. & Carroll, S. *Language and situation*. London: Routledge & Kegan Paul, 1978.

Gulliver, P.H. *Disputes and negotiations*. New York: Academic Press, 1979.

Halliday, M.A.K. *Explorations in the functions of language*. London: Edward Arnold, 1973.

Haynes, J.M. *Divorce mediation: A practical guide for therapists and counselors*. New York: Springer Publishing Co., 1981.

Hoffman, L.R. *The group problem solving process*. New York: Praeger, 1979.

Hollander, E.P. Conformity, status, and idiosyncracy credit. *Psychological Review*, 1958, *65*, 117-127.

Hollander, E.P. Emergent leadership and social influence. In L. Petrullo and B.M. Bass (Eds.) *Leadership and interpersonal behavior*. New York: Holt, 1961.

Hollander, E.P. *Leaders, groups and influence*. New York: Oxford University Press, 1964.

Hymes, D. Models òf the interaction of language and social setting. *Journal of Social Issues*, 1967, *23*, 8-28.

Hymes, D. Toward ethnographies of communication: The analysis of communicative events. *American Anthropologists*, 1964, *66*, 12-25.

Hymes, D. Ways of speaking. In R. Bauman & J. Sherzer (Eds.) *Exploration in the ethnography of speaking*. Cambridge: Cambridge University Press, 1974.

Johnson, D.W. Role reversal: A summary and review of the research. *International Journal of Group Tensions*, 1971, *1*, 318-334.

Kochan, T.A. *Collective bargaining and industrial relations*. Homewood, IL: Irwin, 1980.

Kochan, T.A., & Jick, T. The public sector mediation process: A theory and empirical examination. *Journal of Conflict Resolution*, 1978, *22*, 209-240.

Kressel, K. *Labor mediation: An exploratory survey*. New York: Association of Labor Mediation Agencies, 1972.

Levinson, S.C. Activity types and language. *Pragmatics Microfiche*, 1978, *3*, 3.3.

Lewin, K. *A dynamic theory of personality*. New York: McGraw-Hill, 1935.

Maggiolo, W.A. *Techniques of mediation in labor disputes*. Dobbs Ferry, NY: Oceana Publications, Inc., 1971.

Margerison, C., & Leary, M. *Managing industrial conflicts: The mediator's role*. Bradford, England: MCB Books, 1975.

Massengill, A.D. Mediation models: An integrated approach. In H. Davidson, L. Ray, & R. Horowitz (Eds.) *Alternative means of family dispute resolution*. Washington, DC: American Bar Association, 1982.

McPhee, R.D., Poole, M.S., & Siebold, D.R. The valence model unveiled: Critique and alternative formulation. In M. Burgoon (Ed.) *Communication yearbook 5*. New Brunswick, NJ: Transaction, 1982.

Morton, T.L., Alexander, J.F., & Altman, I. Communication and relationship definition. In G.R. Miller (Ed.) *Explorations in interpersonal communication*. Beverly Hills: Sage, 1976.

O'Donnell-Trujillo, N. Relational communication: A comparison of coding systems. *Communication Monographs*, 1981, *48*, 91-105.

Podell, J.E., & Knapp, W.M. The effect of mediation on the perceived firmness of the opponent. *Journal of Conflict Resolution*, 1969, *13*, 511-520.

Poole, M.S., McPhee, R.D., & Siebold, D.R. A comparison of normative and interactional explanations of group decision-making: Social decision schemes versus valence. *Communication Monographs*, 1982, *49*, 1-19.

Pruitt, D.G. Indirect communication and the search for agreement in negotiation. *Journal of Applied Social Psychology*, 1971, *1*, 205-239.

Pruitt, D.G. *Negotiation behavior.* New York: Academic Press, 1981.

Putnam, L.L., & Jones, T.S. Reciprocity in negotiations: An analysis of bargaining interaction. *Communication Monographs*, 1982, *49*, 171-191.

Raush, H.L. Paradox, levels and junctures in person-situation systems. In P. Magnusson & N.S. Endlev (Eds.) *Personality at the crossroads*: *Current issues in interactional psychology.* Hillsdale, NJ: Lawrence Erlbaum Associates, 1977.

Raven, B.H., & Krnglanski, S.W. Conflict and power. In P. Swingle (Ed.) *The structure of conflict.* New York: Academic Press, 1970.

Rubin, J.Z. Experimental research on third-party intervention in conflict: Toward some generalizations. *Psychological Bulletin*, 1980, *87*, 379-391.

Rubin, J.Z. *Dynamics of third party intervention*: *Kissinger in the Middle East.* New York: Praeger, 1981.

Rubin, J.Z., & Brown, B.R. *The social psychology of bargaining and negotiation.* New York: Academic Press, 1975.

Sanders, G.S., & Baron, R.S. Is social comparison irrelevent for producing choice shifts? *Journal of Experimental Social Psychology*, 1977, *13*, 303-314.

Scherer, K.R., & Giles, H. *Social markers in speech.* Cambridge: Cambridge University Press, 1979.

Searle, J.R. A classification of illocutionary acts. *Language in Society*, 1976, *5*, 1-23.

Sherif, M., Harvey, O.J., White, B.J., Hood, W.E., & Sherif, C.W. *Intergroup conflict and cooperation*: *The robbers cave experiment.* Norman: University of Oklahoma Book Exchange, 1961.

Stein, R.T., Hoffman, L.R., Cooley, S.J., & Pearse, R.W. Leadership valence: Modeling and measuring the process of emergent leadership. In J. Hunt and L. Larson (Eds.) *Crosscurrents in Leadership.* Carbondale: Southern Illinois University Press, 1979.

Stiles, W.B. Classification of intersubjective illocutionary acts. *Language in Society*, 1981, *10*, 227-249.

Stokes, R., & Hewitt, J. Aligning actions. *American Sociological Review*, 1976, *41*, 838-849.

Wall, J.A., Jr. Mediation: An analysis, review, and proposed research. *Journal of Conflict Resolution*, 1981, *25*, 157-180.

Walton, R.E. *Interpersonal peacemaking*: *Confrontations and third-party consultation.* Reading, MA: Addison-Wesley, 1969.

Weiner, M. & Mehrabian, A. *Language within language*: *Immediacy, a channel in verbal communication.* New York: Appleton-Century-Crofts, 1968.

PART III

Overview

10

Communication Competence

The Elusive Construct

JAMES C. McCROSKEY

Communication competence is the current "hot topic" in the field of communication. Over the past several years it has been a rare volume of a major journal that has not included at least one article devoted to this topic. National and regional conventions are replete with papers and programs in this area. The present book is the latest example of the attention scholars in communication are giving to this topic.

The origin of the term "communication competence" and the expansion of the field's interest both coincided with the national "back to basics" movement. Contemporary American society has concluded that our schools must prepare our young people in the basic skills for survival. Testing programs in basic skills or competencies are being implemented for students and teachers in state after state. The central place of communication competence in such programs was assured when federal legislation defined the basic skills as reading, writing, speaking, listening, and mathematics. With four of the five basic skills being communication skills, communication competence becomes a focal point in the education of the young. Communication competence is "hot." Even computer literacy must take a back seat.

A HISTORICAL PERSPECTIVE

While all of this attention may justify our believing that our field has "come of age," it is important that we place this current flurry of attention in perspective. The importance of competence in communication is not a

product of creative insight of people in the 1970s. In fact, we are very open
to the charge that we are placing new wine in old wineskins.

The history of communication competence, under other labels, is a long
and distinguished one. The importance of competence in communication
has been recognized for thousands of years. The oldest essay ever discovered, written about 3000 B.C. consists of advice on how to speak effectively. This essay was inscribed on a fragment of parchment addressed to
Kagemni, the eldest son of the Pharoah Huni. Similarly, the oldest extant
book is a treatise on effective communication. This book, known as the *Pre-
cepts*, was composed in Egypt about 2675 B.C. by Ptah-Hotep. It was written for the guidance of the Pharoah's son.

As early as the fifth century B.C. schools were established in Greece
with communication holding a central place in the curriculum. In the fourth
century B.C. Aristotle wrote the most significant book on communication
ever written, the *Rhetoric*. Over two thousand years later, when schools and
colleges were established in the American colonies, communication was a
central part of the curriculum. One of the early lecturers on communication
at Harvard, John Quincy Adams, was later to become President of the
United States.

This central focus on communication in the education of the young has
continued to the present. Every state in the United States requires instruction
in written composition for all students, and many also require instruction in
oral communication. Similarly, written composition is a virtually universal
requirement in American colleges and universities. Oral communication
requirements, although less common, are far from unusual; and even when
not required, oral communication classes are popular electives for students.

Our current concern with communication competence, then, does not
represent the birth of a new orientation in our field. Rather, it represents a
continuation of a centuries-old tradition. What is new is the term, communication competence.

THE PROBLEM OF DEFINITION

In the title of this chapter I have branded communication competence as
"the elusive construct." If you have read the preceding chapters in this
book, you may be wondering what scholars mean when they use the term
"communication competence." What is the scope of this construct? After
reading these chapters and reviewing the extant literature under this heading,
I must confess I have these same questions. What do competence in understanding commercials and competence in interpersonal interaction have in
common, if anything?

While preparing this chapter I participated in a seminar on communication competence held in conjunction with the 1983 convention of the Speech Communication Association. The participants in this seminar were all scholars who had written and/or done research in this area. We all exchanged papers prior to the formal seminar sessions. One of the main concerns of these papers was this problem of definition. Regretfully, no consensus definition emerged from these essays. Clearly, communication competence means different things to different scholars.

My reading of the literature in this area suggests that the term "communication competence" did not emerge full-blown as a new construct with a research foundation. Rather, it appears that this construct evolved from lay consideration of competence in young people. If my reading of the literature is correct, then, we should not be looking to the scholarly literature for our definition. Instead, we should look to common usage of these words by nonspecialists.

Dictionaries are not authoritative sources for what words mean. However, they do attempt to record what people typically mean when they use a given word. Thus, in this case, a dictionary is useful in our attempt to determine what nonspecialists may have in mind with a term like "communication competence."

Let us begin with the term "competence." The two dictionaries on my shelf provide very similar definitions. In one, competence is "adequate ability." For the other, it is "ability, fitness." Similarly, for the related term "competent," the two are in agreement. One suggests that competent means "fit, suitable" while the other indicates it means "able, fit."

While as a field we have had considerable difficulty agreeing on a definition of communication, my dictionaries indicate little confusion in the lay pubic's mind about the term's meaning. One simply says that communication is the "act or means of communicating." The other says it is the "act or fact of passing along; giving of information by talking, writing." For the term communicate, one says we mean to "impart, transmit, make known." The other says communicate means to "pass along, transfer."

Thus, if the dictionaries are taken as good reporters of what the lay public means by the terms communication and competence, when put together, this construct must mean something like "adequate ability to pass along or give information; the ability to make known by talking or writing." Thus, at the most basic level, those people who pay our salaries and ask that we make their children "communicatively competent" want their young people to acquire the modest ability to talk and write so that others can understand them. It is as simple as that.

Of course, whenever we make something simple we run the risk of making it simplistic. We who pretend to be experts in the field of communication may have difficulty accepting such a straightforward, simple description of what we are about. We will be quick to charge that such an approach is out-dated—it is too "source oriented." Talking and writing are only half of the communication process. Listening and reading are at least as important as talking and writing. And such a simplistic approach to communication competence does not leave room for such important matters as learning to understand commercials and learning to develop good communicative relationships with others.

We are not wrong to stress the complexity of the communication process. We are not wrong to emphasize that there is more to communication than simply talking or writing clearly. However, it may be wrong of us to take the basic construct of "communication competence" and twist it to include our own narrow specializations. When we do that we make the construct itself quite meaningless, and we are likely to fail to accomplish the most basic objectives our society expects from our field.

Without wishing to suggest any qualitative reaction to any other chapter in this book, I suggest that Powers and Lowry most directly speak to the basic issues of communication competence. They are most concerned with the ability of students to talk so that others can understand them. They have clearly operationalized what this means and provided a method of assessing that ability. In the process they have advanced a method which could also be used to asseses receiving skills, but that is beside the point for the moment. The fact that this work first reaches print in this book rather than in our scholarly journals is indicative of how distorted the construct of communication competence has become in our field. In private conversations with Powers, I learned that papers based on this work consistently have been rejected by the professional journals. The essence of the negative reviews has been, What does *this* have to do with communication competence? My answer, as you might surmise, is *everything*. This is the starting point upon which we can build.

I believe that one of the reasons that we, as a field, have generated so much confusion about the meaning of the communication competence construct is that we have tended to confuse competence with excellence—the ability to be unusually good, to be better than others. Excellence certainly must be one of the goals of our field. However, excellence rests on a foundation of competence, it is not the foundation itself. To illustrate, being relationally competent (excellent) rests of the foundation of being able to make one's ideas clear to the other in the relationship. To target excellence in relational competence in the absence of communication competence begs failure in the achievement of that excellence.

A second reason for our conceptual confusion is the extreme diversity of specializations in the field of communication. Whole fields have grown up within the general field: journalism, speech communication, speech pathology and audiology, theatre, broadcasting, advertising, and public relations, to name a few. Within these, dozens of subfields have emerged, as suggested by the subgroupings in our professional associations. Consequently, while we all see ourselves as being in "communication," we all see that field through the blinders of our specializations.

For these reasons I do not believe we can generate a single definition of communication competence that will satisfy everyone in this field, any more than we have been able to generate one definition of communication itself that will satisfy all. Probably the best we can do is to make our definition clear, and recognize that competence to one may include aspects of excellence to some others and irrelevancies to still others. For what it is worth, my definition for the remainder of this chapter will be "adequate ability to make ideas known to others by talking or writing."

UNDERSTANDING AND DOING

Communication is a behavior-based discipline. Unlike some of our sister disciplines, knowing the content of our discipline is not enough—our bottom line is doing.

While this is one of the strengths of our discipline, it has also tightened our blinders as we have looked at communication competence. Often, we have assumed that if we know about communication we will be able to do it. Even more often, we have assumed that if we can do it, we understand it. At the risk of being seen as a latent faculty psychologist, I feel we must reject both of those assumptions.

The equating of understanding and doing is not an original problem stemming from the communication competence literature. The areas of language development and reading have already confronted this problem and, after many years of misdirected effort, handled it. Understanding is not equal to doing.

Scholars in the field of language acquisition have long distinguished between understanding and doing and recognized that the two develop in individuals at different rates. Commonly the understanding element has been referred to as competence and the doing as performance.[1] In some cases competence develops before performance, in others the pattern is the reverse. Many studies have illustrated, for example, that children know more than they can say. If asked to point to point to a picture of an elephant, the child may be able to comply; but if one points to the elephant and asks the child what it is, the child may be unable to answer. In contrast, children can be taught to recite the pledge of allegiance or the Lord's Prayer long before they have any understanding of what they are reciting. One may not infer competence from performance or project performance from competence. Neither is a necessary condition for the existence of the other.

Our colleagues in the field of reading also have come belatedly to the realization that competence and performance are not necessarily related. For many years it was believed that oral reading (performance) was an excellent indicator of reading skill. It is now recognized that many children can perform (read aloud) with considerable skill without understanding virtually anything they perform while others can read to themselves with full understanding while being unable to perform (read orally). Once again, the previously assumed relationship between competence and performance was found wanting.

The importance of the understanding/doing distinction can be illustrated from our experiences in teaching basic courses in speech and writing. Some of our students can present good speeches or essays but do poorly on content examinations. Others do very well on the exams but cannot perform adequately. One might say, as I have been known to, if they can do it that is all that counts, who cares about the exams. Such a position, however, is confounded by the faulty assumption that if a student can do it in the classroom, they also can do it out in the "real world." This often is not the case.

Communication competence requires not only the ability to perform adequately certain communication behaviors, it also requires an understanding of those behaviors and the cognitive ability to make choices among behaviors. When examined closely, the behaviors in which one needs to engage to make ideas clear to others, either in speaking or in writing, are rather simple and mundane. The overwhelming majority (although certainly not all) of our students arrive in both high school and college with the ability to perform those behaviors, even if they seldom demonstrate that ability in the classroom.

In general, students do not engage in behaviors that would lead us to label them as communicatively competent because they do not understand the need for them to do so, because they do not care how we evaluate them, or because they are afraid to engage in the behaviors, not because the behaviors are not in their repertoire. Thus, for those students with true skill deficits, we must continue to teach behavioral skills. But our primary focus, particularly in the upper grades and in college, must be on the cognitive abilities and affective orientations of our students which inhibit their demonstration of communicatively competent behavior.

THE PROBLEM OF MEASUREMENT

Once we have conceptually defined communication competence, our most basic problem becomes how to measure it. This, of course, is the traditional problem of operationalization. In this instance, the problem may be more severe than in some others. We know that behavior is our bottom line, but research in the field may not have reached the level where we can be certain what behaviors we must measure; and we must face the fact that behavior is not always enough, as we noted in the previous section.

In order to determine whether a person is communicatively competent, I suggest that we must measure both their behavior under appropriate circumstances and their cognitive abilities. The former measurement permits a direct assessment of the underlying ability. The latter may enable us to determine how broadly we may generalize from the behavior specimens available, as we can never obtain direct behavior measures for every type of situation possible.

Our field has long known that communication is a transactional process, although that jargon has only crept into our language in the last decade or so. Making ideas and feelings clear *to others* is more than making ideas and feelings clear. Communication does not exist without a receiver, and what is clear to one receiver is not necessarily clear to another receiver. In days gone by we referred to the process of coping with this problem as audience analysis and adaptation. Clearly, then, what we must measure is not what the person does but what impact what the person does has on the receiver. Clarity (or any other outcome variable we might choose) is in the mind of the receiver, not in the mind of an observer or in the behavior of the communicator.

The only promising method of measuring communication competence that I have seen is the one advanced by Powers and Lowry in this book and in their earlier convention papers. This method provides a carefully controlled communication situation with a clearly known (by the researcher and the source) idea to be communicated and a method by which the effectiveness of the source can be quantified. While the method at present is represented by only one type of situation (explaining how to draw a geometric figure), it provides a basic model that can be emulated to provide measures of an unlimited number of situations. The method is not inherently limited to a presentational format, it can be implemented in a dyadic or group context. The geometric shape measure can be replaced, when desired, by other measures such as a cloze test or affective response test. Once we decide what outcomes are going to be operationalized as indicants of communication competence, the Powers and Lowry model can be applied to construct an appropriate measure of each outcome.

Once measures of the type suggested above are available, the door to meaningful research on the nature and components of communication competence will be open. We will be able to distinguish between people who score high and low on such measure and study differences between the groups in terms of both what they do and what they know. Indeed, we will be able to build a behavioral science of communication competence. Such a research program can be expected to tell us both what behaviors young people must be taught and what cognitive material they must be taught.

In order to clarify that for which I am calling, let me contrast such a program with the current state of affairs. Most of our so-called communication competence measures in use today stem from theoretical speculations of their developers and/or from traditional pedagogical prescriptions with little or no empirical base. They characteristically employ either observers who are not a part of the communication transaction from which they are to provide data or untrained subjects who are asked to provide their estimate of the competence of another person in the transaction. Neither can be expected to generate significant knowledge with a solid scientific foundation.

Another major portion of the research in this area is based on self-reports of competence, a data base with even less scientific validity than the two described previously. Self-reports have an important place in communication research, but this is not one of them. Subjects can be expected to provide valid reports of how they feel, their attitudes, orientations, and predispositons. But abundant research has indicated they are unable to regularly provide valid data on what they do, even who they talk to in a given day. I can tell you how competent I feel I am as a communicator, but my response may have more to do with my self-esteem than it does with my true competence.

This negative reaction of self-report data should not be taken as a blanket indictment of the use of self-reports in communication competence research. Depending on how one chooses to define this construct, such reports may be very valuable. However, I suspect that self-reports will be much more useful for judging the competence of others rather than the person completing the report. For example, if the desired outcome in a test of communication competence is for the "other" person to feel comfortable and at ease while communicating with the "subject," a self-report measure provided by the "other" should be a valuable indicant of whether the "subject" accomplished the established goal.

A THEORETICAL APPROACH

For a person to behave consistently in a manner that can be characterized as communicatively competent, four things must occur. First, the individual must acquire certain, modest behavioral skills that are well within reach of all normal individuals in our society. Most children, although not all, will have acquired these skills by the time they leave elementary school. Second, the individual must acquire a moderate level of cognitive understanding of the communication process and the situational constraints placed on communication behavior. In the absence of systematic training, few individuals will acquire these cognitive skills. With the help of a well-designed basic course, however, most individuals can acquire these cognitive skills, at either the secondary or college level.

With the acquisition of these behavioral and cognitive skills, most individuals will be able to behave in a communicatively competent manner in most circumstances. However, many will not be able to do so. For these individuals the behavioral and cognitive skills are inhibited from use by negative affective responses. For this very sizable group a third thing must occur: They must develop a positive affective response toward communication. While many children enter elementary school with such positive affect, many others do not develop it in their entire lives.

Finally, competent behavior must become an habituated, selective response of the individual. Skills that are learned but not used tend to be lost. The old phrases "every teacher is an English teacher" and "every teacher is a speech teacher," are very appropriate. If students learn competent communication behaviors but do not have an opportunity to use them or are not reinforced for them, they are likely to lose them.

Theoretically, then, the communicatively competent individual is the product of a learning environment which permits the development of appropriate behavioral and cognitive skills, shapes a positive affect for communication, and provides opportunities for use and reinforcement of those abilities. One of our functions as communication professionals is to foster the creation of such environments.

Beyond this educational function, in which all of us must play some part, many of us need to perform other functions. One of our primary functions is basic research in communication competence. While as a field we are far from ignorant concerning what constitutes the behavioral and cognitive abilities that lead to communicatively competent behavior, it is also true that we have much more to learn. Few of us would confidently accept the charge to specify for our field what the central behavioral and cognitive abilities are for communication competence. And if we accepted the charge, it is probable that few would agree with our product. On most of our campuses we cannot even get our faculty to agree on what should be included in our basic course!

We also must devote considerably more of our field's efforts to the problems associated with communication affect. Only in the past decade has our field begun to recognize that such affective problems as shyness and communication apprehension really exist and that, because of these problems, teaching of cognitive and behavioral skills is unlikely to modify the behaviors of many of our students.

Finally, we must keep in mind that competence and excellence are not the same thing, as we noted previously. While our efforts in the area of communication competence must be directed toward all students, we can not raise all students to a level of excellence. While it may be hard for some of us to accept, and while our field does indeed have something for everyone, our individual specialities must be reserved for the select few.

PUTTING COMMUNICATION COMPETENCE IN PERSPECTIVE

Just as this book is but one of many books published by Sage Publications, communication competence is but one of many foci in the field of communication. With the pressures of the back-to-basics movement and the demands for certifying competencies for students and their teachers, we must take care that our "communication dog" continues to "wag its competence tail" rather than the other way around.

Over the past several years I have seen some academic departments become so concerned with developing competence standards for their basic communication course that everything else was let slide. In most cases, as such efforts were not based on solid research, the results were professionally embarrassing. But even if the products had been of higher quality, such efforts represent the tail taking over. Although in most schools more students take the basic communication course than all other courses combined, this is far from all that we do.

While we have a responsibility to our society to provide the means by which our citizens may become communicatively competent, this is far from our only responsibility. While in most of our institutions only a small percentage of the students will specialize in communication, excellence for these few is every bit as important, if not more important, than competence for the many. In a similar vein, we must never sacrifice our basic research efforts on the altar of service to the competence needs of ever-increasing numbers of students. If we help one student become communicatively competent, that benefit to society will live as long as does that individual. If our research generates one new insight into communication, that insight will live as long as civilized humans inhabit this planet.

NOTE

1. Note that competence is not being used here in the same sense as it is in the term communication competence. With my definition of communication competence advanced above, the performance aspect is actually closer than the competence aspect.

About the Contributors

JAMES L. APPLEGATE (Ph.D., Illinois) is Associate Professor of Communication at the University of Kentucky. Widely published in the general area of developmental approaches to communication, Applegate's recently edited (with Howard Sypher) *Interpersonal Communication in Children and Adults* will be published by Sage this fall.

ROBERT N. BOSTROM is Professor of Communication and Director of Graduate Study in the College of Communications at the University of Kentucky. He received his Ph.D. from Iowa University in 1961. He has been a member of the International Communication Association since 1961, having originally been affiliated with the NSSC. His latest book, *Persuasion*, was published in 1983 by Prentice-Hall.

RALPH E. COOLEY (Ph.D., Michigan) was Professor of Speech at the University of Oklahoma. Specially trained in linguistics, Cooley's life was given to study of theoretical approaches to language. Professor Cooley died on September 28, 1982.

MARY E. DIEZ (Ph.D., Michigan State) is Assistant Professor of Communication at Alverno College.

THOMAS R. DONOHUE (Ph.D., University of Massachusetts) is Professor of Telecommunication and Chairperson of the Department of Telecommunication at the University of Kentucky. He has published widely in varying areas of telecommunication but is especially well known for his work with children's understanding of television commercials.

WILLIAM A. DONOHUE (Ph.D., Ohio State) is Associate Professor of Communication at Michigan State University. He is widely published in the area of bargaining and negotiation and acts as a consultant in mediating industrial disputes.

H. THOMAS HURT (Ph.D., Ohio University) is Associate Professor of Communication at North Texas State University. His book on basic communication skills will soon be published by Ginn and Company.

KATHY KELLERMANN (Ph.D., Northwestern) is Assistant Professor of Communication Arts at the University of Wisconsin, Madison. She has done extensive work in the mathematical modeling of interpersonal interaction, social cognition, and communication.

MICHAEL KIRKHORN (Ph.D., Missouri) is Associate Professor of Journalism at the University of Kentucky. Widely published in professional journalism, Kirkhorn spent many years as a reporter and editor of the *Milwaukee Journal*.

GREGORY B. LEICHTY (M.A., Kentucky) is a Ph.D. candidate at the University of Kentucky.

DAVID N. LOWRY (Ph.D., Oklahoma) is Assistant Professor of Speech at Oklahoma Christian College.

JAMES C. McCROSKEY (Ph.D., Penn State) is Professor of Communication and Chairperson of the Department of Communication at the University of West Virginia. A former editor of *Human Communication Research*, McCroskey is widely known for his work in communication apprehension and interpersonal communication.

TIMOTHY P. MEYER (Ph.D., Ohio University) is Professor of Communication at the University of Wisconsin at Milwaukee. He has published widely in varying areas of mass communication effects.

WILLIAM G. POWERS (Ph.D., Oklahoma) is Associate Professor of Communication at North Texas State University.

DEBORAH A. ROACH (M.A., Auburn) is a Ph.D. candidate in the Department of Speech at the University of Oklahoma.

MICHAEL E. ROLOFF (Ph.D., Michigan State) is Associate Professor of Communication at Northwestern University. He is the author of *Interpersonal Communication: The Social Exchange Approach* (Sage, 1981).

BEVERLY DAVENPORT SYPHER (Ph.D., Michigan) is Assistant Professor of Communication at the University of Kentucky where she teaches organizational communication. Among her many consulting clients are the IBM Corporation, Connecticut General Life Insurance company, and the Northern Kentucky Development Council.

DEBORAH WEIDER-HATFIELD (Ph.D., Michigan State) is Assistant Professor of Speech Communication at the University of Georgia.